Dokdo

Its History and Facts

Dokdo
Its History and Facts

 NORTHEAST ASIAN
HISTORY FOUNDATION

Northeast Asian History Foundation
12F, NH Nonghyup Bldg., 81, Tongil-ro, Seodaemun-gu, Seoul 03739, Korea

Compiled by Northeast Asian History Foundation
Translated by Sun Jaisang

Copyright © 2019 Northeast Asian History Foundation

ISBN 978-1-62412-131-9

Library of Congress Control Number: 2019957193

Production & Distribution
Seoul Selection U.S.A., Inc.
4199 Campus Drive, Suite 550, Irvine, CA 92612
Phone: 949-509-6584 / Seoul office: 82-2-734-9567
Fax: 949-509-6599 / Seoul office: 82-2-734-9562
E-mail: hankinseoul@gmail.com
Website: www.seoulselection.com

Printed in the Republic of Korea

Dokdo
Its History and Facts

—

Kim Hakjoon

NORTHEAST ASIAN
HISTORY FOUNDATION

The Author's Acknowledgment

I am glad that my book *Dokdo Yeongu* (*Dokdo: Its History and Facts*), originally published in Korean in 2010 by the Northeast Asian History Foundation (NAHF), is translated into English. Dokdo, an island in the East Sea, has been an integral and inseparable part of the Korean territory since ancient times.

Throughout this book, I attempted to prove this undeniable historical and geographical fact utilizing primary sources, thereby rejecting the erroneous Japanese claim that Dokdo is their territory. I wish this book would help the international community understand the true identity of Dokdo.

My thanks are due to Sun Jaisang who translated the book into English and the Northeast Asian History Foundation, who published this translated version. I would like to add that this work is dedicated to the late Chairman Sohn Yeolho (1921–2013), the founder of TCC Steel, who supported my research on this subject.

December 1, 2019
Kim Hakjoon

Preface

1. This book is a complete revision of my earlier book *Dokdo neun Hanguk ttang* (Seoul: Hanjulgi, 1996, first edition, 2003; Haemaji, second edition, 2005). All previous editions of the book, whose title may be translated into English as *Dokdo is Korean Territory*, including the original edition, the first revised edition, and the second revised edition, were written to enlighten the general public rather than present a specialized, academic discourse. Therefore, footnotes were minimized, with but a small number included in the original text. Also, explanations of professional and expert topics were not provided.

Since the first edition of this book was printed, fourteen years have passed, and five years have passed since the second edition was printed. Not only have additional evidence and documents been discovered, but there has also been new research published since the first edition and the second edition. Specifically, the *Ilbon Gukhoe Dokdo gwallyeon girok moeumjip* (Collection of Japanese National Diet records on Dokdo) compiled by the Northeast Asian History Foundation has made me think more deeply about this subject, and I very much wanted to publish a new edition of the book reflecting this collection. Also, more importantly, I wished to transform my work from a publication for general enlightenment to a scholarly text.

Considering that in 1910, more than 100 years ago, Japanese imperialists wrested Korean sovereignty from the Korean people, and that the annexation began with Dokdo, this book takes on greater academic significance. The Northeast Asian History Foundation graciously decided to support the project of publishing a new edition of the book, for which I am forever indebted. However, it should be noted and made clear that this book was not written as propaganda for the Republic of Korea's government.

2. Looking back, numerous books on the Dokdo issue have already been published in South Korea. However, most of those books are collections of papers written on Dokdo or texts that analyzed one side of the issue. In my view, none of the literature on Dokdo has based its analysis on geography, history, and international law together. This edition is not perfect, but it is a careful attempt to combine these three analytical bases.

For this new edition, I selected the method of controversy analysis. To date, the so-called Dokdo issue has been analyzed by the Korean and Japanese governments, and by academics, but never together. The analysis from two different cultures resulted in fierce claims over the territorial rights to Dokdo. My attempts to analyze the controversy between Korea and Japan required extremely careful inspection of the primary sources. The most important of the primary sources are three-fold. First are the documents which the Japanese government sent to the Korean government. Existing literature grouped these documents as shuttle documents, and I have called them *Japanese Government Opinions* or *Korean Government Opinions*. Second are the writings of representative scholars from both countries on the issue of Dokdo. I have carefully reviewed the above two types of sources multiple times, very thoroughly. Third are the historical maps that both sides have presented as historical evidence. These maps are basic primary sources, and I have compared the arguments offered by both sides in judging the validity of the arguments.

In this edition, I have strictly distinguished between the main text and the footnotes. Also, I introduced a wide range of Japanese logic and argument over the island that they call Takeshima. In doing so, I attempted to raise the objectivity of the issue with my conclusion that Dokdo belongs to Korea. Further, I tried my best to introduce the original texts of the primary sources.

3. A new edition could not have come about without the gracious support and help of others. First, I would like to thank a group of scholars who pioneered the study of Dokdo, Bang Jong-hyeon, Shin Sok-ho, Yu Hong-ryeol, Yi Pyong-do, Lee Sungun, Choe Nam-seon, Hong Yi-sup, Park Kwan-Sook, Park Jong-seung, Shin Ki-suk, Shin Dong Wook, Lee Han-key, and Hwang Sang-gi.

I also thank the second generation of Dokdo scholars, who continued the tradition established by their predecessors. These scholars include Song Byeong-Ki, Lee Hyun-jong, Loh Kye-hyun, Lee Chan, Kim Myungki, Kim Chung-Kyun, Kim Chan-gyu, Paik Choong-Hyun, Lee Byung Joe, Lee Jung Birm, Han Hyong-Kon, Kim Byungryull, Kim Young-Koo, Nah Hong-ju, Lee Sang Myeon, Yang Tae-jin, Lee Sang-Tae, Lee Jong-hak, Li Jin-mieung, and Choi Suh-myun.

I would like to pay special gratitude to Shin Yong-Ha, who published a series of Dokdo-related texts that became a foundation upon which the next generation of Dokdo scholars based their research and studies.

Dokdo scholars of the so-called third generation that have contributed to this work are Chung In Seop, Kim Chai-hyung, Kwak Jin-o, Kim Young-soo, Kim Yong-hwan, Bae Chin-Soo, Yu Ha-young, Hong Seong-keun, Kwon O-yub, and Kwon Jung.

Moreover, I acknowledge and thank Korean Dokdo scholars working in Japan whose contributions have been indispensable. They include Park Byeongseob, who has published extensive studies under the pen name Ban Weol-seong. Japanese scholars of Dokdo have also contributed invaluable studies. These scholars include Yamabe Kentarō, Kajimura Hideki, Hori Kazuo, and Naitō Seichū.

I am forever indebted to all those who have helped me to write this book, but I am solely responsible for this book.

I also thank former president of the Northeast Asian History Foundation Chung Jae-jeong, former director of the Dokdo Research Institute Lee Hoon, and all the editors at the foundation. Further, I wish to thank Chang Duckjoon, Kim Haknoh, Soh Young-A, and Yoon Jong-Koo, all of whom helped me to acquire, translate, and understand Japanese sources and texts. Lastly, I wish to pay special thanks to Yoon Youngsup, who spent a great deal of time typing the transcript.

April 1, 2010

In memory of the ninetieth anniversary of the founding of the *Dong-A Ilbo*

Kim Hakjoon

Introductory Remarks

1. There are several points to remember before proceeding to read this book.

First, the names of the islands that we call Ulleungdo and Dokdo today have transformed over time since the Silla period. There were multiple ways of writing the island names in Chinese characters, and old texts contained numerous printing errors, which complicated matters.

Today, we believe that Dokdo is the island that was called Usando during the Silla period. However, there are sources indicating that in the Joseon Dynasty Ulleungdo was Usando, and that Usando was Ulleungdo. These sources are used by the Japanese side to claim that Dokdo was never Usando. Also, there are multiple smaller islands next to Ulleungdo. The Japanese side argues that if Usando and Ulleungdo are divisible, one of the smaller islands is Usando.

Second, names of the islands have changed in Japan as well throughout history. For instance, generally, Japanese people generally called Ulleungdo as Takeshima until the early Meiji period. And they called Dokdo as Matsushima. Only a few people mixed up the two islands. In 1849, when a French whaling ship, the *Liancourt*, found Dokdo, the French named it "Liancourt Rocks," a name that spread throughout

Japan. Some Japanese people were confused that this rock was a new island distinct from the island that they had been calling Matsushima.

In the midst of such "confusion over names" (author's note: this phrase is quoted from the Japanese government), the Meiji government in Japan officially ruled on February 22, 1905, that Ulleungdo was to be called Matsushima, and Dokdo as Takeshima. Because of this official declaration, today, some Japanese scholars argue that the island that Korean people claim to be Dokdo is actually not Dokdo, and that Dokdo is an island adjacent to Ulleungdo.

The principal names that will be used throughout this book are Dokdo and Ulleungdo in Korean, and Takeshima and Matsushima in Japanese. However, because of the name confusion, one must be extremely careful when analyzing texts and records related to these islands. I too admit that I have fallen into this trap of confusion a couple of times. Readers are thus alerted that careful attention is required in reading this text.

In this context, in essence, the entire issue is a controversy of names. The Korean side argues that Usando featuring in the historical records is Dokdo, and the Japanese side argues that that Usando is actually Ulleungdo. A series of arguments like these proves that the Korea-Japan claims essentially constitute a controversy of names or name controversies. Readers are asked to keep in this in mind.

2. The United States government called this island "Liancourt Rocks." I reference the official labeling of the United States with quotation marks. The same rule will be applied to Japan's labeling of the island as "Takeshima." This is not to say that I agree with the labeling or naming of the US or Japan. The proper name of the island is Dokdo.

3. In this book, the term "representatives of the Republic of Korea in Japan" appears often. The Republic of Korea utilized this envoy from January 19, 1949, to December 18, 1965, until the two countries normalized relations. On the day that the normalization treaty went into effect, the statuses of the representatives were elevated to that of embassy.

The Japanese government requested the Korean side to allow the operation of Japanese representatives in Seoul. However, the Korean government denied that request, claiming that such diplomatic operations would only be allowed when the two countries had normalized relations.

4. For the sake of readability, I have decided to shorten official names of lengthy titles of records. For example, the Treaty of Peace with Japan is shortened to the San Francisco Treaty.

Contents

The History of
the Dokdo Issue and
the Geography of Dokdo

Chapter 1

1 Dokdo in Korea-Japan Relations

The History of Japanese Invasions of the Korean Peninsula

Dokdo is clearly Korean land that rightfully belongs to the Korean people. It has been for thousands of years, and it currently belongs to the Republic of Korea.

Japan calls this island Takeshima (Jukdo in Korean) and claims the island as Japanese territory. The difference is that 100 percent of Korean people accept the Korean government's territorial right over Dokdo, whereas only 99 percent of Japanese people accept the Japanese territorial right over Dokdo, with the remaining 1 percent accepting the rightful possession of Dokdo by Koreans.

A small minority of the Japanese acknowledge Korea's territorial right over Dokdo. Among them was Kajimura Hideki. In his article "Takeshima=Dokutō mondai to Nihon kokka" (The Takeshima = Dokdo issue and Japan), which was published in the September 1978 issue of *Chōsen kenkyū*, Kajimura criticized Japan's claim to Dokdo as a manifestation of a spirit of invasion.[1]

---

1 See Kajimura Hideki, "Takeshima = Dokutō mondai to Nihon kokka" [The Takeshima = Dokdo issue and Japan] *Chōsen kenkyū* 182 (September 1978). Kajimura's article was translated into Korean and

Kajimura's conclusion correctly captures the imperialistic basis for Japan's claim to Dokdo. This, in turn, should be seen against the backdrop of the long history of Japanese expansionism on the Korean Peninsula.

There were multiple Japanese invasions of Korea after the Goryeo Dynasty, not counting the invasions during the Three Kingdoms period and the Later Three Kingdoms period. During this period, the people of Goryeo referred to Japanese people as "groups of robbers" because Japanese pirates repeatedly violated Goryeo territory, which had already suffered from a series of Mongol invasions. Fortunately, a few great military commanders joined forces with peasants and soldiers to fight off the Japanese. Among these commanders in the late fourteenth century was Yi Seong-gye, who founded Joseon in 1392.

With the establishment of Joseon, Japanese piracy seemed to halt. However, the lull was short-lived, and thus the fourth king of Joseon, King Sejong, along with his father, King Taejong, implemented policies to end Japanese violations of Joseon territory. In 1419 they sent Yi Jong-mu as supreme commander on a military campaign to Tsushima Island (in Korean, Daemado), and temporarily incorporated the island as part Gyeongsang-do province.[2] They also opened three ports along the South Sea, Busanpo (today, Dongnae), Jepo (today, Jinhae), and Yeompo (today, Ulsan), to the Japanese for trade in such products as rice and dried goods. As time passed, however, the Japanese began to express frustration over the limited quantities of goods traded with them. Frustration eventually turned to violence, and in 1510 the Japanese rebelled

---

published as "Ilbon ttang jujang eun paengchang – singminjuui sosan" [The argument of Japanese possession is a result of expansion and colonization] *Shindonga*, (April 1996), 610–630. The translated version of Kajimura's article will be cited below.

2 Yu Jong-hyeon, *Daemado yeoksa munhwa gihaeng: Daemado neun bonsi uri ttang inga* [Historical and cultural trip to Daemado: Is Daemado originally a part of Korea?] (Seoul: Hwasan Munhwa, 2008), 19–20. After many complaints from Kyushu, the Joseon government returned Daemado to Kyushu in 1420.

in the three ports in Gyeongsang-do province identified above. Despite the suppression of the event, the 1510 riot in the three ports marked only the beginning of Japanese violence. In 1555, the Japanese once again brought violence to the shores of the South Sea.

Japanese incursions on the Korean Peninsula led to full-scale invasion during the reign of Joseon's fourteenth king, King Seonjo. In the fourth month of 1592, on the 200th anniversary of the founding of the Joseon Dynasty and the 100th anniversary of Christopher Columbus' discovery of San Salvador, Toyotomi Hideyoshi landed 200,000 men at Busan. This marked the beginning of the Japanese invasion of Joseon in 1592.

The invasion proceeded badly for Joseon, and King Seonjo had to evacuate to Uiju in Pyeongan-do province in 1592. At that point, however, armies from all eight provinces of Joseon took the invasion into their own hands, and Admiral Yi Sun-sin fought the Japanese at sea. With the help of military aid from Ming China, Joseon pushed the Japanese forces to the edge of Gyeongsang-do province. This did not stop Toyotomi's ambition to invade Korea, however. In 1597, his ships landed again bringing 150,000 soldiers. This second invasion resulted in Japan's defeat and Toyotomi's death.

After Toyotomi's death, Tokugawa Ieyasu became the practical ruler of Japan. He received the title of shogun from the emperor, who then was little more than a figurehead, and established the shogunate in Edo. Thus began the Edo Period.[3]

Tokugawa soon sought reconciliation with Joseon. Therefore, in 1607, nine years after the second invasion, King Seonjo sent ambassadors to Japan. From then on, Joseon sent officials called the Tongsinsa, or the

---

3 The shogunate was the government through which shoguns had dealt with state matters since the Kamakura period. It was the office for the military government. Tokugawa Ieyasu bore only the role of shogun.

Communication Envoy, twelve times to Japan until 1811. (Japan also sent officials to Joseon, but they were never permitted to enter the capital Hanyang). The two nations maintained a peaceful relationship in which Korea was the dominant partner.

The Japanese Imperialist Invasion of Joseon and the Japanese Occupation of Dokdo

The peace between Joseon and Japan was again threatened near the end of the eighteenth century. Japanese nationalistic activism led by intellectuals, who had once perceived Joseon as a nation with a superior culture, had come to hold many anti-Joseon sentiments. By the end of the Edo period and into the beginning of the Meiji Restoration, ideas and theories such as the *seikanron* ("advocacy of a punitive expedition to Korea") debate and the "nearby sea protection theory" spread among Japanese leaders. These views held that Japan must conquer Korea in order to defend Japan from potential invasions by European powers.

At the time, during the reign of King Gojong (r. 1863–1907), the Joseon Dynasty was in a state of collapse due to a long period of seclusion. Japan took advantage of this, and in 1875 Japanese navy vessels shelled the "Hermit Kingdom" at Ganghwado Island, near the Joseon capital, Seoul. Ultimately, Japan forced Joseon to sign a peace treaty in February 1876.

Under Japan's typical gunboat diplomacy, Shin Heon was among the few diplomats who always conducted negotiations wisely with Japan. The peace treaty is often called the Japan-Korea Treaty of 1876 or the Ganghwado Treaty of 1876. This treaty is an example of an unequal treaty forced upon a weaker state by a stronger state.

Afterwards, Japan's invasion of Korea unfolded systematically in many phases. The first phase began with the Sino-Japanese War in 1894, which Japan won. In 1895, Japanese agents murdered Queen Min, who was a strong leader of the anti-Japan faction in Korea. The assassination of Queen Min is also known as the Eulmi Incident. This incident ignited popular unrest and led to the start of the Righteous Army Movement. It was also a factor in the transformation of the Joseon governing system into the Korean Empire in October 1897. King Gojong came to the throne as emperor and Queen Min, who had passed away, was given the posthumous title of Empress Myeongseong.

This did not stop Japan's invasion of the Korean Empire. Winning the Russo-Japanese War in 1904–1905 meant that Japan had successfully defeated the last competitor for the Korean Empire. Riding the wave of victory, Japan took over the Korean Empire's diplomatic and financial rights by forcing Korea to sign the five-article Japan-Korea Treaty of 1905, also known as the Eulsa Treaty. In 1907, Japan confiscated domestic and national defense rights through the Jeongmi Treaty. By unwillingly signing these treaties, the Korean Empire was stripped of its rights, with nothing left but its title. Japan proceeded to strip even the title "Korean Empire," and finally annexed the Korean peninsula in August 1910. Koreans mourned annexation, calling it a national humiliation.

It took nearly thirty-four years from the Japanese imposition of the Peace Treaty of 1876 to full annexation of Korea. From here, those thirty-four years will be regarded as the first phase of Japan's Joseon colonialism policy. We must remember in this context that toward the end of the first phase of Japanese colonialism in Korea, Japan unilaterally claimed Dokdo as part of Japanese territory and changed the island's name to Takeshima. Further details of this will be discussed in Chapter 5. What should be emphasized here is that Dokdo, a small rock island, was the first victim of the Japanese annexation of Korea. Therefore, the Dokdo occupation should be remembered as a symbol of Japan's invasion of Korea not only legislatively but also publicly.

Japan's expansionism did not end in Joseon. Manchuria became the next target of colonialism in 1931, and then China in 1937, ultimately leading to the Pacific War initiated against the United States in December 1941. Japan also challenged other Western powers, such as the French and Dutch in Southeast Asia. Who would have thought that Japan's invasion of a small rock island in the East Sea of Joseon would expand throughout the Asia-Pacific area?

After World War II: Japan's Unchanged Attitude Towards Dokdo

Japanese imperialism continued until August 15, 1945, when the Allied Forces delivered a devastating defeat and forced Japan to leave the Korean Peninsula.

Japan's territorial ambitions on the Korean Peninsula did not end with World War II, however. On January 18, 1952, the Korean government officially announced the Presidential Proclamation of Sovereignty over Adjacent Seas. "Presidential Proclamation on Sovereignty over the Seas Surrounding the Republic of Korea." This proclamation defined the Republic of Korea's maritime boundaries and included Dokdo. In response, the Japanese government protested in a note verbale (an unsigned diplomatic note) to the official representatives of the Republic of Korea in Japan. The Korean representatives refuted the Japanese claims. However, since 1952, the Japanese government has continued to send such notes verbale, averaging twice a year.

The Japanese government did not stop there. It also requested that post-World War II territorial rights over Dokdo be heard by the International Court of Justice. People of the Third World third-party countries, who do not have sufficient knowledge of the history of Dokdo, may be convinced by the Japanese argument, but for the Korean people, this proposal is untenable. If a thief steals something and then offers to take the case to court, the rightful owner would never accept such a request.

Nonetheless, since 1995, the Japanese government has steadfastly asserted its territorial ambition for Dokdo. In 1995, the fiftieth anniversary of Japan's unconditional surrender, Japan should have reflected on its ignoble past, but leaders of Japan instead tried to legitimize Asian colonialism by claiming that the Pacific War liberated Asian nations from Western imperialism. They even asserted that Japan's annexation of Korea ultimately brought modernization to Korea. This is the context in which Japan continues to assert territorial rights over Dokdo.

The most well-known example is the Japanese textbook issue. The Japanese Ministry of Education, Culture, Sports, Science and Technology has presented Dokdo as Takeshima and as Japanese territory in its textbooks. Thus Japanese students have learned since 1996 that Dokdo is Takeshima, a Japanese territory. As Shin Yong-Ha wrote, "The Japanese government strengthened the indoctrination of its students to think that the 'Dokdo invasion' is 'territorial recovery.'"

Japan became more provocative in 1996. In late January of that year, the Japanese government announced an exclusive economic zone (EEZ) of 200 nautical miles off its coast and included Dokdo in that zone. And on February 10, Prime Minister Hashimoto Ryūtarō publicly announced that Takeshima is inherently Japanese territory. Minister of Foreign Affairs Ikeda Yukihiko claimed that the Korean government's attempt to build a dock on Dokdo was an infringement of Japanese sovereignty.[4] Japan even declared a "Takeshima Day." On March 16, 2005, the Shimane Prefecture Assembly passed a bylaw that commemorated February 22, 1905, as the day that Takeshima was incorporated as part of Shimane Prefecture.

Japan's position on Dokdo endures even after the long rule of the Liberal Democratic Party ended in 2009 and the ruling Democratic

---

4 *Ilbon Gukhoe Dokdo gwallyeon girok moeumjip*, vols. 1–2 [Collection of Japanese National Diet records on Dokdo, vols. 1–2] (Seoul: Northeast Asian History Foundation, 2009), vol. 2, 873–877.

Party of Japan assumed power. In these circumstances, the Korean people must confirm their allegiance to Dokdo and promise to protect it unconditionally. As Lee Han-key, a luminary in the Korean legal profession, stated, "Even if the territorial rights to the land are clear, it will never return to those who fail to fight for it."[5]

---

5 Lee Han-key, *Hanguk ui yeongto: Yeongto chwideuk e gwanhan gukjebeopjeok yeongu* [Korean territory: International law on territorial acquisition] (Seoul: Seoul National University Press, 1996), i.

2 Geography, Topography, and the Ecosystem of Dokdo[6]

Geography

Where exactly is Dokdo? According to records collected by the USS *New York* in 1902, the coordinates of this small rock are 37 degrees 9 minutes 30 seconds north latitude, 131 degrees 55 minutes east longitude. On the other hand, according to the 1908 records of the Japanese naval ship the *Matsue Maru*, one of Dokdo's two islands is located at 37 degrees 14 minutes 18 seconds north latitude, 131 degrees 52 minutes 22 seconds east longitude.

What of the coordinates provided by the Korean government? The answer to this question differs according to the institution. However, according to the Korean Government Standard Dokdo State of Affairs, provided by the Commission for Establishing Correct History, the coordinates of Dokdo are as follows: east longitude located between 131

---

6 Regarding the coordinates, the following studies are noted: Dokdo Research Conservation Association, *Dokdo ingeun haeyeok ui hwangyeong gwa susan jawon bojeon eul wihan gicho yeongu* [Basic research on conserving environment and marine resources around Dokdo] (Seoul: Dokdo Research Conservation Association, 1998). Ministry of Maritime Affairs and Fisheries, Korea Institute of Ocean Science & Technology, *Areumdaun seom Dokdo* [Beautiful island, Dokdo] (Seoul: Ministry of Maritime Affairs and Fisheries, Korea Institute of Ocean Science & Technology) is a useful guidebook with detailed information regarding the ecosystem and environment of Dokdo.

degrees 51 minutes 41 seconds and 131 degrees 52 minutes 10 seconds, north latitude located between 37 degrees 14 minutes 24 seconds and 37 degrees 14 minutes 26 seconds.[7]

Discussing the coordinates of Dokdo does not provide a vivid sense of its location. Dokdo is located in the middle of the East Sea, 87 kilometers southeast of Ullengdo. On a clear day, Dokdo is visible to the naked eye from Ulleungdo. From the mainland of Korea, Dokdo is closest to Uljin in Gyeongsangbuk-do province. From the Gulf of Jukbyeon, Dokdo is approximately 210 nautical miles or 215 kilometers due east.

As to the proximity to Japan, the closest Japanese island to Dokdo is Okishima, which is 160 kilometers away. This means that Dokdo is 73 kilometers closer to Ulleungdo, a Korean territory, than Okishima. The fact that Dokdo is visible from Ulleungdo and not from Okishima proves the point.

Regarding administration, until April 7, 2000, Dokdo included the addresses from San 42 to 57, Do-dong, Nam-myeon, Ulleung-gun, Gyeongsangbuk-do. However, from April 8, 2000, the Dokdo administrative zone changed to San 1 to San 37, Dokdo-ri, Ulleung-eup, Ulleung-gun, Gyeongsangbuk-do. Dokdo, a distant, lonely island in the East Sea, is by far the easternmost territory of the Republic of Korea.

Dokdo is comprised of two islands, Dongdo (East Island) and Seodo (West Island), and eighty-nine small rocks. The eastern rocks have been given such names as Gaje Rock (Seal Rock), Dongnipmun Rock (Independence Gate Rock), Gumeong Rock (Hole Rock), Jine Rock (Centipede Rock), and Mireuk Rock (Buddha Rock). In this sense, Dokdo is a small archipelago.

According to the Corean Alpine Club's report dated November 12, 1952, the surface area of Dongdo is approximately 64,698 square meters,

---

7 Li Jin-mieung, *Dokdo: Jirisang ui jaebalgyeon* [Dokdo: New geographical findings] (Seoul: Samin Press, 1998 first edition; 2005 revised edition), revised edition, 29.

and that of Seodo is approximately 91,740 square meters. However, according to the History Correction Planning Group's report from June 28, 2005, the surface area of Dongdo is 73,297 square meters and that of Seodo is 88,639 square meters. Including the surface area of the rocks around Dokdo, the total gross surface area is approximately 187,453 square meters. Such a surface area would fit inside a square 433 meters by 433 meters. Dokdo is a domain of the state, administered by the Ministry of Land, Transport and Maritime Affairs.[8]

The circumference of Dongdo is approximately 1.9 kilometers or one nautical mile, and that of Seodo is about 2.1 kilometers or 1.1 nautical miles. Seodo also has more rocks around it and reaches a higher elevation than Dongdo. The highest point of Dongdo is 98.6 meters, whereas that of Seodo is 168.5 meters. Because of the difference in size, the two islands have been given nicknames. Seodo is often referred to as Namdo (Male Island), and Dongdo as Yeodo (Female Island).

Between the two islands is a waterway 330 meters long. The widest part of this waterway is 160 meters and the narrowest part is 110 meters. Thus, Dokdo is mainly comprised of Dongdo and Seodo. However, from afar, because of a pointy rock on the southeast part of Dongdo, Dokdo looks like a small mountain range with three summits. Dokdo, however, bears a conical shape.

---

8 Ibid. For the international debate over whether Dokdo is an island, see Kim Byungryull, *Dokdo nya Dakkesima nya* [Dokdo or Takeshima] (Seoul: Dada Media, 1996), 69–70. Kim stated, "Generally, Dokdo is regarded as a collection of rocks. However, modern technology allowed people to live on Dokdo, and in 1982, one family declared their residency on Dokdo and lived there. In 1987, some people even registered their family origin as Dokdo. Nevertheless, declaring residency and registering family origin cannot be the sole factors to determine whether Dokdo is an island."

Geological, Topographical Features, and Climate[9]

The geological features of Dokdo are very similar to Ulleungdo. The bottom part of the Dokdo rocks is composed of black turtle agglomerate and the top part is composed of trachyte agglomerate and tuff.

Dokdo is a volcanic island formed by lava that erupted approximately 2,000 meters underwater and is therefore classified as a volcanic oceanic mountain island.

There are some five oceanic mountains in this region, and Ulleungdo and Dokdo are among them. A third such mountain is 38 kilometers due east of Ulleungdo, a fourth is 35 kilometers due southeast of Dokdo, and a fifth is 50 kilometers due southeast of Dokdo. These five oceanic mountains form a seamount chain, marking the northern border of the Tsushima Basin.

It should be made clear here that Dokdo was formed before Ulleungdo. Dokdo was formed over the course of 200 million years of volcanic activity, between 450 million years ago and 250 million years ago. However, Ulleungdo is estimated to have been formed from 270 million years to 10,000 years ago. For reference, Jeju Island was formed between 120 million years ago and 1,000 years ago, making Jeju significantly younger than both Ulleungdo and Dokdo.

Geographically, the two islands of Dokdo are assumed to have been one island. However, coastal erosion caused the gap between Dongdo and Seodo as well as between the smaller rocks of Dokdo. The waves also eroded the once smooth rocks, turning them sharp.

Coastal erosion continued after Dongdo and Seodo were formed. Sharp rocks along the shore of Dokdo and the formation of a sea cliff

---

9 The geological description relied mostly on the following: Jo Hwa-ryong, "Dokdo: Gaegwan, jayeon hwangyeong, eoeop hwangyeong" [Dokdo: The opening, natural environment, and fishery], in *Minjok munhwa daebaekgwa sajeon* [Encyclopedia of Korean culture], ed. Academy of Korean Studies, vol. 7 (Seongnam, Republic of Korea: Academy of Korean Studies, 1991), 48–49.

are evidence of this. The sharp, rocky shoreline makes it difficult to bring a boat alongside the island. Once on shore, one must be extremely careful in moving around because Dokdo is bereft of trees to grab for balance. There is, however, a cozy, grassy flat area where one may rest in the middle of Dongdo.

What about fresh underground water on Dokdo? According to the *Hydrographic Chart of Joseon* (J. *Chōsen engan suiroshi*), a report completed in 1933 by Japan's Department of the Navy, there is a small freshwater source on the southwestern side of Seodo.[10] However, the Corean Alpine Club failed to find this freshwater source during their expedition to Dokdo in August 1947. In 1965, eighteen years later, a freshwater source producing about ten drums of drinkable water was found in a cave five meters above the northeast shore of Seodo. This water source quenches the thirst of fishermen in the region even today. In this context, Dokdo serves not only as an emergency water source for fishermen but also as a rendezvous point.

In short, Dokdo is an island unsuitable for people. It is a very difficult place for anyone to live, and several Dokdo security officers have lost their lives on the island. While this makes Dokdo seem desolate, there are several marine caves on the northeast shore and an arch that is five meters by three meters on Dongdo, and Seodo's rocks and sheer cliffs make for a spectacular view. There is no question that Dokdo has more than enough interesting features to be a significant tourist destination. The climate of Dokdo is very similar to Ulleungdo. It has an oceanic climate with average monthly temperatures above 0° Celsius, along with rain in all four seasons and constant sea winds.

---

10 Li Jin-mieung, *Dokdo: Jirisang ui jaebalgyeon*, 139.

Plant and Animal Life

As mentioned above, Dokdo is ill-suited for trees and grass. There are, however, three types of woody plants that grow here: pinaceae, rosaceae, and fever twigs. These trees are very sparse and very young, and this is why Dokdo appears to be rather treeless. As for grass and herbaceous plants, there are some water peppers, plantains, and goosefoots. However, because of Dokdo's immature soil, and because it is located so far from land, these plants rarely grow beyond the early stage of development, hence the insubstantial state of flora on Dokdo.

Nevertheless, there is an indigenous aster that grows on the island's cliffs. This aster is native to Korea and is also an original seed. The aster grows anywhere from 30 centimeters to 60 centimeters and is only found in Korea and Japan.[11] Including the aster, there are about fifty-three species of plants on Dokdo. There also are many birds on Dokdo, the most typical being Swinhoe's storm petrel, shearwater, black-tailed gull, osprey, and thrush. Among the birds, the black-tailed gull is probably the species that best represents Dokdo. The gulls sound similar to cats, and they come to Dokdo in late February to lay eggs in April. Therefore, around May or June, when the eggs hatch, Dokdo is covered in black-tailed gulls. People joke that the true owners of Dokdo are the gulls.

Dokdo is also an important stopover for many migratory birds. Recently, birds such as scops owls, crested murrelets, pusillas, tristramis, crows, cormorants, and long-eared owls were found on Dokdo. In January 2010, the government officially announced that there are thirty-eight species of birds on Dokdo. As for insects, there are forty-six species in total. These include dragonflies, earwigs, grasshoppers, cicadas, beetles, flies, and butterflies. There are also four distinct species

---

[11] Republic of Korea Ministry of Environment, "Results of the 2009 Dokdo Ecosystem Investigation," press release, 2010.

found only on Dokdo, including a ladybug that eats aphids. There are no native terrestrial mammals on Dokdo. However, in 1973, Dokdo security officers brought more than ten rabbits from the mainland, which have reproduced abundantly over time.

On the rocks on and around Dokdo one used to see many sea lions, which the people of Ulleungdo call *gaje*. This is why, for a time, Dokdo was called Gajedo. A famous rock north of Seodo is named Gaje Rock for this reason. Today, there are few sea lions left on Dokdo due to overharvesting by Japanese fishermen in the early 1900s. This will be discussed further in Chapter 5.

Overall, according to the Korean government's Ministry of Environment, as of January 2010, there were fifty-three species of plants, thirty-eight species of birds, forty-six species of insects, and thirty species of invertebrates on Dokdo, totaling 167 different species living on the island. Because Dokdo is designated Natural Monument number 336, all living species on Dokdo are also considered part of Natural Monument 336. (Some texts state that black-tailed gulls are Natural Monument 336, but this is incorrect.) Dokdo is also commonly known as a natural resource.

The coast of Dokdo, too, is interesting. The coastal surface water temperature is lowest between March and April, at around 10° Celsius, and highest in August, at about 25° Celsius. The salt concentration of the surface water is approximately 33–34 percent and transparency is between 17–20 meters, thus there is a high salt concentration and relatively clear water.

Dokdo is located in uncontaminated waters and there is an abundance of fishery resources nearby. Abalones, conches, crabs, and mussels are among the most typical. There are also many kinds of algae around Dokdo, including seaweed and kelp. There are five species of blue algae, sixty-seven species of red algae, nineteen species of brown algae, and eleven species of green algae. Although farming is limited, some people harvest abalone and conch off the coast of Dokdo.

About seventy kilometers northwest of Dokdo is Daehwatoe (Yamato Shallows) where the warm currents from Tsushima collide with cold currents from North Korea. This explains the ample amount of plankton, which attract migratory fish. In this region, there are even subtropical fish such as the *jaridom* (pearl-spot chromis). The environmental characteristics of Dokdo discussed here make the area a very attractive and important fishing ground for many fishermen. Dokdo is not just an important primary fishing ground, but one of the richest fishing grounds in the East Sea. This is why Japanese fishermen have historically coveted Dokdo. Important fish include squid, pollack, cod, shark, rockfish, salmon, and mullet. According to the Ulleung-gun county office, 90 percent of the fishing boats around Dokdo are from Ulleungdo. These boats fish as far as three hours away from shore.

Counting Ulleungdo boats alone, in 2009, there were about eighty boats that sailed. These boats operate for approximately 100 days a year, which means that there were around 8,000 departures each year, with an annual catch of over 5,000 tons. During June and July, when it is ideal for squid fishing, the lights of countless boats near Dokdo at night make it seem like daylight. Squid season in the summer is quite a scene, with hordes of black-tailed gulls attacking the squid on the decks of the fishing boats.

The mineral deposits in the vicinity of Dokdo are as important as the other resources. Most of the mineral deposits are methane hydrates, a potential alternative to fossil fuels. The Korea Ocean Research & Development Institute calculated that methane hydrate reserves reach 600 million tons, with a market value of 150 trillion won.

Furthermore, around Dokdo are uranium and phosphate minerals containing vanadium. The Republic of Korea is solely dependent on imports for these potential fuel sources. If Korea were to develop these fuels, it would greatly benefit the country. Japan, of course, is also interested in the rich mineral deposits of Dokdo.

Records of Ulleungdo and Usando from Goryeo and Early Joseon

Chapter 2

1 Focus on the Korea-Japan Controversy

For how long has Dokdo breathed with the Korean people? Dokdo has been a part of the Korean national consciousness since the New Stone Age. At that time, according to Korean historians and anthropologists, Korean people inhabited Ulleungdo and founded the small kingdom of Usanguk, which included Dokdo and other surrounding islands.

The Japanese government's interpretation is quite different. Japan argues that, while it is true that there were people on Ulleungdo during the New Stone Age, there is insufficient evidence to conclude that Usanguk included Dokdo.

Which argument is true? This chapter will analyze the records of the Goryeo and Joseon dynasties, with a specific focus on the competing Korean and Japanese interpretations of these records.[12]

---

12 This chapter relies in part upon the following studies: Kim Byungryull, *Dokdo nya Dakkesima nya*; Kim Hwa-hong, *Yeoksajeok siljeung euro bon Dokdo neun Hanguk ttang* [Dokdo is Korean territory in the perspective of historical evidence] (Seoul: Simon, 1996); *Dokdo yeongyugwon yeongu nonjip* [Dokdo territorial right research collection] (Seoul: Dokdo Research Conservation Association, 2002); Shin Yong-Ha, *Dokdo ui minjok yeongtosa yeongu* [Research on Dokdo national territorial studies] (Seoul: Jisik Sanup Publications, 1996); Shin Yong-Ha, *Dokdo, bobaeroun Hanguk yeongto: Ilbon ui Dokdo yeongyugwon jujang e daehan chongbipan* [Dokdo, precious Korean territory: Criticism on Japanese claim over territorial right of Dokdo] (Seoul: Jisik Sanup Publications, 1996); Shin Yong-Ha, *Hanguk gwa Ilbon ui Dokdo yeongyugwon nonjaeng* [Korea and Japan's Dokdo territorial rights controversy] (Seoul: Hanyang University Press, 2003); Yang Tae-jin, *Hanguk dongnip ui sang-*

2 Records from the *Samguk sagi* and the *Samguk yusa*

The oldest history book of Korea is the *History of the Three Kingdoms* (K. *Samguk sagi*), written by Kim Bu-sik, a scholar and government official active in the Goryeo period. The *History of the Three Kingdoms* was completed in 1145. There are two instances in which this text mentions Usanguk, a kingdom with which Dokdo is commonly associated. First, in the "Jijeung Maripgan" section in the "Records of Silla" chapter (K. *Silla bongi*) it is stated:

In the sixth month of 512, Usanguk surrendered and paid tribute to Silla with local goods and products. Usanguk is an island kingdom east of Myeongju, otherwise known as Ulleungdo. This area is 100 leagues large, and its people relied on the high cliffs and deep sea; they were not submissive. Therefore, Ichan Isabu was made governor of Haseulla

jing Dokdo [Symbol of Korean independence, Dokdo] (Seoul: Baeksan, 2004); Lee Sang-Tae, *Saryo ga jeungmyeong haneun Dokdo neun Hanguk ttang* [As evidence shows, Dokdo is Korean territory] (Seoul: Kyongsaewon Publishing Company, 2007); Li Jin-mieung, *Dokdo: Jirisang ui jaebalgyeon*; Lee Han-key, *Hanguk ui yeongto*; Hwang Sang-gi, *Dokdo yeongyugwon haeseol* [Dokdo territorial right explained] (Seoul: Geullo Haksaengsa, 1954). Among these books, Shin Yong-Ha's *Dokdo ui minjok yeongtosa yeongu* was translated into Japanese by Han Seong as *Tokutō Takeshima: Shiteki kaimei* (Kyoto: Inta shuppan, 1997).

Province.

"Jijeung Maripgan" refers to Silla's twenty-second monarch, King Jijeung. *Ichan* was a government position in Silla. And Haseulla, also known as Aseulla, was a Silla province located in today's Gangneung area.

The second mention of Usanguk is in the "Tale of Isabu." Here, Kim Bu-sik wrote that "Isabu was a Silla person with the surname Kim, and the fourth son of King Naemul, governor of Aseulla," who used trickery to steal Gaya as well as Usanguk. It is further written, "He made wooden lions and placed them at the front line. Once he arrived at the shore, he shouted, 'If your people do not surrender, I will release beasts that will stomp you.' The people of then Usanguk surrendered in extreme fear."

The story of King Jijeung and Isabu's conquest of Usanguk is also told in the *Memorabilia of the Three Kingdoms* (K. *Samguk yusa*). This book was written by the great monk Iryeon in 1285. Iryeon wrote about an island two days due east of Haseulla Province, called Ulleungdo or Ureungdo, where King Jijeung used wooden lions to fool the people into submission.[13] However, in the *Samguk yusa*, Park Yi-jong, as opposed to Isabu in the *Samguk sagi*, was rewarded with the title of governor of Haseulla Province for subjugating Usanguk. Korean scholars consider Park Yi-jong and Isabu to be the same person.

The Controversial Interpretations of Korea and Japan

Both the *Samguk sagi* and the *Samguk yusa* explain in detail how Usanguk was subjugated by Silla. But did Usanguk include only Ulleungdo and no other islands?

---

[13] Further explanation of the story in *Samguk sagi* and *Samguk yusa* is found in Lee Sang-Tae, *Saryo ga jeungmyeong haneun Dokdo neun Hanguk ttang*, 160–162.

The Korean government and Korean scholars argue that the Kingdom of Usanguk consisted of Ulleungdo, which was the main capital island, and other islands, one of which was Dokdo. They further argue that in history texts from the Joseon period Ulleungdo had many names, including Ureungdo and Mureungdo, and that Dokdo was also called Usando.

In response, the Japanese government and Japanese scholars asserted the following. Neither the *Samguk sagi* nor the *Samguk yusa* mention Dokdo. Therefore, Usanguk refers to Ulleungdo and to no other islands. And, in the *Annals of King Sejong* (K. *Sejong sillok*) in the *Annals of the Joseon Dynasty* (K. *Joseon wangjo sillok*) there is a statement that reads, "In the Silla period, Usando was called Ulleungdo." Therefore, Usanguk refers to Ulleungdo only. On February 10, 1954, Japan's Ministry of Foreign Affairs delivered a diplomatic note titled *Japanese Government Opinion 2* to the official representatives of the Republic of Korea, reiterating its stance regarding Dokdo. The Ministry also pointed out that none of the extant Joseon-period maps include Dokdo by that name. In the same context, Ueda Toshio argued that there is no evidence from Joseon proving that Usanguk is the same island as Dokdo.[14]

It was pointed out in Chapter 1 that the Japanese historian Kajimura Hideki had published a paper stating that Dokdo is Korean territory. Despite his argument, Kajimura also wrote that there is no physical or real evidence proving Dokdo, an uninhabited island, was part of Usanguk.[15]

---

14 This argument from *Japanese Government Opinion 2* is included in Shin Yong-Ha et al., *Dokdo yeongyugwon jaryo ui tamgu*, vol. 4 (Seoul: Dokdo Research Conservation Association, 2001), 218–219.

15 Kajimura Hideki, "Ilbon ttang jujang eun paengchang – singminjuui sosan," 614.

The Meanings of Ulleung and Usan

Here we should discuss the meaning of the place names Ulleung and Usan. As will be addressed below, (1) Ulleung and Usan are used interchangeably; (2) the Chinese characters of the two place names are different, yet similar; and (3) in some Japanese documents, Ulleung is written as Uruma (ウルマ; as 宇流麻 in Chinese characters) in order to resemble the Korean pronunciation.

According to Yi Pyong-do, who published an article about Ulleung and Usan in 1963, Usan is the former name of Ulleung, and this name originated from the ancient port city of Ujin. Ujin was the name of the current Uljin during the Goguryeo Kingdom. Uljin was the closest mainland city for Ulleung to pay tribute. The "u" in "Usan" and the "ul" in "Ulleung" led to the names "Usando" or "Ulleungdo." Yi Pyong-do theorized that "Ulleung" became the name for the main island, and that "Usan" became the name for the surrounding islands.[16]

Shin Yong-Ha studied this issue in depth. He noted that the central part of the word "Ulleung" is "ul." "Ul" originated from "ureu 우르," which is connected to the words "eoreun 어른" (elder) and "ureoreo 우러러" in ancient Korean. An example of a connection between a modern word and an ancient Korean word can be found in the bureaucratic titles of the Baekje Kingdom. The highest bureaucratic title one could receive in Baekje was "eoraha 어라하." To write "ureu" in Chinese characters, the word eventually had to be written as "鬱 (ul 울)," "蔚 (ul 울)," "亏 (ul 울)," "羽 (u 우)," and "于 (u 우)." Also, there are two Chinese characters, "武 (mu 무)" and "茂 (mu 무)," which sound like "u" in Chinese but are "mu" in Korean.

---

16 Yi Pyong-do, "Dokdo ui myeongching e daehan sajeok gochal: Usan, Jukdo myeongchinggo," [Historical contemplation of different names of Dokdo: The study of names: Usando and Takeshima] (Seoul: Dokdo Research Conservation Association, 2003), 35–43.

Then, what does "*leung*" mean? "*Leung*" means hill [陵: *reung* 릉] or mountain [山: *san* 산]. Therefore, ultimately, the word "*Ulleung*" has the meaning "high mountain." The highest mountain on Ulleungdo, Seonginbong Peak (聖人峰), is the writing in Chinese characters of "peak of *uru*." The "*u*" in "*Usan*" also means "*uru*." Therefore, "*Usan*" is an expression through Chinese characters of "*urumoe* 우루뫼" or "High Mountain."[17]

17 Shin Yong-Ha, "Dokdo – Ulleungdo ui myeongching byeonhwa yeongu: Myeongching byeonhwa reul tonghae bon Dokdo ui Hanguk goyu yeongto jeungmyeong" [Study on Dokdo and Ulleungdo name transformation: Proof of Korean territorial right of Dokdo through name transformation], in *Dokdo yeongyugwon jaryo ui tamgu* 2 [Study on the territorial right over Dokdo], ed. Shin Yong-Ha et al. vol. 2 (Seoul: Dokdo Research Conservation Association, 1999), 294–297.

3 Records from *History of Goryeo*

In addition to *Samguk sagi* and *Samguk yusa*, Usanguk and Ulleungdo are mentioned many times in the *History of Goryeo* (K. *Goryeosa*). King Sejong (r. 1418–1450) of Joseon ordered a committee of scholars led by Jeong In-ji and Kim Jong-seo to compile this text, and the *History of Goryeo* was completed in 1451, during the reign of King Munjong (r. 1450–1452).[18]

According to the *History of Goryeo*, Usanguk pledged its allegiance to Goryeo after witnessing the near collapse of Silla. This occurred in the Later Three Kingdoms period when the Later Baekje and Later Goguryeo kingdoms gained dominance in their respective regions. General Wang Geon of Later Goguryeo eventually dismantled the Later Goguryeo state and founded Goryeo in 918. In 929, he nearly destroyed Later Baekje. Silla, which had essentially lost everything but its name, surrendered to Wang Geon and was incorporated as part of Goryeo in 935. Ulleungdo took note of this and switched its allegiance from Silla

---

18 The text in *Goryeosa* [History of Goryeo] which mentions Ulleungdo may be found in Lee Sang-Tae, *Saryo ga jeungmyeong haneun Dokdo neun Hanguk ttang*, 164–166. Also, further explanations of these passages may be found on pages 225–226 of Lee's book.

to Goryeo.

The following is described in the first volume of the *History of Goryeo*. In 930, "Ureungdo sent their envoys, Baekgil and Todu, to Goryeo. King Taejo (Wang Geon) accepted the tribute and granted Baekgil the title of *jeongwi* and Todu the title of *jeongjo*, which both of them accepted with a bow."[19]

Here, notice how the tributary subject was not called "Usanguk" or "king of Usanguk." This means that Wang Geon considered Ulleungdo and the affiliated islands as part of Silla, not as a separate country called Usanguk. Also, the fact that the envoys from Usanguk were granted Goryeo bureaucratic titles implies that Wang Geon allowed a generous semiautonomous rule of Ulleungdo.[20]

In the *History of Goryeo*, Usanguk was first mentioned in the section concerning records from 1018, during the reign of King Hyeonjong. The text states that the "agriculture of Usanguk was ruined" after the invasion by the Jurchens. Therefore, Yi Won-gu was deployed with gifts of farm tools for the people. The Jurchens in this passage were a group who lived northeast of the lower bank of the Dumangang River (Tumen River). This record proves that the Goryeo government continuously ruled and managed the old Usanguk and its people.[21]

The fact that the Goryeo government ruled over Usanguk is reemphasized in later chapters of the *History of Goryeo*. In passages from the tenth year of King Hyeonjong's reign (1019) it is stated that the "people of Usanguk who evacuated to the mainland during the invasion of Jurchens were ordered to return to the island." In the discussion of the thirteenth year of King Hyeonjong's reign (1022), the text states that

---

19 The original text can be read in Shin Yong-Ha et al., *Dokdo yeongyugwon jaryo ui tamgu* [Research on the territorial right of Dokdo], vol. 1 (Seoul: Dokdo Research Conservation Association, 2001), 20.

20 Ibid., 21.

21 Ibid., 22.

"the Military Council (K. *Dobyeongmasa*) requested that the king build a refugee camp in Yeju and provide travel money and expenses for the Usanguk people who had been affected by the Jurchen invasion, and the king thereby accepted the request."[22]

These two passages use the words "Usanguk" and the phrase "the people of Usanguk," illustrating that the Goryeo government considered Ulleungdo and the attached islands, including Dokdo, as one independent and autonomous entity. This in turn shows that Goryeo implemented indirect administration through landed proprietors. At the same time, the Goryeo government treated the people of Usanguk the same as the people of Goryeo.

Where is Yeju? Explanations and theories vary. However, the argument for Yeju being present-day Deokwon in Hamgyeong-do province is the most convincing.[23]

The semiautonomous, indirect governing of Usanguk turned to direct governing by the Goryeo administration with the ascension of King Deokjong, the ninth king of Goryeo. According to volume 5 of *History of Goryeo*, in 1032 Ulleungdo was called Ureungseong, and the magistrate was called the governor of Ureung. It is thought that Ulleungdo was militarily fortified to fend off the Jurchens and renamed Ureungseong to enhance the sovereignty of the central government.[24] Later, by the time of King Injong, Goryeo's seventeenth king, Ulleungdo was incorporated into Myeongju-do province, present-day Gangwon-do province. Therefore, in 1141, Myeongju-do Inspector Yi Yang-sil was sent to Ulleungdo to collect local products.[25]

Further explanation of Ulleungdo was included in volume 18 of

---

22 Ibid., 22–23.

23 Ibid., 23–24.

24 Ibid., 24–25.

25 Ibid., 25.

History of Goryeo. In the description of the peaceful time during the reign of King Uijong of Goryeo, the monarch is recorded as having sent inspector Kim Yu-rip to Ulleungdo after learning that "Ureungdo is in the middle of the East Sea. The land is wide and the soil is fertile, thus people can live there. Therefore, a local government was installed in the past." Kim Yu-rip returned to report, "The land is full of rocks, and therefore is inadequate for people to live on." The Goryeo government took this report and determined to give up on the idea of resettling people on Ulleungdo.

Kim Yu-rip's inspection trip also appears in government records from the Joseon Dynasty, such as the *Revised and Augmented Survey of the Geography of Joseon* (K. *Sinjeung Dongguk yeoji seungnam*). In 1481, the government printed *Geographical Survey* (K. *Yeoji seungnam*). That text was revised in 1486 as *Augmented Survey of the Geography of Joseon* (K. *Dongguk yeoji seungnam*) and revised again in 1531 as *Revised and Augmented Survey of the Geography of Joseon*. Unfortunately, no copies of *Geographical Survey* or of *Augmented Survey of the Geography of Joseon* are extant.

However, if one reads all of the records mentioned above carefully, one will find that Kim Yu-rip did not state that Ulleungdo is or is not suitable for habitation. What is true is that Kim Yu-rip reported that Ulleungdo is quite large, with evidence of seven settlements and abundant local products.[26] *History of Goryeo* marked the year of Kim Yu-rip's inspection as 1157. However, the *Revised and Augmented Survey of the Geography of Joseon* noted the date as the thirteenth year of King Uijong's reign, or 1159.

Soon, an event that changed the country's fate for the next four generations occurred: the military coup led by Choi Chung-heon. Once in

---

26 Ibid., 30–31.

power, Choi received reports that Ulleungdo had fertile land, rare trees, and plentiful fish. He therefore ordered government officials to move people to the island. However, due to many deadly accidents en route and back, Choi recalled the people he had ordered to Ulleungdo. At this time, Goryeo was a tributary state to Yuan China. When the Yuan officials in Goryeo heard of Ulleungdo and its rare goods, they demanded goods from Ulleungdo to be included as part of the tribute. The Goryeo government requested that the Yuan officials rescind this demand due to the danger involved in collecting items in Ulleungdo.[27]

This fact is found in volume 58 of *History of Goryeo*, a volume dedicated to the geography of Goryeo, hence the title "Jiriji," or geographical gazetteer. In this volume, where discussion of the geography of Uljin-gun county (present-day Uljin-gun, Gyeongsangbuk-do) appears, it is clear that Ulleungdo included other surrounding islands.

> Ulleungdo: It is located due east of Uljin-gun county. During the time of Silla, it was called Usanguk. It was also called Mureung or Ureung. The island is about 100 leagues. [. . .] According to one explanation, Usan and Mureung were originally two different islands, and they are located not far from each other. Thus, on clear days the islands are visible from each other.[28]

The last sentence above is very important. It is the first mention of Usando outside of Ulleungdo in Korean historical texts. Korean scholars draw from the entry the fact that the Usando in this excerpt is today's Dokdo, and historical texts compiled after *Samguk sagi* considered Usanguk the name of a kingdom that included the "Usando" mentioned in this excerpt. Secondly, Ulleungdo and Usando are "mother-child"

---

27 Ibid., 31–32.
28 Ibid., 36–37.

islands, impossible to separate. In a sense, Ulleungdo is the main island, and Usando is Ulleungdo's attached island.[29]

In response to the arguments of Korean scholars, the Japanese government and Japanese scholars make three points. First, the information in the Korean historical texts are not established theories but are based upon rumors. Therefore, neither the Goryeo government nor the Joseon government was certain that Usan and Mureung were two different islands. Second, the statement on the visibility of the two islands is unrelated to truth and may just be a coincidence. Third, the argument that Ulleungdo is the main island and that Usando is an attached island cannot be valid. These arguments by the Japanese government and Japanese scholars will be addressed in later chapters.

---

29 Yi Geun-taek, "1693-1699 nyeon An Yong-bok ui Ulleungdo – Dokdo suho hwaldong: Sutoje 搜討制 silsi wa gwallyeonhayeo" [An Yong-bok's Ulleungdo and Dokdo protection, 1693–1699: In relation to Sutoje 搜討制 implementation]," in *Dokdo yeongyu ui yeoksa wa gukje gwangye* [History of Dokdo territorial rights and international relations], ed. Dokdo Research Conservation Association (Seoul: Dokdo Research Conservation Association, 1997), 69.

4 Records from the *Annals of King Sejong* "Geographical Gazetteer"

Mention of the islands appears again in the *Annals of King Taejong* (K. *Taejong sillok*). The annals' history treats the reign of King Taejong (r. 1400–1418), and Mureungdo and Ureungdo appear frequently. One example is recorded in a passage from 1417.

In the *Annals of King Sejong*, which covers the peaceful reign of King Sejong, Mureung, Mureungdo, and Usan also appear often. Word of the fertile land and rich maritime resources surrounding the island eventually led the government to consider relocating people to the island. On the other hand, the government also considered forcibly returning people who had run away to the island in order to avoid paying taxes or serving in the military. The government also considered the fact that Jurchen and Japanese invasions of the island were increasing. In addition, the government noted that there were reports that people who had drifted to Japan due to typhoons returned to the island after receiving much hospitality from Japanese people.[30]

Despite this complicated background, King Taejong and King Sejong

---

[30] This case may be found in the *Annals of King Sejong*, in an entry from the twelfth month of the seventh year of King Sejong's reign (1425).

both dispatched government officials to the island. These officials generally advised the kings to bring the islanders back to the mainland in order to protect them from invasions by Jurchens in the northeast and by Japanese. Therefore, the Joseon government implemented the *gongdo* policy. Both the Korean government and the Japanese government today translate this policy to mean "the policy of uninhabited islands" or "the policy of evacuation."[31] King Taejong dispatched Kim In-u to Ulleungdo in 1416. As his entourage, Kim brought Yi Man, a man who was knowledgeable of the geography of Ulleungdo. Together, they "searched and arrested people on the island" and returned to the mainland in the second month of 1417.

In the *Annals of King Taejong*, Kim In-u is described as a person who had formerly served as an official in Janggi-hyeon county (K. *jeon pan Janggi-hyeon sa*).[32] Janggi-hyeon was located near today's Yeongil-gun in Gyeongsangbuk-do, thus it was close to Ulleungdo. However, in the *Annals of King Taejong* and the *Annals of King Sejong*, Kim was only described as a navy commander (K. *manho*) in Samcheok-gun, Gang-won-do.[33] The Joseon government had built a naval base in Samcheok, near Ulleungdo, and it seems that King Taejong employed soldiers and sailors who knew the area well.

What is interesting here is that Kim's position was Mureung and other islands pacification commissioner (K. *Mureung deung cheo anmusa*), and not Mureung pacification commissioner (K. *Mureung anmusa*).[34] This shows that King Taejong and his government acknowledged the

---

31 See, for example, the note verbale that the Japanese Foreign Ministry sent to the representatives of the Republic of Korea in Japan on February 10, 1954, in *Japanese Government Opinion 2*, 227. An English translation of the document may be found in Shin Yong-Ha et al., *Dokdo yeongyugwon jaryo ui tamgu*, vol. 4, 216–238.

32 Notes on Kim In-u are found in Lee Sang-Tae, *Saryo ga jeungmyeong haneun Dokdo neun Hanguk ttang*, 167.

33 Shin Yong-Ha et al., *Dokdo yeongyugwon jaryo ui tamgu*, vol. 1, 52.

34 Lee Sang-Tae, *Saryo ga jeungmyeong haneun Dokdo neun Hanguk ttang*, 167.

presence of islands other than Mureung. What then could have been the foundation for such an acknowledgement? It relied upon the report of the second minister of the Ministry of Taxation (K. *Hojo champan*) Park Seup. Park reported to King Taejong that, while he served as governor of Gangwon-do, he had heard about "a small island next to Mureungdo."[35]

King Sejong's case was very similar to that of King Taejong. In the eighth month of 1425, King Sejong again dispatched Kim In-u to Ulleungdo to bring back the people there. Kim was appointed Usan and Mureung royal commissioner of pacification (K. *Usan Mureung deung cheo anmusa*), which makes clear that his administrative jurisdiction extended over both Usando and Ulleungdo. Kim, along with fifty soldiers on two warships, landed on Ulleungdo and returned to the mainland in the tenth month with twenty men and women from the island.

In 1436, eleven years later, Yu Gye-mun, then governor of Gang-won-do, advised King Sejong that "since Ulleungdo has fertile soil, good fishing, and is suitable anchorage for ships, it would be wise to permit people to live on the island and to construct a naval base there, and have the commander of the base be the administrator of the island." Yu also warned that there was a potential for Japanese occupation of the island. The government rejected Yu's request, and instead dispatched government officials from time to time to catch and bring back criminals who had fled to the island.[36]

There are other instances acknowledging the presence of Usando and Mureungdo. In the *Annals of King Sejong*, volume 153, completed in approximately 1454, it is noted that there are multiple annexed islands in Uljin-gun, Gangwon-do. The text focused specifically on the mutual relationship of Usando and Mureungdo, as shown in the following passage.

---

35 This fact is found in the *Annals of King Taejong*. See Shin Yong-Ha et al., *Dokdo yeongyugwon jaryo ui tamgu*, vol. 1, 49.

36 Song Byeong-Ki, *Gochyeo sseun Ulleungdo wa Dokdo* [Rewritten Ulleungdo and Dokdo] (Seoul: Dankook University Press, 2005), 31–33.

于山武陵二島 在縣正東海中

(Usan Mureung ido jaehyeon cheongdong haejung)

二島相距不遠 風日清明 則可望見

(Ido sanggeo bulwon pungil cheongmyeong jeukga manggyeon)

The passage translates as:

The islands of Usan and Mureung are in the middle of the sea due east of the county.

The distance between the two islands is not far, thus on a clear day each [island] is visible from the other.

These excerpts are rather conclusive regarding the presence of the two islands. The "Geographical Gazetteer" (K. *Jiriji*) in the *History of Goryeo* only hinted, "There are rumors of two islands," whereas the "Geographical Gazetteer" in the *Annals of King Sejong* concluded that "there are two islands." The latter text added that "the two islands [. . .] were called Usanguk during the Silla period."[37] In the diplomatic note *Korean Government Opinion 1*, dated September 9, 1953, the Korean government presented this evidence to Japan's Ministry of Foreign Affairs.[38]

The Counterarguments of Japanese Scholars and the Rebuttals of Korean Scholars

In response to the arguments of the Korean government and scholars, Japan's Ministry of Foreign Affairs sent *Japanese Government Opinion 2* on February 10, 1954, and *Japanese Government Opinion 3* on September

---

37 This passage is explained in Lee Sang-Tae, *Saryo ga jeungmyeong haneun Dokdo neun Hanguk ttang*, 168.

38 An English-language translation of *Korean Government Opinion 1* may be found in Shin Yong-Ha et al., *Dokdo yeongyugwon jaryo ui tamgu*, vol. 4, 432–442.

20, 1956. A summary of the two documents follows below.

First, the "Geographical Gazetteer" in the *Annals of King Sejong* was completed in 1432, and the "Geographical Gazetteer" in the *History of Goryeo* was completed in 1451 but not printed. This fact signifies a self-correction by the Joseon government that the conclusive remarks in the *Annals of King Sejong* were based upon a rumor in the "Geographical Gazetteer" in the *History of Goryeo*. This is a clear indication that the Joseon government was uncertain of the presence of the two islands.

Second, no maps from the Joseon period depict an island named Dokdo.

Third, King Taejong's empty island (K. *gongdo*) policy is proof that the Joseon government virtually abandoned Ulleungdo and placed the islands outside of its administrative jurisdiction. It is difficult to believe that the Joseon government exercised administrative jurisdiction on islands located farther away than Ulleungdo.

Fourth, there is a sentence in the *Annals of King Taejong* that reads, "Kim In-u, upon returning from Usando, offered local goods such as large bamboo, water buffalo hide, unbleached ramie cloth, cotton seeds, fruits, etc. And he brought three islanders with him, who testified that there are fifteen families or eighty-six people living on the island." This record is proof that Usando was not a deserted island, but an inhabited island with people living on it.[39]

Taijudō Kanae made the same argument, emphasizing the report of Kim In-u and stressing that Usando cannot be today's Dokdo.[40]

The Korean government and scholars countered these claims. In *Korean*

---

39 The Japanese- and English-language translations of the original documents may be read in Shin Yong-Ha et al., *Dokdo yeongyugwon jaryo ui tamgu*, vol. 4, 216–231 and 324–364.

40 Taijudō Kanae, "Takeshima funsō," *Kokusaihō gaikō zasshi* 64 (March 1966), 114.

Government Opinion 2, dated September 25, 1954, they asserted that King Taejong's "*gongdo* policy on Ulleungdo is not at all the renunciation of its territorial right." Koreans also pointed out that in old Japanese maps the name "Ulleungdo" was written and Romanized as "Jukdo." Furthermore, "Ulleungdo" was written in katakana as チユクド, which is based upon the Korean-language pronunciation, not the Japanese-language pronunciation. They also argued that these facts signify that Joseon's sovereignty over the island was accepted by Japanese in the past. Noting that Dokdo is Ulleungdo's attached island, Koreans argued that the *gongdo* policy included the evacuation of Dokdo, as well.[41]

As will be addressed in Chapter 4, the *Korean Government Opinion 2* stressed that the Joseon government dispatched a series of government officials and soldiers to Ulleungdo, showing that the Joseon government exercised "the administrative jurisdiction over territory."[42] Shin Yong-Ha described the *gongdo* policy as a territorial administration policy.[43]

Second, "Ulleungdo" and "Usando" were used interchangeably in Joseon. In this case, Usando referred to the name of Usanguk used after the Silla Kingdom. The legal expert Hwang Sang-gi interpreted Kim In-u's report in the *Annals of King Taejong* as follows:

> This entry in the Annals of King Taejong was written with an understanding that Usanguk is Ulleungdo, and therefore Usando. In this sense, by the end of the Joseon period, after finding the misuse of the titles on documents and maps, a correction was made to use Ulleungdo

---

41 Shin Yong-Ha et al., *Dokdo yeongyugwon jaryo ui tamgu*, vol. 4, 226 (Korean), 285 (English); Yu Hong-yeol, "Dokdo neun Ulleungdo ui sokdo: Yeongyugwon eul jungsim euro," in *Dokdo*, ed. Daehan Gongnonsa (Seoul: Daehan Gongnonsa, 1965), 193–198.

42 Shin Yong-Ha et al., *Dokdo yeongyugwon jaryo ui tamgu*, vol. 4, 286 (English).

43 Shin Yong-Ha, *Dokdo ui minjok yeongtosa yeongu* [Research on Dokdo national territorial studies] (Seoul: Jisik Sanup Publications, 1996), 316.

and Usando as the name, as it is today.[44]

Third, when the issue of bringing people on Ulleungdo back to the mainland was addressed at King Sejong's court, the monarch concluded that the "people of Ulleungdo did not go into a foreign country." This means that Ulleungdo, as well as its attached island, Usando, were not considered as foreign islands, but as islands of Joseon.[45]

44 Hwang Sang-gi, "Dokdo munje yeongu" [Study of Dokdo issues], in *Dokdo*, ed. Daehan Gongnonsa (Seoul: Geullo Haksaengsa, 1954; Seoul: Daehan Gongnonsa, 1965), 227; Hwang published "Dokdo munje yeongu" in 1954, making it the first Korean publication addressing Dokdo issues. He received a master's degree in law from Seoul National University with the same publication in 1955.

45 *Annals of King Sejong*, eulyu day, tenth month, year 7; Shin Yong-Ha, "Dokdo – Ulleungdo ui myeongching byeonhwa yeongu: Myeongching byeonhwa reul tonghae bon Dokdo ui Hanguk goyu yeongto jeungmyeong," 309.

5 Records from *Revised and Augmented Survey of the Geography of Joseon* and the Attached Map

Records showing that there are two different islands in the sea near Uljin-gun county are not only found in the *Annals of King Sejong* "Geographical Gazetteer" and the *History of Goryeo* "Geographical Gazetteer," but also in the *Revised and Augmented Survey of the Geography of Joseon*. In volume 45 of this third text, it is noted that Ulleungdo had other names, such as Mureungdo or Ureungdo, and also that there were two islands east of Uljin-gun, called Ulleungdo and Usando. The original text is introduced below.

于山島 鬱陵島

一云武陵, 一云羽陵, 二島在縣正東海中, 三峯岌嶪撑空, 南峯稍卑, 風日清明則峯頭樹木及山根沙渚, 歷歷可見, 風便則二日可到[46]

This passage in the *Revised and Augmented Survey of the Geography of Joseon* may be translated as follows.

---

[46] This part is printed in Lee Sang-Tae, *Saryo ga jeungmyeong haneun Dokdo neun Hanguk ttang*, 172.

Usando, Ulleungdo

Also known as Mureung and Ureung, the two islands are located in the middle of the sea, due east of [Uljin-gun] county. Three peaks reach toward the sky, and the southern peak is slightly lower than the others. On clear days, tree lines of the peak and sandy beaches are clearly visible, and if the wind permits, it takes two days to arrive there.

This passage concludes that there are two different islands called Usando and Ulleungdo. It further records that the islands are clearly visible and one can reach the islands in two days with a good wind. The descriptions are essentially the same as those in "Geographical Gazetteer" in the *Annals of King Sejong*. As noted above, *Korean Government Opinion 2* emphasizes this fact and states that "[it] goes without saying that Usando and Ulleungdo are two different islands."[47]

Objections by the Japanese Government and Japanese Scholars

In the *Revised and Augmented Survey of the Geography of Joseon* is a passage which states, "According to one report, Usan[do] and Ulleung[do] are one island."[48] This passage, like the passage in the "Geographical Gazetteer" in the *History of Goryeo*, gives the impression that the two-island theory was not an established theory. The Japanese government reiterated this in its *Japanese Government Opinion 2*.

Japanese scholars also raised issue with maps included in the *Revised and Augmented Survey of the Geography of Joseon*, these being the *Map of the Eight Provinces* (K. *Paldo chongdo*) and the *Map of Gangwon-do*

---

47 The passage may be found in Shin Yong-Ha et al., *Dokdo yeongyugwon jaryo ui tamgu*, vol. 4, 252 (Korean), 270 (English).

48 The passage may be found in Lee Sang-Tae, *Saryo ga jeungmyeong haneun Dokdo neun Hanguk ttang*, 172.

Province (K. *Gangwondo jido*). They claimed that Usando was drawn approximately the same size as Ulleungdo, and not very much smaller. They argued that Usando was not drawn to the east of Ulleungdo, rather to the west, therefore, near the middle of the Korean Peninsula. They concluded that all of these claims show the lack of understanding and ignorance of the Joseon government.

At the head of Japanese objections is Kawakami Kenzō, who served as the deputy director of the Treaties Bureau in the Ministry of Foreign Affairs. In August 1953, he submitted a report titled "Territorial Right of Takeshima." Since then, he has been consistently developing the logic that Takeshima (Dokdo) is Japanese territory. In 1966, a compilation of his arguments was published as *Studies in the Historical Geography of Takeshima* (J. *Takeshima no rekishi chirigaku-teki kenkyū*). This book became the most referenced book among Japanese scholars and government officials in arguing that Dokdo is Japanese. Kawakami concluded, "As it seems, the Usan and Ulleung Two Island Theory is completely abstract, and is in no way based on any historical facts or real knowledge."[49] This Japanese argument is called the "One-Island Theory" or the "One-Island Two-Names Theory," and has been the position of the Japanese government in diplomatic cables since 1954.

---

49 Kawakami Kenzō, *Takeshima no rekishi chirigaku-teki kenkyū* [Studies in the historical geography of Takeshima] (Tokyo: Kokin shoin, 1966), 114. Kawakami Kenzō was born in Taipei in 1909. He graduated from Kyoto Imperial University's faculty of letters in 1933. He worked as a teacher in Taipei, and towards the end of World War II he worked as a civilian in the headquarters of the Japanese army. In the postwar period, he entered the Ministry of Foreign Affairs and eventually served as Japanese minister to the Soviet Union. After his death in 1995, Kokin Shoin, which had published *Takeshima no rekishi chirigaku-teki kenkyū*, printed a new edition. Kim Young-Koo, "Dokdo yeong-yugwon e gwanhan gibon ipjang ui jaejeongnip" [Re-correction of the basic position on the territorial rights over Dokdo], in *Dokdo yeongyugwon yeongu nonjip* [Dokdo territorial right research collection], ed. Dokdo Institute (Seoul: Dokdo Research Conservation Association, 2002), 95 footnote 7.

The Counterarguments of the Korean Government and Korean Scholars

In *Korean Government Opinion 2*, the Korean government argued that the Japanese government was using the *Revised and Augmented Survey of the Geography of Joseon* and the "Geographical Gazetteer" of the *Annals of King Sejong* inappropriately because it had failed to analyze the contexts from which these documents had appeared.[50]

The Korean government noted that during a period when geographical knowledge was less developed, it is only natural that the same region was given different names. They noted that a leading figure in Japanese academia studying Dokdo, Tabohashi Kiyoshi, wrote that "during the early Meiji, a time of deficient geographical knowledge, Matsushima (Songdo) and Takeshima (Jukdo) both were names of one island, Ulleungdo, which was later called Ulleungdo and Takeshima. Simultaneously, Takeshima, a name for Ulleungdo, was designated." [51]

Lee Han-key's argument against the Japanese government's position follows the same line of reasoning. His explanation is as follows:

> During former times of underdeveloped geographical knowledge, it is inevitable that different names are created to name an identical place, and that the names are then used interchangeably as the real or official name. This often leads to a two places-two names phenomenon. There are so many instances in which this happens that it is virtually impossible to fully enumerate every instance. [. . .] Dokdo is one of those instances in which Ulleungdo and Usando combined to form Usanguk, and once Usanguk collapsed, naturally the name changed to "Usando," which was interchangeable with "Ulleungdo" until Usando was separated to

---

50 The text cited may be found in Shin Yong-Ha et al., *Dokdo yeongyugwon jaryo ui tamgu*, vol. 4, 253.

51 Tabohashi's article was cited in *Korean Government Opinion 2*. Ibid., 254.

refer to Dokdo. Therefore, the development of the Usan-Ulleung same island theory accurately reflects the state of knowledge from the period when "Ulleungdo" was used to refer to as "Usando."[52]

Also, on the problem of maps, Lee Han-key stated the following by referencing Choe Nam-seon's article:

In the beginning, Usan was the name of the country, and Ulleung was the name of the island recorded in the *History of the Three Kingdoms*. By the time of Goryeo, heterogeneous use of the name led to the creation and use of different names, such as Mureung (武陵), Ureung (羽陵), Mureung (舞陵), and Ulleung (蔚陵). Moreover, along with the development of real maps and documents, the different names were used interchangeably, which made the content of the name different from person to person. This is why Usan, the original name of Ulleungdo, was changed and used to name another island. It is hypothesized that Usan was probably the name of Dokdo, which is located due southeast of the main island, Ulleungdo. Therefore, the expressions "Usando" and "Ulleungdo," as used in the mid-Joseon period, were attached to Ulleungdo. And the expression "Dokdo" was attached to Usando by the late Joseon period. In this way, the fact that the name Usando was applied to Dokdo is very natural.[53]

On the issue of incorrect expressions on maps, Shin Yong-Ha blamed "immature map development and lack of geographical knowledge." He noted that scholars drew these maps without having actually been to

---

52 Lee Han-key, *Hanguk ui yeongto*, 236.

53 Ibid., 237; Choe Nam-seon, "Ulleungdo wa Dokdo" [Ulleungdo and Dokdo], *Seoul Shinmun*, August 10–September 7, 1953.

the islands.[54] Furthermore, he stressed that all Joseon maps drawn after the eighteenth century placed Usando to the east of Ulleungdo, where Dokdo lies. Maps will be discussed in detail in Chapter 4.

Westerners Influenced by the *Map of the Eight Provinces* on the Question of Ulleungdo and Usando

The *Map of the Eight Provinces* in the *Revised and Augmented Survey of the Geography of Joseon* seems to have influenced Westerners. Note again that this map placed Usando to the west of Ulleungdo and placed the two islands very close to each other.

A map of Joseon drawn by a French cartographer and known as *Carte de la Corée, sans titre* placed both Ulleungdo and Usando close to the mainland. Although it is uncertain who drew the map, Li Jin-mieung suggested that the map was compiled between 1550 and 1600.[55]

Considering that the *Map of the Eight Provinces* was published in 1531, if *Carte de la Corée, sans titre* was indeed drawn between 1550 and 1600, it is possible that the latter map was influenced by the *Map of the Eight Provinces*. At any rate, *Carte de la Corée, sans titre* is the first map drawn by a foreigner that confirmed the close proximity of Ulleungdo and Usando to the mainland.

Roughly around the same time period, a reproduction of *Map of the World* (C. *Tianxia yuditu*; K. *Cheonha yeojido*) compiled by Wang Pan, a high-ranking official in the Ming China government, was brought to Joseon by Korean envoys to the Ming court. This map was revised by Joseon cartographers between 1603 and 1650 to become *Map of the World, Korean Version* (K. *Joseon-bon Cheonha yeojido*). This map

---

54 Shin Yong-Ha, *Hanguk gwa Ilbon ui Dokdo yeongyugwon nonjaeng*, 61.

55 Li Jin-mieung, *Dokdo: Jirisang ui jae balgyeon*, 175.

shows Usando to the west of Ulleungdo, and both islands are located near the mainland.[56]

Later, under the direction of Qing China's Kangxi Emperor, Jean-Baptiste Regis, a French priest in China, surveyed China and drew the *Atlas of the Chinese Empire* in 1717. Based on this map, J. B. d'Anville, the renowned French geographer, drew *Carte du Royaume de Corée* in 1732. This was the first map of Joseon compiled by a Westerner. Because *Carte du Royaume de Coree* was based on the *Atlas of the Chinese Empire*, in which Ulleungdo was called "Balleungdo," and Usando as "Cheonsando," those islands were expressed in the map as Fan-ling-tao and Tchian-chan-tao, respectively. *Carte du Royaume de Coree* also places Usando to the west of Ulleungdo and both islands close to the mainland.[57]

D'Anville's map influenced many later mapmakers. The British geographer Emanuel Bowen's *Map of Joseon*, compiled in 1752, the French navy hydrographer Jacques N. Bellin's *Carte de la Corée*, and the French mathematician Rigobert Bonne's *Chinese Tartary*, all referenced d'Anville's work. Therefore, Ulleungdo and Usando were depicted in the manner of d'Anville.[58] Maps of China or Joseon compiled after these works were almost always compiled in the same way as their predecessors. As Chapter 4 will address, it was not until Westerners discovered Ulleungdo in the late 1700s and Usando in the mid-1800s that the names and locations of the islands were corrected.

---

56 Ibid.

57 Ibid., 175–179; Lee Sang-Tae, *Saryo ga jeungmyeong haneun Dokdo neun Hanguk ttang*, 133.

58 Ibid., 135–137.

The Korea-Japan Controversy Over Specific Passages

Let us consider again the "Geographical Gazetteer" in *History of Goryeo* and the "Geographical Gazetteer" in the *Annals of King Sejong*. How do the evaluations of the excerpts from these two gazetteers, which mention Dokdo being visible from Ulleungdo in good weather, differ from the respective arguments of Korea and Japan?

The Korean government and scholars argue that the references in these texts are undeniable evidence showing that the Joseon government understood Dokdo and Ulleungdo to be two different islands. They explain that their arguments are conclusive in nature because it is true what they say about the visibility of Dokdo from Ulleungdo and, also, the fact that it really is possible to sail to Dokdo from Ulleungdo in two fair days.

However, the Japanese government and Japanese scholars interpret the texts differently. For instance, Kawakami argued that Dokdo is not, as a practical matter, visible from Ulleungdo. He argued that Dokdo is only visible from a certain peak on Ulleungdo at a certain elevation, which, during the Joseon period, was too overgrown for people to access. Moreover, even if a person reached that elevation, it would not have been possible for him to see Dokdo due to thick tree lines.

Kawakami arrived at this conclusion via a mathematical equation, $D = 2.09$, that calculated visibility, in which D represents nautical miles, H represents the height (in meters) of an object above the surface of the water, and h represents the height of optical visibility. Kawakami first calculated the highest point of Dokdo, Seodo peak, as 157 meters. Then he calculated the height of optical visibility as 4 meters, considering a person whose height is 1.5 meters is standing on top of a 2.5 meter-high stand. These figures give a final distance between Dokdo and Ulleungdo of 30 nautical miles.

$$D = 2.09(\sqrt{157}+\sqrt{4}\,)$$
$$\approx 2.09(12.5 + 2)$$
$$\approx 30.305$$

This equation therefore shows that at the time when the Joseon texts were being compiled, visibility was only thirty nautical miles. Therefore, Dokdo, at forty-nine nautical miles away, was not visible. In other words, Usando, an island that Joseon gazetteers recorded as visible from Ulleungdo, is not actually Dokdo. Kawakami added that a person is able to see Dokdo from twenty nautical miles due southeast from Ulleungdo.[59] The Japanese government accepted Kawakami's claims unequivocally. Later, Ōkuma Ryōichi also presented the same argument.[60]

In response, Lee Han-key used a figure from the Corean Alpine Association for the highest point of Dokdo, 174 meters, instead of the 157 meters used by Kawakami. Lee's calculation for h also differed. While Kawakami's figure was four meters, Lee's calculation was 985 meters since a person is staring at Dokdo from the highest point of Ulleungdo. In this case, $D = 2.09(\sqrt{174}+\sqrt{985})=2.09(13.19+31.39) \approx 93.17$.

In other words, from the highest point on Ulleungdo, the farthest visible range is ninety-three nautical miles, which guarantees the visibility of Dokdo, only forty-nine nautical miles away. Even if one does not climb the highest peak on Ulleungdo, and only climbs 120 meters and looks to the southeast, according to this equation, one is able to see Dokdo. Also, because it is possible to see Dokdo from twenty nautical miles from Ulleungdo, Lee stated that it is only logical to accept the visibility comments made in the *Annals of King Sejong* "Geographical

59 Kawakami, *Takeshima no rekishi chirigakuteki kenkyū*, 279–283.

60 Ōkuma Ryōichi, *Takeshima shikō: Takeshima (Dokutō) to Utsuryūtō no bunkenshi-teki kōsatsu*, Tokyo: Hara shobō, 1968.

Gazetteer."[61]

A series of arguments and counterarguments by both sides continued. A different case was made by Shimojō Masao. He first criticized Kawakami and Okuma, stating that both scholars approached the problem from the incorrect premise that "Dokdo is visible from Ulleungdo." Shimojō believed that the visibility comment in the *Annals of King Sejong* "Geographical Gazetteer" should be read as describing the view of Ulleungdo from the mainland. His interpretation was that "Usan and Ulleung are one island, starting at three magnificent peaks. When the sea is clear, the trees on the mountain are immediately visible." Shimojō argued that the correct interpretation of the text is, "From the mainland coast of the East Sea, Ulleungdo is visible along with its neighboring islands." And he pointed out that there is an island called Jukseo, a much smaller island, next to Ulleungdo. He therefore argued that the Korean argument is incorrect and inconceivable.

Shimojō referred to the *Chungwanji* (春官志), an encyclopedic text compiled by Yi Maeng-hyu and requested by King Yeongjo himself in 1745 that discusses Yeongjo's executive and legal duties and precedents. Using this text, he argued that Usan, Ureung, Ulleung, Mureung, Gijuk, and others were all used as names of Ulleungdo. Furthermore, he asserted that scholars from the late Joseon period, such as An Jeong-bok and Yi Yu-won, should be read as stating that Ulleungdo and the island next to it are visible from the mainland, not from Ulleungdo.[62]

---

61 Lee Han-key, *Hanguk ui yeongto*, 232–234. A Korean scholar of Dokdo calculated the distance between Ulleungdo and Dokdo using many different mathematical equations and argued that one can see the top of Dokdo from an elevation of 86 meters on Ulleungdo. (Chung Tae-Man, "Dokdo munje ui suhakjeok jeopgeun: Dokdo neun wae jirijeok yeoksajeok euro uri ttang i doel su bak e eomneunga?" [A mathematical approach to the Dokdo issue: Why is it inevitable that Dokdo is our land geographically and historically?], *Dokdo yeongu* 5 [December 2008], 177–178.)

62 Shimojō Masao, "Takeshima mondai kō" [Considerations on the Takeshima issue], *Gendai Koria* 361 (1996), 66; Shimojō Masao, "'Jukdo' ga Hanguk ryeong iraneun geungeo neun waegok dwaeeo itda" [Evidence of Korean possession of 'Jukdo' is fabricated], *Hanguk nondan* (*Monthly Korea Journal*) (May 1996), 148–150. Originally published in Japanese, Shimojō's article was translated into Korean by the journal *Hanguk nondan* and published in the May 1996 issue, pages 144–159. Shimojō

Kim Byungryull, an expert in international law, responded to Shimojō's argument. He noted that the text in the *Revised and Augmented Survey of the Geography of Joseon*, which reads, "Also known as Mureung and Ureung [. . .] it takes two days to get there," can be interpreted to mean that the two islands are visible from the mainland, or that the two islands are visible from each other. However, Kim maintained that it is only logical and sensible if the quote is interpreted in the second way, that is, that the two islands are visible from each other. As will be shown in Chapter 3, texts written before An Yong-bok's expedition, in which An proved that Usan and Ulleung are two different islands, are in error.

Shimojō's interpretation of *Chungwanji* was also challenged by Park Byoungsup, a prominent Korean Dokdo researcher. He examined in detail comments in the *Chungwanji* which explain that Usan was Usanguk in the Silla period. Park argued that Usan and Ulleung should be interpreted as the same island.[63]

---

pointed out that about 40 percent of the original text was not translated in the version printed in translation.

63 The debate between Shimojō and Kim Byungryull is introduced in detail in Kim Byungryull, *Dokdo nya Dakkesima nya*, chapter 12, 285–376. Kim's rebuttal to Shimojō's statement may be found on page 318. Park Byoungsup, "Simojo Masao (下條正男) ui nonseol ul bunseok hada (2)" [Examining Shimojō Masao's arguments (2)], *Dokdo yeongu* 7 (December 2009), 122–124.

6 Records from the *Annals of King Seongjong*

So far, we have discussed the two-island theory which states that Usando and Ulleungdo are two different islands. Nonetheless, it is necessary to point out that there are historical records that use names other than Usando.

The Joseon Government Acknowledges Sambongdo as Dokdo

Since the coronation of King Seongjong, the ninth King of Joseon, there were rumors about an island called Sambongdo, a three-peaked island, in the middle of the East Sea within Gangwon-do. King Seongjong therefore appointed Park Jong-won[64] as Sambongdo inspector (K. *Sambongdo gyeongchagwan*) and ordered him to find the island. In 1472, Park Jong-won, along with an entourage composed of Japanese-language and Chinese-language translators, sailed from Uljin Port. However, according to the thirty-first volume of the *Revised and*

---

[64] Park Jong-won's military career began during the reign of King Seongjong. Later, he was a key figure in the dethronement of King Yeonsangun and the enthronement of King Jungjong.

Enlarged Edition of the Reference Compilation of Documents on Korea
(K. *Jeungbo munheon bigo*), Park failed to reach Sambongdo due to
strong rain and waves and had to spend a night on Ulleungdo.[65] This
record proved that Sambongdo indeed existed beyond Ulleungdo and
supports the two-island theory.

Despite the failure of Park's expedition, interest in Sambongdo did not
waver. On the contrary, according to a phrase from that time, interest in
the "island that no one has set foot on" increased. In addition, because of
a rumor that people of Gangwon-do were living on this island to avoid
taxes and compulsory military service, interest did not fade. This worried
the Joseon government, which formed a special expeditionary group to
search for the island. This group failed to find the island, however.

King Seongjong continued the search. In 1476, the governor of
Yeongan-do (present-day Hamgyeong-do province) Yi Geuk-gyun
sent people to search for Sambong. The results of the expedition were
reported to the Joseon government in the following manner:

In accordance with the central government's order, the people of Yeon-
gando deployed by the provincial governor Yi Geuk-gyun, including Kim
Ja-ju, Song Yeong-ro, Kim Heung, Kim Han-gyeong, Yi Oh-eul-mang,
and twelve others, sailed from Ong-gumi Port on five military-grade
ships provided by Yi Geuk-gyun on the sixteenth day of the ninth
month. On the same day, the group arrived at Jicheongam, Buryeong
[County], and spent the night. On the eighteenth day, the group arrived
in Maleungdae, Gyeongwon [County]. On the twenty-fifth day, the
group anchored at a location approximately 7–8 nautical miles west of
Sambongdo and stared at the island.

---

65 *Revised and Enlarged Edition of the Reference Compilation of Documents on Korea* is a revised version
of *Dongguk munheon bigo* and was composed by King Yeongjo. The text was published in 1908
during the reign of King Sunjong. The original text is transcribed on page 185 of Lee Sang-Tae,
Saryo ga jeungmyeong haneun Dokdo neun Hanguk ttang.

According to Kim Ja-ju's reports, when the group stared at Sambongdo from where they were anchored, there were three rocks in line on the north side of the island. Next, there was a small-sized island and rocks in line, then a middle-sized island. To the west of the middle-sized island there was another small-sized island. All of the islands have flowing seawater, and thirty or so doll-like figures are in between the islands. Kim Ja-ju and the other twelve people were afraid of the rocks, so they did not attempt to land on the island. Instead, they drew the shape of the island and brought it back.[66]

The important point that should be noted about this report in the *Annals of King Seongjong* (K. *Seongjong sillok*) is the fact that the existence of Sambongdo was proven. In other words, questions and theories on the existence of Sambongdo were answered.

An additional point to be addressed is the fact that this record provides compelling proof that Sambongdo is today's Dokdo. As described in Chapter 1, Dokdo appears as if there are three peaks in line. Also mentioned in Chapter 1, there were many sea lions around Dokdo in the past. Perhaps the expedition mistook sea lions as "doll-like figures."

Combining these points, the Korean representatives argued in *Korean Government Opinion 1* that the Sambongdo which Kim Ja-ju saw is today's Dokdo. They added that Kim Ja-ju's report is also recorded in the *Augmented Survey of the Geography of Joseon*.[67] Korean historians such as Shin Sok-ho and Shin Yong-Ha also have concluded that Sambongdo is Dokdo.[68]

---

66 This report was recorded in volume 72 of *Seongjong sillok*. See Ibid., 171.

67 The English-language manuscript of *Korean Government Opinion 1* may be found in Shin Yong-Ha et al., *Dokdo yeongyugwon jaryo ui tamgu*, vol. 3 (Seoul: Dokdo Research Conservation Association, 2000), 432–442. Mention of Kim Ja-ju is found on page 435.

68 Shin Sok-ho, "Dokdo ui naeryeok" [The origin of Dokdo], in *Dokdo*, ed. Daehan Gongnonsa (Seoul: Daehan Gongnonsa, 1965), 21–22; Shin Yong-Ha, *Dokdo ui minjok yeongtosa yeongu*, 87.

An exception among Japanese scholars, Kajimura supported the Korean government's interpretation and suggested that Sambongdo is Dokdo. He wrote, "After comparing the drawings from records, [Sambongdo seems to] match the shape of Dokdo. [...] Staring at Dokdo from the east, Dongdo and Seodo overlap, therefore the 'middle-sized island' includes both islands, and the mention of 'flowing seawater' means that the waves are high enough to cover the small islands or rocks around Dokdo."[69]

The Counterarguments of Japanese Scholars and the Rebuttals of Korean Scholars

The majority of Japanese scholars and government officials denied the Korean arguments. In *Japanese Government Opinion 2*, they stated that the assertion that Kim Ja-ju's report was recorded in the *Augmented Survey of the Geography of Joseon* is "erroneous." They added that "Kim Ja-ju's report is only recorded in the *Annals of King Sejong*."[70]

On this point, both sides were wrong. The argument that Kim Ja-ju's report was included in the *Augmented Survey of the Geography of Joseon* is erroneous. However, the Japanese government's argument that Kim's report is found only in the *Annals of King Sejong* also is incorrect. As discussed above, Kim's text is recorded in the *Annals of King Seongjong*.

Kawakami speculated that the Sambongdo that Kim Ja-ju supposedly saw was not Dokdo, but rather was the northern cliffs of Ulleungdo. Other Japanese scholars, including Ueda, Taijudō, and Tabata Shigejirō, agreed and stated that there are a number of islands with three peaks

---

69 Kajimura, "Ilbon ttang jujang eun paengchang – singminjuui sosan," 616–617.

70 The following passage may be found in Shin Yong-Ha, *Dokdo yeongyugwon jaryo ui tamgu*, vol. 4, 218.

near Ulleungdo.[71] During the reigns of King Jeongjo and King Gojong in the late Joseon period, Jeong Won-yong composed *Munheon chwallok*, in which he wrote that Ulleungdo is Usando and also Sambongdo. In detail, he wrote, "Ulleungdo is located in the sea east of Uljin. [. . .] Much bamboo is collected from that island; thus, it is also known as Jukdo. And due to the three peaks of the island, it is also known as Sambongdo. Usan, Ureung, Ulleung, Mureung, Gijuk, and others are names that originated from the pronunciation of the name." The Japanese government and scholars used this record as evidence to support an argument that Ulleungdo, Usando, and Sambongdo are all the same island.[72]

In response, the Korean government and Korean scholars claimed in *Korean Government Opinion 2* that Jeong Won-yong's *Munheon chwallok* is but a personal diary, thus it need not be considered seriously.[73]

The rebuttal by the Japanese side provided other records as evidence, such as Yi Su-gwang's *Topical Discourses of Jibong* (K. *Jibong yuseol*), completed in 1614 during the reign of King Gwanghaegun. In the second volume of this book, Yi Su-gwang wrote, "Ulleungdo is also known as Mureung or Ureung. [. . .] It was called Usanguk during the Silla period."[74] Using this statement, the Japanese government argued that Ulleungdo and Usanguk are the same island. Moreover, it is not justified or appropriate to argue against using or referencing personal records as opposed to government records. Japanese scholars asserted that "it

---

71 Ueda Toshio, "Dakesima ui gwisok eul dulleossan Il-Han bunjaeng" (in Japanese) [Japan-Korea controversy over the return of Dokdo], 29; Kim Byungryull, "Dokdo yeongyugwon e daehan Ilbon cheuk ui jujang jeongni (整理)" [The collection of Japanese arguments on territorial rights over Dokdo] (Seoul: Dokdo Research Conservation Association, 2002), 211.

72 The section referencing *Munheon chwallok* may be found in ibid., 218–219.

73 Verbale note from the representatives of the Republic of Korea in Japan sent on September 25, 1954. Ibid., 254.

74 The original text may be found in Shin Yong-Ha et al., *Dokdo yeongyugwon jaryo ui tamgu*, vol. 1, 153. Yi Su-gwang held the post of headmaster of National Academy ([*Seonggyungwan*] *daesaseong*) during the reign of King Gwanghaegun. After King Gwanghaegun was dethroned and King Injo enthroned, Yi held the post of minister of rites (K. *Ijo panseo*).

is obvious and necessary to study, compare, and analyze all sources, personal or official, to determine history."[75] In response, Lee Han-key argued, "It is not right to put so much weight on personal records when proving history."[76]

Korean scholars demonstrated that official records of the Joseon government show that Ulleungdo and Usando are two different islands and that it takes at least one day to reach Sambongdo from Ulleungdo. More importantly, they pointed out that the adjacent smaller islands around Ulleungdo, including Jukseo, are very close to Ulleungdo. These islands are visible from Ulleungdo regardless of the weather conditions and therefore are very different from the descriptions of Sambongdo. Combining such arguments, Korean scholars concluded that Sambongdo is not an island adjacent to Ulleungdo.

For example, Lee Han-key carefully explained that "among the Joseon people, there was a clear indication that Sambongdo was located some-where in the East Sea, and that it was a separate island from Ulleungdo. Moreover, there are only Ulleungdo and Dokdo in the East Sea. There are no other islands. While the geographical knowledge of Koreans was vague, they were not ignorant."[77] Shin Yong-Ha also stated that Sambongdo was then called Usando and now is called Dokdo.[78]

Did the Joseon government in fact find Sambongdo? After Kim Ja-ju's group returned from their expedition with a diagram of Sambongdo, King Seongjong continued to send expeditions in search of the island. However, many inspectors ordered to sail were afraid of the treacherous waters and never boarded their ships. This did not stop King Seong-jong's orders to search for the island, although his efforts were fruitless.

---

75 Lee Han-key, *Hanguk ui yeongto*, 239.

76 Ibid.

77 Ibid.

78 Shin Yong-Ha, *Hanguk gwa Ilbon ui Dokdo yeongyugwon nonjaeng*, 62 footnote 31.

In 1483, thirteen years after the Kim Ja-ju expedition had returned, the Joseon government finally concluded that Sambongdo was a non-existent island.

The Joseon government then executed Kim Han-gyeong, the first person to spread rumors about Sambongdo, and Kim's ten-year-old daughter, Kim Gwi-jin, was made a government slave. This tragedy is recorded in the *Annals of King Seongjong*. Shin Yong-Ha lamented "the brave people who worked only for their country and the King and died under false accusations, victims of an absolute monarchy and the tyranny and plots of a dirty *yangban* bureaucracy."[79]

---

79 Shin Yong-Ha et al., *Dokdo yeongyugwon jaryo ui tamgu*, vol. 1, 147.

7 Summary

Records from the Joseon government show that Usando and Ulleungdo are two different islands that belonged to Joseon. The Korean government and Korean scholars use this evidence as the foundation of their argument that Ulleungdo and Usando have been Korean territory since the Silla period. They argue that Usando is Dokdo.

Some records state that Usando and Ulleungdo are the same island. The Japanese government and Japanese scholars use these records as the evidential base to argue against their Korean counterparts. As will be addressed in the next chapter, An Yong-bok, who was active in the mid-Joseon period, proved that Ulleungdo and Usando are two different islands. From that time on, the Joseon government aggressively investigated these islands to spread confidence that the two islands belong to Joseon.

The Conflict between Joseon and Japan over Ulleungdo and Usando, and An Yong-bok's Confrontation with Japan

Chapter 3

1 The Genesis of the Ulleungdo Dispute, or the "Takeshima Incident"

The Korean-Japanese Controversy over "Acknowledgement"

Since the reign of King Taejong, the Joseon government has developed policies toward Ulleungdo and its adjacent islands. The resource-rich coastal waters were a common fishing ground for those who sought to circumvent government control. However, after the Japanese invasion of Joseon in 1592, the Joseon government lost some influence in the region compared to before the war. This ultimately led to Japanese fishermen establishing themselves in these waters.

Joseon people considered the Japanese fishing in the region as aggressive and invasive. This was detailed in Yi Su-gwang's *Topical Discourses of Jibong*. Yi explained, "Recently, Japanese have occupied Gijukdo, which is also known as Ulleungdo." During this period, Japanese knew Ulleungdo as Takeshima or Iso Takeshima.[80]

On September 25, 1954, Japan's Ministry of Foreign Affairs sent a diplomatic message called *Japanese Government Opinion 3* part III (2) to the representatives of the Republic of Korea in Japan. The Ministry of

---

80 The original text may be found in Shin Yong-Ha et al., *Dokdo yeongyugwon jaryo ui tamgu*, vol. 1, 153.

Foreign Affairs asserted that Korea could not prove that it had exercised sovereignty over Takeshima "in the old days." The Japanese, however, have not only controlled Ulleungdo, but also used Ulleungdo since the "old days." The summary of their argument is as follows:

First, according to *Gonki,* an ancient Japanese text written in 1004, the Japanese knew Ulleungdo as Uruma-no-shima, or Uruma Island. According to the *History of Goryeo,* Japanese people visited the island from 1379.

Second, after Joseon evacuated Ulleungdo, virtually abandoning it, many Japanese people frequented the island. After the Bunroku no eki (that is, the Imjin War) in 1592, and lasting for approximately 100 years, Ulleungdo was used as a base of operations for fishing and hunting by Japanese.

Third, at this time, another island, Matsushima, was used as a way station for trips to and from Japan. Matsushima provided moorage, abalone fishing, and sea lion hunting, as well. This island is known today as Takeshima.

These facts have been proven by many historical documents, but a map prepared by the Ikeda family during the Edo period following the Shogun's order clearly supports the above. This map shows Matsushima as an island composed of two small islands opposite one another separated by a waterway. This supports the theory that Matsushima is today's Dokdo. Furthermore, this evidence supports the idea that Japanese people of those days already knew Matsushima as Takeshima.[81]

The Korean government's counterargument followed. In *Korean*

---

81 The English-language text and the Japanese-language text from *Japanese Government Opinion 3* may be found in Shin Yong-Ha et al., *Dokdo yeongyugwon jaryo ui tamgu,* vol. 4, 330–332 and 346–348.

Government Opinion 3, January 7, 1959, the representatives of Korea addressed the historical documents presented by the Japanese government. The Opinion stated that those documents show that the "Usando" in the old Joseon documents is in fact today's Dokdo. The representatives added that the Japanese record *Matsushima no ki* makes this point "without a doubt." The Korean representatives argued that because "there is no original map there is no way to counter the Korean government's opinions."[82]

The Fixation of the Tsushima Daimyō: The Ulleungdo Territorial Rights Plans

Let us consider the Japanese fishing industry in the Ulleungdo area. Once the Tsushima daimyō (J. *hanshu*; governor of Tsushima)[83] clearly understood that Joseon was unable to govern Ulleungdo and its adjacent islands, he sought to officially declare Ulleungdo as a part of Japanese territory and to commence Japanese migrations to the island. His plan did not stop there. He thought that once Ulleungdo was officially declared Japanese territory, he should expand the influence of Tsushima in the East Sea further north. He attempted to legitimize his plan to occupy Ulleungdo based upon a historical instance during the Imjin War (1592–1598), when Japanese soldiers, who were falling back from the Joseon-Ming unified forces, used Ulleungdo as a rallying point during the retreat.[84]

---

82 The English-language part of *Korean Government Opinion 3* may be found in pages 330–332, 346–348, 377–378, and 394–395.

83 Some texts have "Tsushima tōshu" (島主) instead of "Tsushima hanshu," but both terms have the same meaning. In an administrative sense, *hanshu* is the correct term, but *tōshu* also was used interchangeably. This position was held by the island's governing family from the fourteenth century at the latest.

84 Yang Tae-jin, *Hanguk dongnip ui sangjing Dokdo*, 65–67.

Thus, in the sixth month of 1614, the Tsushima daimyō sent a document (equivalent to today's diplomatic cable; used as a letter of credence or visa) to the Joseon government office in Dongnae-gun county requesting a guide to Iso Takeshima for the purpose of exploration in accordance with the Edo Shogunate's order.[85]

The Joseon Government Notifies the Tsushima Daimyō that Ulleungdo is Joseon Territory

Yun Su-gyeom, the magistrate of Dongnae-gun, reported this to the central government. The report was soon relayed to the Border Defense Council (K. *Bibyeonsa*), a government office that dealt with diplomatic and border issues. The council ultimately decided to deny the Tsushima daimyō's request by issuing a notice to Tsushima in the ninth month of 1614.

The denial notice concluded that "in [Joseon], the island is known as Ulleungdo," and as shown in the *Augmented Survey of the Geography of Joseon*, "The island belongs to our country." This notice cautioned that the very fact that the Tsushima daimyō wanted to "explore" the island was enough to suspect Japan's intent for the island. The Joseon government made clear that no Japanese person is authorized to live on the island.[86] Several times in this document the Joseon government affirmed that Iso Takeshima, as it was known in Japan, was in fact Ulleungdo, and Joseon territory. This shows that the Joseon government

---

85 See *Byeonnye jipyo*, vol. 17, 502, and *Daily Records of Gwanghaegun* (K. *Gwanghaegun ilgi*). Detailed descriptions based on these primary sources may be found in Kim Byungryull, *Dokdo nya Dakkesima nya*, 109–111; Shin Yong-Ha, *Dokdo ui minjok yeongtosa yeongu*, 97–105; and Yang Tae-jin, *Hanguk dongnip ui sangjing Dokdo*, 65–80.

86 This document was published in 1614 in *Joseon tonggyo daegi* (朝鮮通交大紀). It was referenced in Shin Yong-Ha et al., *Dokdo yeongyugwon jaryo ui tamgu*, vol. 2, 188–191. Records from the Joseon side may be found in Shin Yong-Ha et al., *Dokdo yeongyugwon jaryo ui tamgu*, vol. 1, 155–156.

was explicit in its response vis-à-vis the "Ulleungdo Dispute."

The notice was soon delivered to the Tsushima daimyō. However, Japanese envoys visited Dongnae-gun in 1615 and again "requested authorization to explore the geography of Iso Takeshima." The magistrate of Dongnae-gun at the time, Park Gyeong-eop, in accordance with the central government's policy, denied the request. At this time, Park wrote that, as with the earlier denial, "It is a fact that you are not ignorant of Ulleungdo being a Joseon territory, yet you still come over and scout. What are we to make of this?" He also wrote that the "Iso Takeshima that you speak of is actually Ulleungdo." Park provided a map from China as evidence to prove that Ulleungdo belonged to Joseon.[87]

The Edo Shogunate Authorizes Japanese Fishermen to Enter the Coastal Waters of Ulleungdo and Dokdo

The Japanese government persisted. Three years later, in 1618, the Edo Shogunate accepted the requests of two families, those of Ōya Jinkichi and Murakawa Ichibei, of Yonago, Hōki Province,[88] in present-day Tottori Prefecture, to be issued a "passage to Takeshima license" (that is, a fishing license) to fish in Ulleungdo waters. This government-sanctioned act allowed Japanese fishermen to enter Joseon waters. In 1656, the Edo Shogunate issued the same type of license to the Ōya and the Murakawa families, officially allowing them to fish off the coast of Dokdo.[89]

The Korean legal expert Lee Sang Myeon noted that not once did the

---

87 These passages may be found in the documents composed by Japanese. The original texts may be found in Shin Yong-Ha et al., *Dokdo yeongyugwon jaryo ui tamgu*, vol. 4 (Seoul: Dokdo Research Conservation Association, 2001), 39. Park Gyeong-eop was mentioned in the following, as well: Ōnishi Toshiteru, *Dokdo*, translated by Kwon O-yub and Kwon Jung (Seoul: JENC, 2004), 163.

88 Tottori Province and Shimane Province are in western Honshu.

89 This information may be found in *Japanese Government Opinion 3*. Also see Kawakami, *Dakesima ui yeoksa jirihakjeok yeongu*, 71–72.

Edo Shogunate consult the Joseon government during this process.[90] According to *Japanese Government Opinion 3* part III (2) from 1956, the current Japanese government thought that there was no need for the Edo Shogunate to consult the Joseon government. It stressed that Ulleungdo is an island known to Japanese people from old, and the Joseon government had practically abandoned it. Japan's Ministry of Foreign Affairs repeated this same argument in *Japanese Government Opinion 4*, sent on July 13, 1962.[91]

Let us move now to the fishing practices of the Ōya and Murakawa families along the coast of Ulleungdo. According to *Japanese Government Opinion 4*, the third-generation leader of the Ōya family, Ōya Kyūemon Katsunobu, wrote in a letter dated the thirteenth day of the fifth month of 1681, stating, "[Ships that belong to my family] are docked at an islet on the way to Takeshima. [Takeshima in this period is today's Matsushima in Japanese and Ulleungdo in Korean.] This is a rocky islet with neither grass nor trees." Ōya continued that "our family was granted this island twenty-five years ago (1656) by Abe Shirōgorō and have obtained a small quantity of sea lion oil from it."[92] In *Japanese Government Opinion 4*, the Japanese government asserted that this island was an island where Japanese fishing boats temporarily docked on their passage between Yonago and Ulleungdo. In other words, this island was used as a point of "anchorage" for Japanese fishing vessels leaving the fishing village of Fukuura, Tottori domain, en route to Ulleungdo.

Japanese argue that this Matsushima is known today as "Takeshima" by Japanese people and "Dokdo" by Koreans. *Japanese Government*

---

90 Lee Sang Myeon, "Dokdo yeongyugwon ui jeungmyeong" [Proof of territorial rights over Dokdo], in *Hanguk ui Dokdo yeongyugwon yeongusa* [Research history of Korea's territorial rights over Dokdo], ed. Dokdo Institute (Seoul: Dokdo Institute, 2003), 285.

91 The English-language manuscript of *Japanese Government Opinion 4* may be read in Shin Yong-Ha et al., *Dokdo yeongyugwon jaryo ui tamgu*, vol. 4, 423–462.

92 Ibid., 425 (Japanese), 442 (English).

Opinion 4 suggested that the Ōya family was issued a "passage to Matsu-shima license" [93] by the Edo Shogunate in 1656. The Japanese Ministry of Foreign Affairs stressed the word "issued."

Controversial Interpretations of the Issuance of Fishing Licenses

The Japanese government considers the Takeshima sailing license and the Matsushima sailing license to be evidence that the two islands are Japanese. Specifically, on the topic of the Matsushima sailing license, those issued the license received "the exclusive right to management of the island, including fishing." Therefore, the Ministry of Foreign Affairs argues that Japanese "managed" the island "under official approval" by the government. Moreover, the Ministry of Foreign Affairs argues that Japanese have always known of these islands and considered them to be Japanese territory. [94]

The Japanese government claims that Japanese maintained "effective control and management" of the islands for seventy years beginning in 1618. This is the year in which the Takeshima sailing license was issued. In addition, the Japanese government stressed that even after the Edo Shogunate admitted that Takeshima is Joseon territory and decided "not to manage" the island in the first month of 1696, this did not stop people from going to the island. The Japanese government argued that the fact that the Edo government did not stop people from visiting Matsushima indicates that the Edo Shogunate considered Matsushima to be Japanese territory. Furthermore, the Japanese side stated, "The Korean govern-ment has yet to provide examples and evidence of Joseon management

---

93 Ibid.

94 Ibid., 227–228.

and acknowledgment of Matsushima."[95]

Some Japanese researchers have explained the word "issued" as "received territory" or as "received domain." For instance, Tamura Seizaburō and Ōkuma Ryōichi argued that the two families were issued the licenses, which means that they were given the territorial rights to the islands.[96] In short, the Japanese government argues that the Edo Shogunate effectively controlled and managed Matsushima through the fishing licenses and that the Korean government cannot provide evidence of Joseon's effective control and management. In the words of the international law expert Park Hyun-jin, the Japanese government considered, and attempted to ensure, that this moment in history is the "critical date" in the territorial rights issue.[97]

Korean scholars counter by pointing out that, during the period when the licenses were issued, the Edo Shogunate forbade overseas travel (J. *kaikin seisaku*; K. *haegeum jeongchaek*). The fact that the licenses were issued to the families for travel implicitly means that the Edo Shogunate considered the two islands to be foreign territory. Therefore, these licenses act as evidence supporting the view that the Edo Shogunate knew that the islands were part of Joseon territory.

Second, in written communications between the two families, the expression "Matsushima within Takeshima" (K. *Jukdoji nae Songdo*) was used. This is translated as "Dokdo within Ulleungdo." For instance, they recorded the location of Matsushima in Takeshima by using the statement, ". . . from next year on, in case your ships go to Matsushima within Takeshima. . . ." Also, the two families recorded Matsushima as

---

95 Ibid., 423–427.

96 Tamura Seizaburō, *Shimane-ken Takeshima no shin kenkyū* [New research on Takeshima, Shimane Prefecture] (Shimane-ken, 1963), 4; Ōkuma, *Takeshima shikō*, 83.

97 Park Hyun-jin, "Yeongto, haeyang gyeonggye bunjaeng gwa jido, haedo ui jeunggeo jiwi, gachi: Dokdo gwanllyeon jido, haedo ui beop, jeongchaek, oegyo reul jungsim euro" [The legal status and probative value of maps and charts in international adjudication on territorial/boundary disputes], *Gukjebeop hakhoe nonchong* (*Korean Journal of International Law*) 53, no. 1 (April 2008), 82.

"a small island near Takeshima" (J. *Takeshima kinjō jisodo*), or "Matsu-shima near Takeshima" (J. *Takeshima kinpen Matsushima*). These records show that the families themselves understood Matsushima, or Dokdo, to be an island adjacent to Ulleungdo.[98] It may be extrapolated that since a license to travel to Ulleungdo was already issued, Koreans therefore interpreted this to mean that the Edo Shogunate had issued such a license to travel overseas to Dokdo.[99]

Third, the Korean side argues that the word "issued" was incorrectly interpreted. The word means no more than "respectfully accept with a bow." They state that focusing too much attention on this single word and attributing it too much meaning in explaining the larger picture is an inappropriate application of its significance.[100]

Fourth, the Japanese argument that "Japanese people have managed Matsushima and Takeshima since olden times and considered them part of Japanese territory" fails to take into account the presence of Japanese piracy along the Korean coast during this period. Korean representatives made this observation in *Korean Government Opinion 3*, delivered to the Japanese Ministry of Foreign Affairs on January 7, 1959. This document points out that Japanese pirates had invaded and looted Korean villages on the coast as well as further inland since the Three Kingdoms period. "The fact that Japanese people invaded the coasts . . . is no basis to argue for possession of territorial rights."[101]

Fifth, Park Hyun-jin highlighted a 1998 verdict from the Permanent Court of Arbitration, which held that "a fishing license is not a license

98 Shin Yong-Ha et al., *Dokdo yeongyugwon jaryo ui tamgu*, vol. 2, 221–222.

99 For example, see Shin Yong-Ha, *Hanguk gwa Ilbon ui Dokdo yeongyugwon nonjaeng*, 24. Also see Kim Myungki, "Dokdo ui yeongyugwon e gwanhan Ilbon jeongbu jujang e daehan beopjeok bipan" [Legal criticism of the Japanese government's opinion regarding the territorial right over Dokdo], in *Hanguk ui Dokdo yeongyugwon yeongusa*, ed. Dokdo Hakhoe (Seoul: Dokdo Research Conservation Association, 2003), 248–253.

100 Yang Tae-jin, *Hanguk dongnip ui sangjing Dokdo*, 73.

101 Shin Yong-Ha et al., *Dokdo yeongyugwon jaryo ui tamgu*, vol. 4, 379.

authorizing exploitation of natural resources on land, and thus, the act of issuing a fishing license cannot be deemed an act of establishing effective control and management of territory."[102] This case involved Eritrea, a country in the northeastern part of Africa, and Yemen from the south of the Arabian Peninsula. Eritrea filed the case with the Permanent Court of Arbitration on the issue of territorial rights of islands in the Red Sea. Park stated that this verdict is interesting in the context of the Japanese argument that Dokdo and Ulleungdo are Japanese territories based on the Matsushima and Takeshima sailing licenses discussed above.[103]

---

102 Park Hyun-jin, "Yeongto, haeyang gyeonggye bunjaeng gwa jido," 62–63.
103 Ibid., 63, footnote no. 3.

2 Explanations Drawn from the Official Japanese Government Text *Inshū shichō gakki* (Collection of Survey Records on Oki Province)

The First Appearance of Matsushima in Official Japanese Documents

In 1667, nearly ten years after the Edo Shogunate issued the Matsu-shima sailing license, the official Japanese document *Inshū shichō gakki* (Collection of Survey Records on Oki Province) was compiled.[104] This text has the oldest mention of Matsushima in an official government document. This can be interpreted as the Japanese government's recognition of Matsushima in 1656, the year the Matsushima sailing license was issued.

The author of the book, Saitō Hōsen, also known as Saitō Kansuke, was a bureaucrat in Izumo Province,[105] Matsue domain. He was appointed as a district administrator (J. *gundai*) of Oki Province by the Matsue domain daimyō. *Gundai* was a government post held by a regional official who administered a city under the direct control of the shogunate. At that time, Oki Province was under such direct control.

---

104 The description of Dokdo is in Lee Sang-Tae, *Saryo ga jeungmyeong haneun Dokdo neun Hanguk ttang*, 210.

105 Unshū was called Izumo no kuni and Izumo Province.

Oki Province was composed of an island called Okishima. "Inshū" [Oki Province] and "Okishima" were used interchangeably.[106]

Saitō compiled the *Collection of Survey Records on Oki Province* in 1667, on orders from the daimyō. This book includes a discussion of Japan's northwestern border that has become a controversial topic between the governments of Korea and Japan. Therefore, it is important to provide the original text before discussing the issue.

隱州在北海中 故云隱岐島 [...]
從是南方至雲州美穗關三十五里
辰巳至伯州赤崎浦四十里
未申至石州溫泉津五十八里
自子至卯無可往地
戌亥間行二日 一夜有松島 又一日程有竹島
(俗言磯作島 多竹魚海鹿 按神書所謂五十猛歟)
此二島無人之地 見高麗如自雲州望隱州
然則 日本之乾地以此州爲限矣

This passage mentions two islands. One is Matsushima and the other is Takeshima. Again, at the time, Japan called Dokdo as Matsushima, and Ulleungdo as Takeshima. This should be kept in mind while reading the following passage:

Oki Island is in the middle of the North Sea. Thus, it is called Okishima.

To the south, Mihoseki in Unshū [Izumo Province] is 35 nautical miles away, to the southeast, Akajakiura of Hakushū [Hōki Province] is 40 nautical miles away, and to the southwest, Yunotsu in Iwami Province is

---

106 Hong Seong-keun, "Ilbon ui Dokdo yeongto baeje jochi ui seonggyeok gwa uimi" [Characteristics and meanings of Japan's territorial exclusion of Dokdo], in Dokdo wa Han-Il gwangye: Beop yeok-sajeok jeopgeun [Dokdo and Korea-Japan relations legal and historical approaches], ed. Northeast Asian History Foundation (Seoul: Northeast Asian History Foundation, 2009), 95.

58 nautical miles away. There is no passage that connects them north and east, and to the northwest is [. . .] Matsushima [Songdo in Korean], about two days away. Takeshima is another day away. (According to people, it is called Iso Takeshima [K. Gijukdo], and there is much bamboo, fish, and sea lions. Perhaps this is the Isotake god from *Nihon shoki*.)

These two islands are uninhabited islands and looking at Goryeo is just like looking at Inshū [Oki Province] from Unshū [Izumo Province]. Therefore, the northwest border of Japan ends at this province.

The Different Interpretations of Korea and Japan

The core issue here is that "the northwest border of Japan ends at this province." The Korean government and Korean scholars state that "this province" refers to "Inshū" and, therefore, "Oki Province." The two islands of Takeshima and Matsushima, which are located beyond the border, are Joseon territory. Thus, the *Collection of Survey Records on Oki Province*, which is considered an official document of Japan, recognized Dokdo as part of Joseon territory in 1667.

However, the Japanese government does not understand the document in that way. The Ministry of Foreign Affairs discussed *Collection of Survey Records on Oki Province* for the first time in *Japanese Government Opinion 2*, submitted on February 10, 1954, in which they argued that Matsushima, an island that Koreans call Dokdo, is actually Japanese.[107] Furthermore, through the *Japanese Government Opinion 3*, in which the Ministry of Foreign Affairs addressed *Collection of Survey Records on Oki Province* three times, they interpreted the passage as follows:

---

107 The English-language text may be found in Shin Yong-Ha et al., *Dokdo yeongyugwon jaryo ui tamgu*, vol. 4, 216–231.

First, because directions and distances were marked with Inshū [Oki Province] at the center, Matsushima (Dokdo) and Takeshima (Jukdo) are included in Inshū [Oki Province].

Second, considering the point of view from the expression "looking at Goryeo is just like looking at Inshū from Unshū," it is evident that the islands are Japanese.

Third, "province" does not represent Inshū. "Province" has the same meaning as an island, and therefore the "province" in the book is Ulleungdo.

Fourth, Ulleungdo was compared to the Isotake god in *Nihon shoki*, therefore, the northern border of Japan is Ulleungdo.

Fifth, Japan issued the travel ban policy with regard to Ulleungdo in 1696. Therefore, in 1667, when this text was written, Ulleungdo naturally was thought to be Japan's territory.[108]

Which interpretation is correct? The Korean government, through *Korean Government Opinion 3*, which it sent to Japan on January 7, 1959, stated that the Japanese government "greatly misinterpreted" the passage. In addition, the Korean side concluded that it is clear that when Saitō wrote "province" he really meant "Inshū" (Oki Province; K. *Eunju*) as the title of the text suggests.[109]

Lee Han-key also posed the same argument in criticizing the Japanese government's argument.[110] Kajimura pointed out that the Japanese government's interpretation is incorrect. He stated that the expression from the *Collection of Survey Records on Inshū* should be interpreted in the manner of the Koreans.[111] Needless to say, numerous other Korean

---

108 Ibid., 330.

109 Ibid., 378.

110 Lee Han-key, *Hanguk ui yeongto*, 243 (1996 second edition).

111 Kajimura, "Ilbon ttang jujang eun paengchang – singminjuui sosan," 620.

experts criticized the "misinterpretation" of the Japanese government. Kim Byungryull answered the Japanese government's argument point-for-point.

> First, it is not valid to argue that the marking of distances and directions from Inshū requires that the islands be included in Inshū territory.
>
> In the original text, it is stated that Inshū Mihoseki (reportedly 35 nautical miles away), Hakushū Akajakiura (reportedly 40 nautical miles away), and Sekishū Unotsu (reportedly 58 miles away) are all marked around Inshū, but not as part of Inshū territory. This makes any further review futile. If regions marked with exact distances away from Inshū are not even included in Inshū, how is it possible to include Ulleungdo and Dokdo islands as part of Inshū? The line of thought is not logical. By this logic, the Korean government can argue that Japan is only a couple of days away from Busan, therefore Japan is Korean territory.[112]

Kim Byungryull stated that the second Japanese argument that reads, "'looking at Goryeo is just like looking at Inshū [Oki Island] from Unshū [Izumo],' it is evident that the islands are Japanese[,]" is also illogical and nonsensical. Kim claimed, "This kind of expression originated from oral history and the rumors of Inshū fishermen who worked along the coast of Ulleungdo, not from objective fact. If one records that Busan is visible from Daemado (Tsushima), is Busan then Japanese land? This is absolute nonsense."

The third point was that "province" does not represent Inshū. "Province" also means "island," and therefore the "province" in the book is Ulleungdo. Kim admitted that the word "province" is used interchangeably with the word "island." However, he added, "Such a case

---

112 Kim Byungryull, *Dokdo nya Dakkesima nya*, 176.

of interchangeability is only applied to archipelagos or an island with a governing body." Kim's example of such a case came from *Seongho saseol yuseon*, compiled by An Jeong-bok in the late Joseon period. In the text there is the statement, "Due to An Yong-bok's achievements, a territory was regained." This expression means that the result of An's work was regaining Ulleungdo, Jukseodo, and Dokdo, not merely Ulleungdo.

Kim, in response to the fourth point, argued that "it is wrong to argue that Ulleungdo is Japanese territory because of the name Gijukdo." He wrote that "Seonginbong Peak" of Ulleungdo was also called "Gomsuri" and "Gomsul" by Koreans, and that those two names in Chinese characters are "Gungsung." This means "frightful holy" peak. Even today, the peak is called "Seonginbong Peak." The importance of this will be further unpacked. Yi Pyong-do previously wrote in 1963, that *"gung"* originated from *"gom"* (熊; K. *ung*, meaning bear) and *"sung"* originated from *"sul"* (上; K. *sang*) meaning "up." In this context, "Gungsung" is "Gomsuri" and means "High Mountain" or "Holy Mountain."[113]

Kim's interpretation continued as follows below.

The expression "Gungsung" to refer to Ulleungdo reached Japan, and eventually was written in "Chōsen-koku saiken zenzu" (朝鮮國細見全圖), which was produced by Naniwa Shorin in 1789, in "Chōsen hachidō chizu" compiled by Hayashi [Shihei] in 1860, and in "Chōsen-koku saiken zenzu" (朝鮮國細見全圖) composed in 1870. "Gungsung" is translated too liberally by writing it in katakana as イソタケ and later transferring it back to Chinese characters as Gijukdo (磯竹島), which means that the name did not originate from the name of the Isotake god.

---

113 Yi Pyong-do, "Dokdo ui myeongching e daehan sajeok gochal: Usan, Jukdo myeongchinggo" [Historical contemplation of different names of Dokdo: The study of names: Usando and Takeshima], in *Jo Myeong-gi baksa hwagap ginyeom Bulgyo sahak nonchong* (1963). This article was re-published in *Dokdo*, ed. Daehan Gongnonsa (Seoul: Daehan Gongnonsa, 1965), 67–76, and *Hanguk ui Dokdo yeongyugwon yeongusa*, ed. Dokdo Hakhoe (Seoul: Dokdo Research Conservation Association, 2003), 40–41.

If the name of the island came from the name of the Isotake god, then the islands adjacent to Ulleungdo should have been named in the same manner, yet this did not happen. This fact alone, and the fact that there is not a single island in Japan named after a holy being from Nihonseki, proves the fact that Gijukdo was not named after Isotake.[114]

Kim also criticized the fifth point in reference to the 1696 travel ban policy. His detailed counterarguments were seen also in counterarguments made by other Korean experts, such as Lee Han-key and Shin Yong-Ha. These are summarized below.

At the approximate period when the *Collection of Survey Records on Inshū* was written, Japan was clearly aware that Takeshima and Matsushima were Korean territory. Evidence of this fact is the Edo government's issuance of travel licenses, which were authorizations to conduct trade with foreign countries. The Japanese government states that when the Edo Shogunate issued these licenses, "the owners of this license were also issued 'stamps' (K. *juin*), which allowed those possessing a license to go to sea and fish." This point is reiterated by Kajimura, who argued that it was needless for Japanese fishermen to possess such licenses or stamps for fishing in domestic waters.[115] Conclusively, the fact that the licenses were issued to the Japanese fishermen who wanted to fish in the waters of Ulleungdo and Dokdo proves that Japan understood the two islands to be foreign territory.

To counter this interpretation, the Japanese government redefined the meaning of the stamps. In *Japanese Government Opinion 3*, the Ministry of Foreign Affairs argued that while it is true that the stamps can be regarded as equivalent to a passport, in the case of Takeshima and Matsushima it should be understood as a pass authorizing people

---

114 Kim Byungryull, *Dokdo nya Dakkesima nya*, 176–179.

115 Kajimura, "Ilbon ttang jujang eun paengchang – singminjuui sosan," 620.

to travel to uninhabited islands.[116] Taijudō offered the same interpretation. He stated that it is impossible to equate the sailing license allowing travel to Luzon, in the Philippines, with sailing licenses to unpopulated islands such as Takeshima and Matsushima.[117] However, as shown above, it is undeniable that the stamps had the function of a passport or for permitting foreign trade. This is generally regarded as the Japanese government admitting that, at the time, the islands were under Joseon jurisdiction.

How did the *Collection of Survey Records on Inshū* (隱州視聽合記) Treat Ulleungdo and Dokdo?

The ways in which the *Collection of Survey Records on Inshū* portrayed Takeshima and Matsushima illustrate that the islands were not part of Japanese territory at the time the text was composed. Divided into four volumes, this text described many districts in Oki Island in detail but included not a single word on Matsushima. Concerning Takeshima, the book briefly mentions that "[people from Oki Island] going to Iso Takeshima (Ulleungdo) monitored the weather and wind at a town called Fukuu [on Oki Island] and prayed to the gods for safe return." What does this mean? Hong Seong-keun, a Korean expert on Dokdo, stressed the fact that the author of this text only briefly mentioned Takeshima, unlike other details on actual parts of his area, and this means that Japan did not consider Dokdo and Ulleungdo as part of its territory.[118]

---

116 Japanese and English manuscripts of this document may be found in Shin Yong-Ha et al., *Dokdo yeongyugwon jaryo ui tamgu*, vol. 4, 324–342 and 342–363.

117 Taijudō, "Takeshima funsō," 113.

118 Hong Seong-keun, "Ilbon ui Dokdo yeongto baeje jochi ui seonggyeok gwa uimi," 98.

With regard to the *Collection of Survey Records on Inshū* and territorial rights to Dokdo, Japanese scholars state that even if one concludes that Inshū is located northwest of Japan, this does not mean that Matsushima (Dokdo) becomes Joseon territory. In other words, Japanese scholars acknowledge that "it is wrong to use this record—a record with no single reference to territorial rights—in a controversy over territorial rights."

In response, Hong Seong-keun admitted, "There is no document that explicitly states that Dokdo is Korean territory." He continued, "However, despite the lack of a direct statement, it is wrong to judge the records as completely irrelevant to the discussion of Dokdo territorial rights. As seen earlier, the Japanese government already presented writings with no substantive records as evidence."[119]

---

119 Ibid.

3 An Yong-bok's Negotiation with Japan

Who was An Yong-bok?

As seen in the previous section, in accordance with decisions made by the Edo Shogunate, Japanese fishermen began fishing off the coast of Ulleundgo. As might be expected, skirmishes arose between Joseon and Japanese fishermen. In the spring of 1693, a skirmish occurred between Ulsan fishermen from Joseon and Ōya family fishermen from Japan. These Japanese were fishing with seven boats, and all of the crew members were from Hōki Province, an area in today's Tottori Prefecture. As the fight escalated, the Japanese fishermen requested that representatives from Joseon meet and discuss the matter peacefully. When the Joseon fishermen sent the representatives An Yong-bok and Park Eo-dun, the Japanese kidnapped them and took them to Oki Island. This was the beginning of the An Yong-bok negotiations with Japan.

Unfortunately, there is no document available for confirming An's date of birth, his place of birth, and how he died. There are eleven distinct clans—different lineages known as *bongwan*—in the An family, but his *bongwan* is not known and no one has come forward as his descendant.[120] This is understandable because An was a house servant of Oh Chungchu of Seoul. There is no way to determine under what circumstances he became a servant. All that we know about his birth and youth is that he was born in Dongnae-gun and grew up under a single mother in 3-ho, 14-dong, 1-ri, Jwajacheon, which is today's Jwacheon-dong, Dong-gu, Busan.

The fact that he grew up in Jwacheon-dong, in the Busan area, was significant to An's future. Yi Ik, a Silhak scholar active at that time, wrote in his *Seongho saseol*, "An Yong-bok, from his adolescent years, went in and out of the Japan House (K. *Waegwan*), thus he was fluent in Japanese."[121] Considering that Jwacheon-dong was where the Japan House was located, Yi Ik's records are considered to be more accurate. In *Takeshima zasshi* published in Japan in 1874, it is noted that An spoke Japanese when he first encountered the Japanese sailors.[122] If this is the case, An must have negotiated with the Japanese with the language skills he obtained while he was young by frequenting the Japan House.

An originally served in the navy as an oarsman (or *neungnogun*, the term used at the time) in the Left Gyeongsang Province Naval Base (K. *Gyeongsang Jwasuyeong*). According to the *Revised and Enlarged Edition of the Reference Compilation of Documents on Korea* (K. *Jeungbo munheon bigo*), "Oarsman An Yong-bok of Dongnae spoke Japanese well."[123]

The naval base was located in today's Suyeong-gu, Busan. It was

---

120 The entry in *Sukjong sillok* may be found in Shin Yong-Ha et al., *Dokdo yeongyugwon jaryo ui tamgu*, vol. 1, 205. A detailed study of An Yong-bok is Kim Eui-hwan, and Lee Tae-gil, eds., *An Yong-bok janggun: Ulleung-do – Dokdo ui yeoksa*, expanded edition (Seoul: Chipyeong, 1996). The two examples regarding An Yong-bok's two visits [to Japan] for negotiations are treated in detail in Song Byeong-Ki, *Ulleungdo wa Dokdo: Geu yeoksajeok geomjeung* (Seoul: Yeoksa Gong-gan, 2010), chapters 2–3.

121 The original text may be found in Shin Yong-Ha et al., *Dokdo yeongyugwon jaryo ui tamgu*, vol. 1, 292.

122 Yang Tae-jin, *Hanguk dongnip ui sangjing Dokdo*, 85.

123 The original text may be found in Shin Yong-Ha et al., *Dokdo yeongyugwon jaryo ui tamgu*, vol. 1, 230.

responsible for defending the southwest coast, from the east side of the Nakdonggang River to the Gyeongju area. Due to this, An must have been well aware of coastal geography in the East Sea. It is likely that he later fished in the Ulleungdo waters with fishermen from Ulsan after leaving the military.

An Yong-bok Confronts the Head of Oki Island and the Governor of Hōki Province

As mentioned above, accounts of the An Yong-bok Incident are preserved in Joseon records such as the *Annals of King Sukjong* (K. *Sukjong sillok*), *Daily Records of the Royal Secretariat* (K. *Seungjeongwon ilgi*), *Records of the Border Defense Council* (K. *Bibyeonsa deungnok*), and the *Revised and Enlarged Edition of the Reference Compilation of Documents on Korea*.[124] As will be discussed below, An was arrested for traveling beyond the Joseon border without government authorization and interrogated by the Border Defense Council. He provided a statement.

The An Yong-bok Incident was also noted in Japanese records, such as the *Sangoku tsūkō ichiran*. In May 2005, another document from the Murakami family of Oki Island was discovered. This document, "Genroku kyū heishinen Chōsen fune chakugan ikkan no oboegaki" (hereafter "Murakami Documents"), is a historical account of the investigation of An and other Koreans who arrived in Oki Island in 1693 and 1696.[125]

---

124 Lee Sang-Tae, *Saryo ga jeungmyeong haneun Dokdo neun Hanguk ttang*, 174–185; An Yong-bok's activities in Japan are recorded in detail in *Jeungbo munheon bigo*, vol. 31, "Yeojigo 19: Usan, Ulleungdo jo." This text may be read in Shin Yong-Ha et al., *Dokdo yeongyugwon jaryo ui tamgu*, vol. 1, 230–235.

125 Examples from both the Joseon side and the Japanese side may be read in Lee Sang-Tae, *Saryo ga jeungmyeong haneun Dokdo neun Hanguk ttang*, 206–208. The original text and a translation of the document found in May 2005 may be read in "Jaryo: 2005 nyeon e balgyeon doen An Yong-

At this time, An first confronted the governor of Oki Island[126] stating, "Ulleungdo is only one day away from our country, but is five days away from Japan. Therefore, it is our island." (K. *Ja Ulleung geo aguk il-il jeong geo Ilbon oil jeong bisok aguk ja ho*; 自鬱陵距我國一日程 距日本五日程 非 屬我國者乎). Why is it that you kidnapped Joseon people who set foot in Joseon territory?"

According to An's testimony recorded in volume 31 of the *Revised and Enlarged Edition of the Reference Compilation of Documents on Korea*, the governor of Oki Island understood that he was unable to make a determination with regard to An. Therefore, he sent An and Park to his superior, the governor of Hōki Province. However, before the case reached the governor of Hōki Province, An continued to assert that Ulleungdo was Joseon territory and requested that Japanese sailors who cross the border without the Joseon government's authorization be stopped.[127] According to the "Murakami Documents," An Yong-bok was born in 1654, and at the time of the incident, he was a tall, thirty-nine-year-old man [Korean age],[128] and had dark skin with a pockmarked face. The documents described Park Eo-dun as being from Ulsan and thirty-one [Korean age] years of age at that time.

The governor of Hōki Province was well aware that Ulleungdo belonged to Joseon. Therefore, he treated An and Park well. When he sent An and Park to his superior in Edo, he even delivered a special request, pleading for the two men, stating that "since Ulleungdo is not Japanese territory, An and Park deserve favorable arrangements." The Edo Shogunate accepted the request. Afterward, upon the release of An

bok ui jinsul jaryo" [Document: Testimony of An Yong-bok, found in 2005], *Dokdo yeongu (The Journal of Dokdo)* (December 2005), 231–310.

126 Due to its small geographical size, Oki Province could not form a domain (J. *han*). Thus the highest government official in Oki Province did not hold the title of *hanshu* (藩主).

127 The original text may be found in Shin Yong-Ha et al., *Dokdo yeongyugwon jaryo ui tamgu*, vol. 1, 230.

128 "Jaryo: 2005 nyeon e balgyeon dwen An Yong-bok ui jinsul jaryo," 290.

and Park, the governor of Hōki Province gave them a note which stated that "Ulleungdo is not Japanese territory."

In Japan, the incident involving the Joseon fishermen An and Park is known as the "Takeshima Incident of Genroku," or simply as the "Takeshima Incident."[129] Here, Genroku is the era name that the Edo Shogunate used at that time. The first year of the Genroku era was 1688.

Different Interpretations of the An Yong-bok Incident

The Japanese government and Japanese scholars have refuted the official Joseon court records regarding An. In *Japanese Government Opinion 2* and *Japanese Government Opinion 4*, the Ministry of Foreign Affairs argued that "An Yong-bok's testimony has many errors." The Ministry continued, "It is clear that An Yong-bok exaggerated his testimony and added false information to make it seem grandiose" as an excuse for his wrongdoings. The Ministry concluded that "numerous aspects of this testimony are false and erroneous in many respects," therefore, it is "fictitious."[130]

Shimojō argued that volume 17 of *Byeonnye jipyo* (邊例集要) shows that An and Park were not actually kidnapped during the confrontation with the fishermen. He asserts that the two men were captured rather than kidnapped because they failed to escape with the other fishermen who quickly fled.[131] However, this is not true. In fact, it is recorded in

---

129 Original documents regarding the "Takeshima Incident" may be found in Shin Yong-Ha et al., *Dokdo yeongyugwon jaryo ui tamgu*, vol. 4, 11–26.

130 Ibid., 330, 348, and 429.

131 Shimojō Masao, "'Jukdo' ga Hanguk ryeong iraneun geungeo neun waegok dwaeeo itda," 144–159. This paper was cited in Kim Byungryull, *Dokdo nya Dakesima nya*, 286–312. There have been numerous papers written in response to Shimojō. These include (1) Kim Byungryull, "Ilbon gojido edo Dokdo neun Hanguk ttang ira myeongsi" [Dokdo labeled Korean on an ancient Japanese map], *Hanguk nondan (Monthly Korea Journal)* (June 1996), 160–173; and (2) Kwak Chang-kwon, "Simojo-ssi ui jujang busil, buranjeong gadeuk" [Shimojō's arguments, full of flaws and weakness-

Japanese documents that the Oki Island fishermen themselves reported that they had used trickery to kidnap An and Park.[132] Also, according to a Japanese book published in 1801, "The Japanese fishermen offered drinks to the Joseon fishermen and kidnapped them while they were drunk."[133]

Shimojō also questioned the validity of the alleged note that the governor of Hōki Province wrote to An, in which the lord stated, "Ulleungdo is not Japanese territory." Shimojō's argument is that the governor of Hōki Province understood that the territory is inherently Japanese. Therefore, it is impossible that such a note was written. Shimojō offered as evidence the fact that "An stated that 'Ulleungdo became Joseon territory' and this statement is not mentioned by the Japanese." He therefore doubts the existence of a note.

Ikeuchi Satoshi also denies the theory of the alleged note. He argues that there is no record showing that An was sent to Edo, and that it is illogical to claim that a general of the shogunate discussed territorial issues with a mere fisherman.[134]

Concerning this issue, Ōnishi Toshiteru likewise argued that An and Park were never sent to Edo. Instead, he claimed that An and Park were transferred to Yonago, where they were interrogated for one month and then transferred again to a holding facility in Tottori, where they were interrogated again for one week. Ōnishi argues that the details of the

---

es], *Hanguk nondan (Monthly Korea Journal)* (June 1996), 174–183.

132 Ōnishi, *Dokdo*, 213.

133 Yang Tae-jin, *Hanguk dongnip ui sangjing Dokdo*, 208–209.

134 Shimojō Masao, "Jeunggeo reul deureo siljeung hara" [Verify with evidence], *Hanguk nondan (Monthly Korea Journal)* 84, no. 1 (August 1996), 226–235. More detailed elaborations of Shimojō's arguments may be found in the following: Shimojō Masao, "Zoku: Takeshima mondai kō (jō)," *Gendai Koria* 371 (May 1997), 62–78; Shimojō Masao, "Zoku: Takeshima mondai kō (ge)," *Gendai Koria* 372 (June 1997), 38–57. Ikeuchi Satoshi's view may be found in Ikeuchi Satoshi, "Ilbon Edo sidae ui Dakesima, Masseusima insik" [Understanding of Takeshima and Matsushima during Japan's Edo period], *Dokdo yeongu (The Journal of Dokdo)* 6 (June 2009), in Japanese, 181–197; in Korean, 199–221.

interrogation were of course reported to the Edo Shogunate. Nonetheless, An was mistaken when he said that he had been transferred to Edo and interrogated there. Furthermore, Ōnishi wrote that the alleged note given to An was real, but the Japanese people who wrote it thought that Ulleungdo and Takeshima were different islands.[135]

However, considering that the high-ranking Joseon government official Nam Gu-man[136] affirmed that An's testimony was true lends it further credibility. Regarding the note, could it be that the governor of Hōki Province really thought that Ulleungdo was Japanese territory, as Shimojō argued? In response to this question, Kim Byungryull answered that "at the time, the governor of Hōki Province did not think Ulleungdo was their territory." Kim presented documents showing that Tottori, then in charge of Hōki Province, did not officially regard Takeshima and Matsushima as part of its territory, as evidence of his claim.[137] This document will be discussed in detail below.

At the time when the governor of Hōki Province provided the disputed note to An, the Edo Shogunate was trying to rejuvenate diplomatic relations with Joseon. Tokugawa had followed Toyotomi, who had died in 1598 during the war against Joseon. Tokugawa wanted to establish diplomatic ties with Joseon in order to affirm the legitimacy of his regime and bring advanced culture from Joseon to Japan. Thus, the shogunate did not want to create discord with Joseon. The governor of Hōki Province was well aware of the shogunate's intentions. This was the background in which the governor of Hōki Province wrote the note to An. In this context, Kim Byungryull, who debated with Shimojō, concluded that

---

135 Ōnishi, *Dokdo*, 220–221.

136 Nam Man-gu was an elder official who held the posts of first royal secretary (K. *doseungji*), censor-general (K. *daesagan*), and minister of military affairs (K. *Byeongjo panseo*). He is well known to Koreans for his poem, "Dongchang i balgatneunya nogojiri ujijinda."

137 Kim Byungryull, *Dokdo nya Dakkesima nya*, 357–358.

"the probability of the existence of this note is very high." [138]

The Tsushima Daimyō's Plan to Seize Ulleungdo and the Joseon Government's Conciliatory Gesture

According to An, he carried the note with him when he left Edo on the voyage home through Nagasaki and Tsushima. This itinerary was the only route to Joseon. [139] However, Sō Yoshimichi's plan for this disputed territory did not parallel that of the shogunate. As the highest-ranking person in Tsushima, a mere fishing island, Ulleungdo was an opportunity. According to An's testimony, the Tsushima daimyō not only arrested An and Park as criminals who had trespassed on Ulleungdo, but also took the note from the governor of Hōki Province into his possession.

As discussed above, Shimojō had doubts about the note. He also doubted An's testimony that the Tsushima daimyō had stolen the note from him. Shimojō pointed to the text[140] in the *Annals of King Sukjong* regarding a Joseon official suggesting a deeper investigation of An's testimony due to its weak credibility.

Shimojō believed that the Tsushima daimyō's actions in arresting and interrogating An and Park were appropriate. He argued that the Tsushima daimyō intervened as the Edo Shogunate placed Ulleungdo under the jurisdiction of Tsushima. And he insisted that the Joseon fishermen had trespassed on what was clearly Japanese territory. In

---

138 Ibid., 323.

139 Ōnishi Toshiteru argued that An Yong-bok was transported directly to Nagasaki from Tottori, then to Tsushima, and then finally back to Joseon (Ōnishi, *Dokdo*, 213–214). The Japanese side's explanation of the process of An Yong-bok and Park Eo-dun's return to Joseon may be found in Shin Yong-Ha et al., *Dokdo yeongyugwon jaryo ui tamgu*, vol. 4, 11–12.

140 This record is found in the *Annals of King Sukjong*.

short, Shimojō criticized the Korean theory that the Tsushima daimyō had plotted to seize Ulleungdo, as well as the interpretation of An Yong-bok's testimony.[141]

However, it is true that the Tsushima daimyō wanted to receive an official acknowledgment from the Joseon government that Ulleungdo was part of Tsushima. It is evident that the arrest of An was not the first time that Japanese had attempted to acquire Ulleungdo. In 1407, the Tsushima daimyō requested that the Joseon government allow many of his people to relocate to Ulleungdo. The Joseon government refused this request.[142] An and Park were eventually transferred to the Japan House in Busan, Dongnae-gun, after having been charged with trespassing. It had been fifty days since the two men had set foot on Joseon. Of those fifty days, they spent forty days locked up in Busan before finally being transferred to the Joseon government in Dongnae-gun.

An and Park explained in detail to the Dongnae-gun officials their false imprisonment on charges fabricated in Japan. However, Dong-nae-gun officials affirmed the charge of trespassing. An and Park's confinement was soon reported to Tsushima. Concurrently, the envoy who had delivered An and Park to Dongnae-gun forwarded the confis-cated note to the Joseon government. The envoy explained that "Joseon fishermen, such as An and Park, have repeatedly violated the boundary between the two countries to fish. And so, they were originally going to set an example with An and Park, but the Edo Shogunate graciously released the two men. The Joseon government must no longer allow this to happen."[143]

Upon receiving the request, the Joseon government responded in

---

141 Shimojō, "Jeunggeo reul deureo siljeung hara," 231–232.

142 *Annals of King Taejong*; Song Byeong-Ki, *Gochyeo sseun Ulleungdo wa Dokdo*, 50–51.

143 The Japanese request may be found in *Annals of King Sukjong* and in Shin Yong-Ha et al., *Dokdo yeongyugwon jaryo ui tamgu*, vol. 1, 161–162.

a conciliatory manner. The tenor of the response was dictated by the exigencies of domestic politics. At the time, King Sukjong's beloved consort Lady Jang and her Southerner supporters had seized power within the administration. The Northerner officials, led by the second state councillor (K. *jwauijeong*) Mok Naeseon and the third state councillor (K. *uuijeong*) Min Am, remembering the lessons learned from the Imjin War, considered that fighting Japan would be to Joseon's loss. The words of Mok Naeseon and Min Am reminded the King that "this island has been empty for 300 years. [It is] an island for which we cannot possibly risk diplomatic relations with Japan and bring chaos to Joseon." King Sukjong followed their advice.[144]

Despite the conciliatory gestures, the Joseon government could not concede Ulleungdo, thereby recognizing it as Japanese territory. The Joseon government decided to be clear that "Ulleungdo is Joseon territory." Yet, at the same time, the government simultaneously made vague statements implying that Takeshima and Ulleungdo might be different islands. The government wrote that "Takeshima at the border is an important island." In the eleventh month of 1693, the reply was delivered to Tsushima. That letter was a reply from the Ministry of Rites (K. *Yejo*) and was preserved in the *Annals of King Sukjong* as follows:

> We have very strict regulations regarding sea travel. Therefore, coastal residents cannot sail into the open sea. We even ban them from traveling to Ulleungdo, a Joseon territory. Thus, traveling beyond Ulleungdo is not permitted. We are grateful for your hospitality as a good neighbor to send two of our people who set foot on Jukdo (Takeshima) located on your border without having punished them. It is true that many fishermen often escape from harsh weather conditions to a nearby island,

---

144 This was recorded in *Annals of King Sukjong*, in the eleventh month of 1693. The entry may be found in Shin Yong-Ha et al., *Dokdo yeongyugwon jaryo ui tamgu*, vol. 1, 157.

but if it is deemed clear to us that they are intentionally fishing in foreign waters, we will charge and try them by strict standards. We promise to enforce a stricter regulation of the sea.[145]

Again, this letter reveals Joseon's intent to hide its understanding of Ulleungdo's one-island two-name theory. At the same time, by declaring Ulleungdo as Joseon territory, yet also acknowledging Jukdo (Takeshima) as Japanese territory, the Joseon government walked a diplomatic line of ambiguity. Furthermore, the Joseon government forced fishermen who sailed to Ulleungdo to move elsewhere, showing the Joseon government's weak response to the issue of territorial rights.

An official from Tsushima received the letter at the Japan House in the port of Busan. He thought the Tsushima daimyō's plan was already halfway to accomplishment. This was due to Jukdo having been acknowledged as Japanese territory. Yet, the phrase "Ulleungdo, a Joseon territory" rendered the situation muddled and vague. In the second month of 1694, the envoy requested that the Joseon government "delete the word 'Ulleungdo' from the note since [the Japanese envoy] only discussed Takeshima." The envoy was very persistent; he stayed for more than fifteen days arguing with the Joseon government.[146]

The Joseon Government Hardens

During this same period in 1694, Queen Inhyeon, who had been deposed by Lady Jang, was restored to her status. This event, called the Gapsul Oksa, led to the elimination of the Southerners, who had opposed the

---

[145] Ibid., vol. 4, 13–14.

[146] Shin Yong-Ha et al., *Dokdo yeongyugwon jaryo ui tamgu*, vol. 4, 17–18; Kim Byungryull, *Dokdo nya Dakkesima nya*, 114; Shin Yong-Ha, *Dokdo ui minjok yeongtosa yeongu*, 100–101; Lee Han-key, *Hanguk ui yeongto*, 245.

restoration of Queen Inhyeon, and to the rise of the Soron faction.

The Joseon government, now in the control of the Soron faction, was extremely critical of the Southerners who were dovish toward Japan. The Soron leaders, following the lead of the Tsushima daimyō, argued that the last note must be returned. Nam Gu-man criticized the irony in the last note, highlighting that the government "treated guests as owners." Shin Yeo-cheol was another official who supported a tougher stance on the issue of territorial controversies with Japan. Shin warned, "If Japanese occupy the island, the [security of] neighboring areas would be damaged." Accordingly, King Sukjong ordered the return of the last note.[147]

Unaware of the Joseon government's change of stance, in the eighth month of 1694 the Tsushima daimyō once again requested that the controversial phrase from the note be deleted. However, this time, the Soron officials responded with a new note that superseded the first and reaffirmed that Jukdo (Takeshima) is Ulleungdo and thus is Joseon territory.

According to the *Annals of King Sukjong*, the new note accused the Japanese of an "invasion" and of the abduction and the rendering of An to Edo. In addition, the Joseon government strongly urged that the matter be brought to the Edo Shogunate in order to ensure that no Japanese person illegally crossed the border and stepped ashore on Ulleungdo.[148] The Joseon government official Yu Jip-il understood that the Tsushima daimyō had ulterior motives for Ulleungdo that differed from those of the Edo Shogunate after having met An in confinement. Thus, Yu was able to be frank with the Japanese envoy. Yu wrote that he asked the envoy, "If the Joseon government directly contacted the Edo

---

147 *Annals of King Sukjong*; Shin Yong-Ha et al., *Dokdo yeongyugwon jaryo ui tamgu*, vol. 1, 169.

148 The creation and the delivery of this document are elaborated upon in detail in Shin Yong-Ha et al., *Dokdo yeongyugwon jaryo ui tamgu*, vol. 4, 18–21.

Shogunate regarding the wrongdoings of Tsushima, would the heads of the envoy and the daimyō be safe?"[149]

Despite the firm ground that the Joseon government held on Ulleungdo, the envoy remained persistent and requested that minor details be changed in the new note. The envoy remained at the Japan House for one year and returned only after learning that the daimyō Sō Yoshimichi had died.

The Edo Shogunate Accepts the Joseon Government's Arguments

When Sō Yoshimichi died, his younger brother, Sō Yoshitaka, succeeded him. This in turn changed the course of the Ulleungdo dispute. In the first month of 1696, the *kanpaku* of the shogunate along with Yoshitaka and four local lords discussed the Takeshima problem. The Kanpaku asked which country Takeshima is closer to, Joseon or Japan. The new daimyō answered, "Takeshima is closer to Joseon and is not a Japanese territory." The new Kanpaku added that this was exactly why they cannot debate the issue any further, though the debate continued only to conclude that Ulleung is Joseon territory. Needless to say, this conclusion was led by the Kanpaku. In what circumstances did the Kanpaku seek such a result? He had the An Yong-bok Incident in mind while sending seven questions to Tottori on the twenty-fourth day of the twelfth month of 1695. From among the seven questions, the two below pertain to Ulleungdo and Dokdo.

1. From when has Takeshima been part of both Inshū [Inaba Province] and Hakushū [Hōki Province]? (The term *ryōgoku* referred to Inaba and

---

149 Shin Yong-Ha et al., *Dokdo yeongyugwon jaryo ui tamgu*, vol. 1, 172–173.

Hōki provinces.) Did this occur before [King] Seonjo was granted the territory? Or after?

7. Are there any other islands besides Takeshima that belong to both Inshū [Inaba Province] and Hakushū [Hōki Province]? Also, do the fishermen of both domains go there for fishing?

The following is the response from Tottori, which came the next day, on the twenty-fifth day of the twelfth month.

1. Takeshima does not belong to both domains . . . .

7. There are no islands that belong to both domains, including Takeshima and Matsushima.[150]

The Kanpaku thought that Takeshima belonged to both Inshū [Inaba Province] and Hakushū [Hōki Province], and asked Tottori. However, Tottori replied clearly that Takeshima did not belong to either Inshū [Inaba Province] or Hakushū [Hōki Province]. Also, Tottori stated that Matsushima does not belong to Inshū [Inaba Province] or Hakushū [Hōki Province].

In response, the Kanpaku ordered the following four points of Tsushima:

First, Takeshima is about 160 miles away from Hōki Province, whereas it is forty miles from Joseon. Therefore, it is fair to see it as Joseon territory.

Second, it is prohibited for Japanese people to travel to the island.

---

150 Documents such as this were discovered from the family of Ikeda Tsunakiyo, descendants of the *hanshu* of Tottori domain at that time. Detailed description by a Japanese scholar may be found in Ōnishi, *Dokdo*, 224–227. Scholarly explanations by Korean experts may be found in Kim Byung-ryull, *Dokdo nya Dakkesima nya*, 178–179; and Hong Seong-keun, "Ilbon ui Dokdo yeongto baeje jochi ui seonggyeok gwa uimi," 100. This issue was also addressed in *Gijukdo saryak*. That text addressed the tension between the Joseon government and the Edo Shogunate over the issue of possession of Ulleungdo. See Kim Hwa-gyeong, "*Gijukdo saryak* ui haeseol" [Explanation of *Gijuk-do saryak*], *Dokdo yeongu* (*The Journal Of Dokdo*) 2 (December 2006), 241–254.

Third, the Tsushima daimyō will deliver this message to Joseon.

Fourth, upon the daimyō's return to Tsushima he will officially announce the decision to Joseon and report the results to the *kanpaku* of the shogunate.[151]

This order is also recorded in the Ministry of Foreign Affairs National Archives of Japan, where documents from the Edo Shogunate are held. The document above is regarded as very important because it is an acknowledgment and acceptance by the Edo Shogunate that Ulleungdo is Joseon territory.[152] To conclude, the Japanese people's term "Takeshima Incident" showed that Japanese people conceded that Takeshima, that is, Ulleungdo, is Joseon territory.

The new daimyō of Tsushima, Sō Yoshitaka, used a delaying tactic by which he delivered an abbreviated message reporting the Edo Shogunate's decision to the Joseon official, Namgung Eung. Further, this daimyō never formally announced the decision.

---

151 A detailed explanation may be read in Shin Yong-Ha et al., *Dokdo yeongyugwon jaryo ui tamgu*, vol. 4, 82–83, and in Kim Byungryull, *Dokdo nya Dakkesima nya*, 120. In Japan, "*gyōbu taifu*" was equivalent to today's minister of justice. The Korean title *daebu* was used only in Goguryeo and Silla, and not in China. In the case of Goguryeo, it is thought to have been used as a title for the prime minister. Tsushima probably inherited the title under the influence of Silla.

152 Shin Yong-Ha et al., *Dokdo yeongyugwon jaryo ui tamgu*, vol. 1, 246.

4 An Yong-bok Returns to Japan and Negotiates

An Yong-bok Claims "Japan's Matsushima is Joseon's Usando"

At approximately the same time as the *kanpaku*'s order, An was released after two years of confinement in Dongnae-gun. He decided that he should decide the island controversy himself. Thus in the spring of 1696 he gathered sixteen others from Joseon, including a monk, oarsmen, and fishermen to sail to Ulleungdo from Ulsan.

When they approached Ulleungdo, they spotted five Japanese fishing boats. According to the *Annals of King Sukjong*, An ran to the bow of the boat and screamed, "Ulleungdo is Joseon territory. How dare you Japanese trespass. It would be proper to tie you people up." The Japanese side responded, "We live on Matsushima, and we accidentally floated to Ulleungdo while we were fishing; we will return soon." An answered, "Matsushima is Jasando (子山島), our island. How dare you say you live on our land."[153]

In the *Annals of King Sukjong*, Usando was recorded as Jasando. Most

---

[153] *Annals of King Sukjong*. This text may be found in Shin Yong-Ha et al., *Dokdo yeongyugwon jaryo ui tamgu*, vol. 1, 205–206. A Japanese document found in May 2005 stated that Noeheon was the head monk at Heungwangsa Temple.

Korean scholars understood Jasando as a corruption of Usando. This view is supported in volume 31 of the *Revised and Enlarged Edition of the Reference Compilation of Documents on Korea* (*Jeungbo munheon bigo*), where Usando is printed as 芋山島, not 子山島. Many scholars speculated that the name Jasando originated from the mother-child understanding of Usando and its nearby islands. However, in the Murakami Documents discovered in May 2005, Jasando was recorded as Sousando (ソウサント), matching a phonetic pronunciation of Jasando in Japanese. This is interpreted as An's understanding that Ulleungdo was Daeusando, and of Usando, for the adjacent islands were regarded as the child islands. In fact, in the Murakami Documents, it is stated that An, while explaining the eight provinces of Joseon, told the Japanese officials that Ulleungdo and Usando are islands that belong to Gangwon-do.

Returning to An's testimony, he and his crew arrived at Usando early in the morning. The Japanese fishermen that he had confronted the day before were roasting fish. An confronted them again and broke what they had prepared with sticks. The Japanese fishermen then left the island.

An chased the fishermen, but ran into a great storm along the way, which forced them to port at Oki Island. When the governor of Oki Island asked An why he had come to Oki Island, An complained that "Japanese fishermen still trespass and fish in our waters even though I had received a note that Ulleungdo and Jasando are Joseon territory." The governor of Oki Island responded that he would receive an answer soon from the governor of Hōki Province. However, there would be no answer.

According to An, he had decided to discuss the matter directly with the governor of Hōki Province. Therefore, he went to Hōki Province with eleven other people. What is interesting here is that among the eleven other people was Yi In-seong, a writer. (Some texts have his name as Gye In-seong, but Yi In-seong is correct.) It seems that An determined that he needed a skilled writer who would make a written record of the negotiation.

It is written in the *Annals of King Sukjong* that An was later arrested for illegally crossing borders and interrogated. He stated, "I could not control my anger so I immediately sailed to Hōki Province pretending to be inspector of Ulleung and Jasan dispatched by the government, wearing a navy robe, a black cap, and leather shoes. Others with me all rode horses to the governor's office." The navy robe that An supposedly wore was only worn by military officials of the third rank and above. It is apparent that An wanted to impersonate a high government official and negotiate with the governor of Hōki Province at the same level.

What does An's fabricated title of inspector of Ulleung and Jasan suggest? As seen above, "Jasan" meant "Usan." Thus, "Ulleung Jasan Yangdo" must mean both Ulleungdo and Usando.

However, in *Takeshima kō*, written by Kosekiryo of Inaba in 1828, it is stated that An Yong-bok used the title "Jo-Ul Yangdo Gamsejang Andongji" (朝蔚兩島監稅將安同知).[154] Korean scholars argue that if this is true, then it clearly illustrates that An saw Ulleungdo as the main island and Dokdo as an adjacent island. "An" in "Andongji" is without doubt "An," and "*dongji*" refers to a position in the Joseon government.

The Governor of Hōki Province Claims the "Two Islands are Already Part of Your Country"

Let us return to An's negotiations. According to the testimony of An given to the Joseon government, he supposedly pointed out that "despite the fact that [he] had received a note on the issue of the two islands

---

154 Ōnishi, *Dokdo*, 240; Shin Yong-Ha et al., *Dokdo yeongyugwon jaryo ui tamgu*, vol. 4, 27.

three years ago, the *hanshu* of Tsushima not only stole the note but also forged it." Furthermore, An threatened the governor of Hōki Province to report the Tsushima daimyō for lying to the *kanpaku*.[155]

The threat must have worked, because the father of the Tsushima daimyō, Sō Yoshizane, begged An not to report the daimyō. The father said, "If a report reaches the *kanpaku*'s table in the morning, my son will die in the evening." The governor of Hōki Province also determined that the report would be as bad for him as it would be for the daimyō. A few months prior to An's arrival, the governor of Hōki Province attended a meeting during which the *kanpaku* concluded that Ulleungdo is Joseon territory. Therefore, such a report would be bad for him.

Thus, the governor of Hōki Province promised An, "The two islands already belong to your country. If any Japanese person is to trespass again, or if the Tsushima daimyō once again attempts to illegally invade, please send a formal government complaint and an interpreter. Then the criminals will be punished harshly." The point of importance is in the first sentence: "The two islands already belong to your country." This passage further shows that Japan admitted that Japan's Takeshima and Matsushima or Joseon's Ulleungdo and Usando are Joseon territory.

While An's effort was admirable, when he returned to Joseon, everyone in his crew, including An himself, was arrested by Inspector Sim Pyeong of Gangwon-do. As mentioned above, they were charged with illegally crossing the border. The members of An's crew were interrogated in the ninth month of 1696 at the "Special State Council."[156]

For An, the chief state councilor (K. *yeonguijeong*) Yu Sang-un argued for capital punishment for "a low-class merchant impersonating a government official and illegally crossing borders in order to raise

---

155 This passage was recorded in *Jeungbo munheon bigo*, vol. 31. The original text may be found in Shin Yong-Ha et al., *Dokdo yeongyugwon jaryo ui tamgu*, vol. 1, 230–231.

156 Ibid., vol. 1, 205.

a diplomatic controversy." The Special State Council did not know whether An was a servant or a slave and instead thought that he was a low-class merchant.

An's life was at stake. However, other high-ranking state councilors such as Yun Ji-wan and Nam Gu-man argued for a less severe punishment. Their logic was that "if they kill An Yong-bok, Tsushima will be happy. And instead of separating his skin and bones . . . we should use him elsewhere some other time." Also, they praised An for ensuring that "Japan cannot anymore call Ulleungdo its island."[157] Eventually, the Joseon government decided to rule after first observing the Japanese reaction.

The Japanese Side Takes Issue With An Yong-bok's Testimony

The historian Tabohashi Kiyoshi remained rather positive in stating that "An Yong-bok's testimony is believable."[158] Although Tabohashi argued that Dokdo is Japanese territory, he is fair in evaluating An.

However, most Japanese scholars and government officials state that An's testimony is fictitious and fabricated to avoid being punished. The Japanese side presents five points in support of this argument: (1) The official title, which An assumed, was not used in the Joseon government; (2) The governor of Hōki Province, with whom An supposedly negotiated, was in Edo at the time of the negotiation; (3) Sō Yoshizane, the father of the Tsushima daimyō, who supposedly begged for his son's life, had already died at the time of the negotiations; (4) An's testimony regarding Japanese fishing ships being present in the sea near Ulleungdo is false due to the shogunate's order banning fishing off the

---

157 Ibid., vol. 1, 230–231.

158 Song Byeong-Ki, *Ulleungdo wa Dokdo*, 61–62.

coast of Ulleungdo in the first month of 1696;[159] and (5) At the time of An's interrogation, Yu Jip-il questioned the validity of An's testimony.[160] Kawakami also continued to argue that An's account of his second visit to Japan was false.

These Japanese point out that An testified that the Japanese fishermen had answered, "We live on Matsushima, to where we will soon return." But since Dokdo is an uninhabited island, it could not have been Matsushima. Therefore, when An said that "Matsushima is Usando," Usando cannot be today's Dokdo. Shimojō argued that An's Usando is an island near Ulleungdo.[161] And he criticized Korean scholars who interpreted the Tsushima daimyō's Ulleungdo plans as a plot to take over Ulleungdo, saying that the plan was an obvious attempt by someone who truly understood Ulleungdo to be Japanese territory.

Lastly, the Japanese side stresses that An was a commoner, not a public person. In *Japanese Government Opinion 3*, the Japanese government argued that, because An was a commoner, his actions cannot be the basis of the Korean side's argument over territorial rights. Taijudō stated that even if one accepts the veracity of An's actions, "Because those actions were not sanctioned by the government, the government holds no binding power."[162]

Ōnishi presented a distinct interpretation. He stated that An's actions and so-called negotiation was an act of personal ambition to expand his business, not an act of securing fishing grounds or borders. The gist of his argument is that while illegal trade between Joseon and Japan

---

159 This argument was first introduced in *Japanese Government Opinion 2*. It was repeatedly used and favored by Kawakami Kenzō. See Kawakami, *Jukdo ui yeoksa jirihakjeok yeongu*, 168–169.

160 This point was made clear by Shimojō. See Shimojō, "Jeunggeo reul deureo siljeung hara," 231; Kim Byungryull, *Dokdo nya Dakkesima nya*, 342.

161 Shimojō, "'Jukdo' ga Hanguk ryeong iraneun geungeo neun waegok dwaeeo itda," 155.

162 This argument, originally found in *Japanese Government Opinion 3*, can be read in Shin Yong-Ha et al., *Dokdo yeongyugwon jaryo ui tamgu*, vol. 4, 330. Taijudō's opinions may be found in his book, *Takeshima funsō*, 114.

was growing in Busan, An, an anarchist, was interested in the flow of commerce, which led him to Japan to acquire silver, silk, linen, and other goods. Supposedly, the people An took on his second trip were merchants. Ōnishi added that the fact that An impersonated a government official is the very reason why An had a profit-motivated mind in Japan.[163]

The Korean Counterargument

Koreans countered. Above all, they argued that the Murakami Documents discovered in May 2005 show that An's first and second trips to Japan did in fact occur. They note that the Murakami Documents pertaining to An's second visit to Japan are very detailed. Therefore, Kawakami's argument that the second visit is false is circumstantial and thus should not stand.

Even before the Murakami Documents were discovered, the Korean government and Korean scholars argued that An's trips were recorded in depth in the Joseon government's official records. For instance, in *Korean Government Opinion 3*, the Korean government argued that An's negotiation was recorded not only in the official records of the Joseon government but also in private records as well.[164] In the same context, Lee Han-key pointed out that "the fact that the shogunate was shocked shows that the Edo Shogunate believed that An's actions had a diplomatic effect."[165] Also, the Korean side stressed that An's trips to Japan were acknowledged by the Joseon government after a series of debates. Thus, King Sukjong acknowledged An's acts, and that is suffi-

---

163 Ōnishi, *Dokdo*, 236–241.

164 Shin Yong-Ha et al., *Dokdo yeongyugwon jaryo ui tamgu*, vol. 4, 380.

165 Lee Han-key, *Hanguk ui yeongto*, 248.

cient to state that An's actions were real.

In addition, the Japanese government at the time of An's second visit reacted and treated An as if he were an official government envoy. Naitō Seichū and Ōnishi Toshiteru have agreed that the Japanese officials did not know that An was impersonating a government official. Even 150 years after An's return to Joseon, the Tottori domain official Okajima Masayoshi, while writing about An, identified An as "Joseon Messenger" (J. *Chōsen tsūshi*).[166]

Based upon all of these arguments, the Korean representatives submitted *Korean Government Opinion 2* on September 25, 1954, to Japan's Ministry of Foreign Affairs. The Korean side argued that the Japanese government's efforts to "label An's testimony as printed in the *Annals of King Sukjong* as a 'fictitious story not based on evidence' is an attempt to discredit the value of a historical text."[167]

The Korean side also argued that the Japanese fishermen's statement that "they live on Matsushima, to which they would return," is a fabricated excuse. Although Dokdo is uninhabitable, it is entirely suitable for a short visit. Therefore, it is illogical to argue that Matsushima is not Dokdo. Specifically, in response to the Japanese argument that An's testimony on seeing Japanese fishermen on the coast of Ulleungdo was false due to a travel ban, the Korean side noted that the ban was in effect nearly two months after An arrived at Ulleungdo in the fifth month of 1696.[168]

What of Ōnishi's argument that An's trips to Japan were purely "personal business and profit motivated"? It is true that there are some passages in An's testimony that might be so interpreted by individuals

---

166 Ōnishi, *Dokdo*, 239.

167 The Korean text and the English-language translation of this document may be found in Shin Yong-Ha et al., *Dokdo yeongyugwon jaryo ui tamgu*, vol. 4, 251–290.

168 For example, Song Byeong-Ki, *Ulleungdo and Dokdo*, 59–60.

who would like to discredit An's testimony. During the first visit to Japan, An himself testified that he was treated well with "grand communion and money." Ōnishi takes this quote and speculates that An went again to Japan to get more money. Also, An himself testified that he had told [the monk] Noeheon, "'Let us go to a place where there is much seaweed,' and Noeheon gladly followed." To Ōnishi, this comment was evidence that An was not only motivated by profit, but also that his entire group had the same mindset to bring home a great quantity of goods. Nonetheless, An stated that although he was greeted with "grand communion and money" by the governor of Hōki Province, he did not accept it. Furthermore, An concluded that he told the governor of Hōki Province, "It is not money that I want, rather a promise by Japan not to enter Ulleungdo ever again." [169]

---

169 Shin Yong-Ha et al., *Dokdo yeongyugwon jaryo ui tamgu*, vol. 1, 230–231.

5 An Yong-bok Avoids Death as the Territorial Rights Dispute Officially Ends

The Edo Shogunate Sends a Note Officially Acknowledging Ulleungdo as Joseon Territory

In the first month of 1697, Tsushima domain announced the Edo Shogunate's decisions to the Dongnae-gun official Yi Se-jae through his aide (J. *Taifu shūi*) Taira Yoshizane, to Taira Naritsune. This is accurately recorded in the Joseon-period text *Byeonnye jipyo*, a collection of documents regarding Joseon-Japan relations.[170]

Also, around the same time, the Edo Shogunate composed a diplomatic document that reaffirmed that Ulleungdo is Joseon territory. In this document, the shogunate stated that because "Takeshima is very far away from Japan, yet close to Joseon," it acknowledged that Takeshima was Joseon territory. The shogunate added that "it is likely that there will be some sort of black-market activity when the people of the two countries mix on the island." Thus they will "soon permanently ban Japanese people from traveling or fishing there." This note was delivered

---

170 Lee Sang-Tae, *Saryo ga jeungmyeong haneun Dokdo neun Hanguk ttang*, 173; Shin Yong-Ha et al., *Dokdo yeongyugwon jaryo ui tamgu*, vol. 1, 239–240.

to Dongnae-gun in the second month.[171]

Upon receiving this document through Dongnae-gun, the Joseon government discussed the Ulleungdo matter again in the fourth month. In the *Daily Records of the Royal Secretariat*, it is written that Chief State Councillor Yu Sang-un reported to King Sukjong that the "Ulleungdo dispute has ended completely and the Japanese side promised to ban its people from fishing there."

The Joseon Government Sends a Document to Japan Confirming Ulleungdo is Joseon Territory

More official documents were exchanged later. In the third month of 1698, the Joseon government ordered its Ministry of Rites Third Minister Yi Seon-bu to confirm with Japan that Ulleungdo is Jukdo and is accepted as Joseon territory. He was also to assure that no future controversies would arise regarding this territory. This document was delivered to the Tsushima daimyō in the fourth month. Later, this document was considered to be a fortunate affirmation of friendship between the two countries. In response to this, the Tsushima daimyō accepted the position of the Joseon government directly in the first month of 1699. This was later delivered to the Edo Shogunate. A note confirming this delivery was sent to Yi Seon-bu. This was the end of the territorial rights controversy between the two countries.[172]

---

171 Shin Yong-Ha et al., *Dokdo yeongyugwon jaryo ui tamgu*, vol. 2, 213–216.
172 Ibid., 216–222.

The Korean-Japanese Controversy

Korean scholars who reviewed the diplomatic document exchanges concluded that Japan admitted that today's Ulleungdo and Dokdo are Joseon territories. The note sent by the Edo Shogunate in the second month of 1697 reflected the acknowledgment by the governor of Hōki Province that Takeshima and Matsushima were Joseon territories.[173]

The Japanese government and scholars offer a different interpretation. They claim that only Ulleungdo was admitted to being Joseon territory. Dokdo was not part of the acknowledgment. In the *Japanese Government Opinion 2*, they stressed that the Japanese fishermen were issued the "Passage to Matsushima License." That island referred to as Matsushima is today's Dokdo, which was abandoned by the Joseon government. The Japanese managed the island since it had been abandoned, which ultimately led to Japan's *inherent* possession of the island.[174] Therefore, under international law, Japan not only has *original* title, but also *historical* title to the island.[175] This Japanese argument will be examined in greater detail in later chapters.

The Evaluation of An Yong-bok

The end of the territorial controversy had a direct effect on the fate of An Yong-bok. Instead of the death penalty, An was punished with a beating and exiled, and then freed from exile. However, there is no written record of where An lived in exile, when he was freed, or what became of

---

173 For example, Lee Han-key, *Hanguk ui yeongto*, 246; Shin Yong-Ha, *Dokdo ui minjok yeongtosa yeongu*, 126–127.

174 Shin Yong-Ha et al., *Dokdo yeongyugwon jaryo ui tamgu*, vol. 4, 217–231.

175 Lee Han-key, *Hanguk ui yeongto*, 271–274.

him subsequently.

The Japanese government and scholars use this fact as evidence in denigrating An's activities. Their argument is that An was exiled because the Joseon government never formally accepted his testimony. In *Japanese Government Opinion 2*, they claim that the Joseon government arrested An for illegally leaving the country and exiled him. This, they argue, shows that An's testimony is not based on facts.[176] In the case of Shimojō, he asserted that An was supposed to be executed, but since that would only make Japanese people happy, he was exiled instead.[177] Kajimura, who is an exception among Japanese scholars, took a contrary view regarding attempts to discredit An's testimony and activities. He wrote, ". . . it is shameful to see derogatory explanations of An's bold activities."[178]

In response to Japanese mainstream academics, the Korean government in *Korean Government Opinion 2* argued that "the Joseon government's exile of An Yong-bok was a fair and appropriate judgment for illegally crossing the border and is irrelevant to the territorial controversy."[179] Despite the Japanese disparagement of An, the historical evaluation of him has neither diminished nor changed. Yi Ik praised An as "a hero's hero" in *Seongho saseol*. He wrote that An was "a mere oarsman who had risked his life on multiple occasions to face a strong enemy in ending a controversy that had continued for generations."[180] It is in this regard that the Gyeongnam An lineage erected a statue (155 cm × 91 cm × 31 cm) commemorating An with an obituary written by the poet Yi Eunsang.

---

176 Shin Yong-Ha et al., *Dokdo yeongyugwon jaryo ui tamgu*, vol. 4, 219.

177 Shimojō, "'Jukdo' ga Hanguk ryeong iraneun geungeo neun waegok dwaeeo itda," 151.

178 Kajimura, "Ilbon ttang jujang eun paengchang – singminjuui sosan," 618.

179 Shin Yong-Ha et al., *Dokdo yeongyugwon jaryo ui tamgu*, vol. 4, 258.

180 The original text may be found in Shin Yong-Ha et al., *Dokdo yeongyugwon jaryo ui tamgu*, vol. 1, 299.

As noted above, the home of An's descent group is not known. What, then, to make of the Gyeongnam An lineage? Because he was born and raised in Busan, An families in the region used the name Gyeongnam An clan in commemoration of An. In naming the statue, they decided that it was no overstatement to title An as a general.

In 1965, an organization for commemorating An Yong-bok was established, and in 1966 the monument to him was placed in Suyeong Park in Busan. President Park Chung-hee granted him the title of general. The commemoration organization holds an annual memorial service and a rite on April 18, as the eighteenth day of the fourth month was the day he was exiled.

The Meiji Government Concludes upon Investigation that Takeshima and Matsushima are "Irrelevant to Our Country"

Chapter 4

1 The "Ulleung-Usan Separation Theory" is Settled as a Result of Regular Patrol Governance

Regular Patrols Establish the "Ulleung–Usan Separation Theory"

Looking back, one of An Yong-bok's most noteworthy contributions is that he clearly proved that Ulleungdo and Usando are two separate islands. His outstanding legacy was to completely disprove the so-called "one-island two-name theory."[181] This revelation stimulated the Joseon government, and in the ninth month of 1694, it ordered Jang Han-sang, the ranking military official in Samcheok-gun county in Gangwon-do province, to patrol Ulleungdo. Jang took 149 men in six ships to Ulleungdo for thirteen days from the twentieth day of the ninth month through the third day of the tenth month. On the sixth day of the tenth month, the day on which he returned, Jang submitted a report regarding his expedition, which was included in the *Annals of King Sukjong*.

Jang also wrote the text *Ulleungdo sajeok*.[182] According to this text, he verified the existence of an island now called Dokdo. Jang wrote, "If one stares to the west [from Ulleungdo], there is the twisted pass of

---

181 See Ōnishi, *Dokdo*, 250.

182 The important parts of *Ulleungdo sajeok* may be read in Lee Sang-Tae, *Saryo ga jeungmyeong haneun Dokdo neun Hanguk ttang*, 175.

Daegwallyeong, and to the east there is an island in the middle of the sea which is located in a cozy direction." What he meant by "cozy direction" is the southeast direction. In this case, the only island located in a cozy direction is Dokdo.

The crucial fact here is that the island about which Jang wrote cannot possibly be other islands near Ulleungdo. Kawakami and other Japanese scholars argued that islands other than Ulleungdo recorded in texts printed in the early and mid-Joseon period cannot be Dokdo. Rather, they are other islands adjacent to Ulleungdo. This argument extended to the argument that Joseon people did not know Dokdo at the time. However, Jang's record proves that Joseon people were well aware of the fact that there is an island in the "cozy direction" from Ulleungdo.

Jang was quite specific about the island. He mentioned particular dimensions and locational data. He stated that the island was one-third the size of Ulleungdo and located no more than 300 nautical miles away. In fact, Dokdo is much smaller than one-third the size of Ulleungdo. To be exact, it is 1/391 the size of Ulleungdo. It is speculated that because he observed Dokdo from a great distance he must have made an error in sizing the island.[183]

Within the context of affirming the identification of Usando as Dokdo, as examined in the previous chapters, the Joseon government patroled Ulleungdo after having received notification from the Edo Shogunate acknowledging Ulleungdo as Joseon territory. According to the entry dated the thirteenth day of the fourth month of 1697 in the *Daily Records of the Royal Secretariat*, Chief State Councilor Yu Sang-un suggested that although it is difficult to dispatch patrol officers every year to Ulleungdo, it may be possible to do so periodically. Following suit, King Sukjong suggested that it might be wise to divide the task

---

183 Song Byeong-Ki, *Gochyeo sseun Ulleungdo wa Dokdo*, 53–54.

over two years. However, the period fell to once every three years for patroling the island.[184]

According to this decision, in the sixth month of 1699, Jeon Hoe-il, the military official in charge of Wolsong port in Pyeonghae-gun county, was sent to Ulleungdo. In addition, in 1702, King Sukjong sent Yi Jun-myeong, a general from the Samcheok military base. This was the second time in which a high military official was sent to Ulleungdo as an patrol officer. Jang and Yi both collected bamboo trees, juniper trees, and other local flora in order to pay tribute to the king.[185] Here, it is important to note that the patrol officers were the highest-ranking military officials from the ports of Samcheok and Wolsong on the East Sea coast. This is known as the "frontier generals' patrol rotation."[186]

The patrol was very successful. Most importantly, the forgotten geography of Ulleungdo provided valuable information to the Joseon state. In 1714, Secret Royal Inspector Jo Seok-myeong reported that he had heard that "an island to the east of Ulleungdo is near the border with Japan."[187] This is one of many comments that illustrate growing interest and geographical knowledge. Naturally, this kind of interest and cognizance regarding Dokdo expanded. Ultimately, the confusion created by many theories about Ulleungdo and Usando was simplified to that of Ulleung and Usan as separate islands. Usando is located due east of Ulleungdo.

184 Ibid., 63–65

185 *Annals of King Sukjong*, eulyu dasy, fifth month, year 28; Shin Yong-Ha, "Dokdo – Ulleungdo ui myeongching byeonhwa yeongu," 39.

186 Song Byeong-Ki, *Gochyeo sseun Ulleungdo wa Dokdo*, 66.

187 *Annals of King Sukjong*, sinyu day, seventh month, year 40.

Ulleungdo and Usando are Accurately Depicted in Maps and Writings of Korean Silhak Scholars

As seen above, the developing knowledge of Ulleungdo and its adjacent seas affected cartographic production directly. For instance, a map titled *Dongguk daejido* compiled by Jeong Sang-gi (1678–1752), a Silhak scholar active in the eighteenth century, is an exemplary case. Jeong developed contacts with another Silhak scholar, Yi Ik, who expanded his interest and knowledge in geography. This interest eventually led to personal expeditions throughout the Joseon territory. As a result, the *Dongguk daejido* was compiled. During its drafting, Jeong used a unique scaling method in order to more accurately portray distances on the map. He also used color on the map to differentiate between regions. And he placed Usando to the east of Ulleungdo, and the two islands quite a distance apart.

The son Jeong Hang-ryeong (1700–unknown) disseminated his father's work and also supplemented the maps with additional data.[188] In fact, some scholars believe that Jeong Hang-ryeong, not Jeong Sang-gi, compiled *Dongguk daejido*. Although partial supplements to the map are extant, it is apparent that the son's work differed from that of the father and left unaltered the portions containing Ulleungdo and Usando. The maps and supplements were a Jeong family affair and were never influenced by other Korean maps such as *Map of the Eight Provinces* (K. *Paldo chongdo*), or Chinese maps such as *Map of the World* (Ch. *Tianxia yuditu*) and *Atlas of the Chinese Empire*. As already seen in Chapter 2, these maps positioned Usando to the west of Ulleungdo, and both islands very close to each other.

---

188 Jeong Sang-gi and the explanation of his *Dongguk daejido* were recorded from a phone interview with Lee Sang-Tae, the author of *Saryo ga jeungmyeong haneun Dokdo neun Hanguk ttang* (March 8, 2010).

Jeong Sang-gi's *Dongguk daejido* had an enormous influence. Many maps were compiled in the late eighteenth century, such as the anonymous *Joseon jeondo, Joseon paldo jido, Haedonjido,* and volume 6 of *Yeojido.* All of these important documents placed Usando east of Ulleungdo and depicted its size as very small. Additionally, these maps clearly demarcated the islands as Joseon territory.[189]

The Joseon people's new geographical understanding and awareness were found in other types of writings, as well. The best example is *Ganggyego,* written by the Silhak scholar Shin Gyeong-jun in 1756. In this text, Shin referenced *Yeojiji,* compiled in 1656 by the Silhak scholar Yu Hyeong-won, to explain that Ulleungdo and Usando are two different islands. In *Yeojiji,* according to Shin's reference, Yu wrote, "There is a theory that claims Usando and Ulleungdo to be the same island. However, considering numerous maps, they are two separate islands. [Among those two islands] one is called Matsushima by Japanese, and both of these islands belong to Usanguk." Also, Shin detailed An Yong-bok's two trips and repeated An's quote, "Songdo is Usando. Have you never heard that Usan, too, belongs to us?"

In *Yeojigo* in *Dongguk munheon bigo,* compiled in 1770, Shin Geyong-jun clearly stated his expert opinion without reference to *Yeojiji.* He concluded, "Usan is what Japanese refer to as Songdo." Shin once again described An's two expeditions in great detail in seeking to reiterate that the islands are Joseon territory.[190]

Shimojō evaluated the writings regarding Usando, which appears in many texts, including *Yeojigo* in *Dongguk munheon bigo.* He argued that by using Yi Maeng-hyu's *Chungwanji,* in which An was mentioned, and *Yeojiji,* for which the author and its sources are unclear, the *Dongguk*

---

189 These maps may be found in Lee Sang-Tae, *Saryo ga jeungmyeong haneun Dokdo neun Hanguk ttang,* 43–47.

190 Ibid., 67–71.

munheon bigo provided the contemporary foundation to falsely interpret Usando as Dokdo.[191] This, however, is Shimojō's revisionist theory supporting *Dongguk munheon bigo*.

In response, Hosaka Yūji, a Korean citizen born in Japan, criticized Shimojō's argument. First, Hosaka suggested that Japanese "probably began distorting facts because they felt a sense of crisis due to the text identifying Usando, or Matsushima, as Dokdo." He concluded, "Such an argument is no more than Shimojō's speculation. Shin Gyeong-jun wrote of Usando out of the awareness that Usando is an island of Usan-guk, and Usando is what Japanese refer to as Matsushima." In addition, Hosaka stated that the "Joseon government obviously concurred with An Yong-bok's testimony declaring that Usando is what Japanese call Matsushima. And while it may be true that it was once confusing and divisive, Joseon reaffirmed that Usando is Dokdo. Therefore, the assertion that Usando is Matsushima and Dokdo is not Shin Gyeong-jun's personal opinion. Rather, it is the Joseon government's official opinion." Hosaka concluded, "Even by looking at how the Joseon government approved the records written by [Shin Gyeong-jun], it can be proven that the Joseon government at the time understood Dokdo as its own territory."[192]

The Korean-Japanese Controversy over Gajido

As discussed above, the Joseon government continued to patrol the Ulleungdo region in the midst of expanding its regional knowledge. Only a drought in Gangwon-do prompted the King to permit the patrols

---

191 Shimojō, "Jeunggeo reul deureo siljeung hara," 233. This part was discussed in Kim Byungryull, *Dokdo nya Dakkesima nya*.

192 Hosaka Yūji, *Uri yeoksa Dokdo: Han-Il gwangyesa ro bon Dokdo iyagi* [Dokdo, our history: The story of Dokdo from the perspective of Korea-Japan relations] (Seoul: BM Seongandang, 2009), 275–276.

to be postponed or rescheduled. Otherwise, regional patrols continued unabated.

Even in the case of King Jeongjo (r. 1776–1800), who respected academics and the arts over all others, regional patrols did not cease. When King Jeongjo received indications that both Koreans and Japanese hid on Ulleungdo to illegally harvest the abundantly growing ginseng and participate in black market activities, he redoubled his support of the periodic patrols. The result of the monarch's continuous effort toward patrols is recorded in the *Annals of King Jeongjo*, which was printed in 1805. According to this official history, Gangwon-do Governor Sim Jin-hyeon ordered Han Chang-guk to explore the Ulleungdo area. Based on Han's reports, Governor Sim reported the results of their patrol to the central government as below:

> Han Chang-guk and his crew of eighty divided among four ships departed from Wolsong Port on the twenty-first day of the fourth month. They arrived in Jangjakji Port, Ulleungdo, on the twenty-fifth day of the fourth month. The center of the island was a fertile land, which could be converted to farmland able to support many types of plants.
>
> They saw three adjacent islands very close to Ulleungdo: Bangpaedo, Jukdo, and Ongdo. The islands were within view. The crew remained on the main island and headed to Gajido on the twenty-sixth day of the fourth month. At Gajido, a few sea lions (K. *gajieo*) were surprised to see the crew and fled. There were animals, which looked like water buffalos. Some hunters of the crew immediately took aim and killed two of them. [. . .] The crew set sail on the thirtieth day of the fourth month and arrived at Wolsong Port on the eighth day of the fifth month.[193]

---

193 The original text may be found in Shin Yong-Ha et al., *Dokdo yeongyugwon jaryo ui tamgu*, vol. 1, 279–280; Lee Sang-Tae, *Saryo ga jeungmyeong haneun Dokdo neun Hanguk ttang*, 179; Yang Tae-jin, *Hanguk dongnip ui sangjing Dokdo*.

Gajido appears in this record apart from Ulleungdo and its adjacent islands. The historian Choe Nam-seon saw Gajido as Dokdo. He argued that it is clear that *gaji* is the *gaje* that lives in groups on Dokdo.[194] This is evidenced through the Ulleungdo people calling *gaje* as *gaji*.

"*Gaje*" is a Korean word for sea lion. In Chinese characters, this word is written as "*haeryeo*" or "*haeryong*." As seen in Chapter 2, Korean scholars assumed that the "doll-like figures" that Kim Ja-ju's crew saw were *gaje*, and that "the island with doll-like figures standing" was Dokdo. The Gajido that Han Chang-guk observed is speculated by Korean scholars to be Dokdo, as well.

The Japanese do not accept such assumptions. According to Kawakami, Ōkuma Ryōichi, and other Japanese scholars, *gaje* are also seen on islands around Ulleungdo other than Dokdo. Therefore, it is not certain that Dokdo is Gajido. Further, Han Chang-guk could have named any of the adjacent rocks near Ulleungdo such as Gwaneumdo, Jukseo, or Samhyeongjeam in a similar way. Assuming that Gajido is Dokdo, Japanese scholars doubt that it would have been possible for Han and his crew to arrive on Dokdo from Ulleungdo in four days considering the level of sailing technology.[195]

The response to this question is quite simple. First, using Japanese logic and arguing that Gajido can be any island near Ulleungdo, then it would have been impossible for Han and his crew to make the round trip in four days to other islands from Ulleungdo. Even if Joseon's navigation technology and techniques were poor, it would have been possible to complete the round trip in four days. Second, considering Han Chang-guk's report that he saw three other islands near Ulleungdo, it can be

---

194 Choe Nam-seon, "Dokdo neun eomyeonhan Hanguk yeongto" [Dokdo is clearly Korean territory], in Dokdo (Seoul: Daehan Gongnonsa), 151.

195 Kawakami, *Jukdo ui yeoksa jirihakjeok yeongu*, 137–138. Ōkuma's paper on Takeshima was published in Japan's Liberal Democratic Party of Japan's *Seisaku geppō* [Policy monthly], in the October 1967 issue, page 121.

inferred that Gajido was not one of these islands.[196]

Kajimura, a historian highly regarded in Japanese academia with regard to the Dokdo issue, stated, "With the help of a fair wind, it is quite possible to make a round trip to Dokdo in three days. Thus, it is [possible] that Gajido is [. . .] Dokdo."[197] A scholar with a diametrically opposite view stated that it could have been possible to make a round trip in four days. Ōnishi wrote that Yi Gyu-won's Ulleungdo patrol only took two days, thus "Han Chang-guk's round trip [to Dokdo] could have been possible."[198]

The Joseon government administered Ulleungdo and the area where today's Dokdo is located through a regular series of patrols. The Korean government and Korean scholars maintain that this is proof that the Joseon government did not abandon the islands but administered them.[199] In response, Japanese countered that the Joseon government's patrols only reached Ulleungdo and not all the way to Dokdo.[200] Kim Byungryull, in response, argued that Joseon people were well aware of Dokdo even at that time and offered reports by Jang Han-sang and Jo Seok-myeong as evidence.[201]

Texts Printed in Joseon after the Discovery of Gajido

Upon Han Chang-guk's return after affirming the separate geographies

---

196 Lee Han-key, *Hanguk ui yeongto*, 241–242.

197 Kajimura, "Ilbon ttang jujang eun paengchang – singminjuui sosan," 619.

198 Ōnishi, *Dokdo*, 259.

199 The argument by the Korean side was included in *Japanese Government Opinion 3*. The Japanese government made such inclusions in order to argue against the Korean side. That portion is included in Shin Yong-Ha et al., *Dokdo yeongyugwon jaryo ui tamgu*, vol. 4, 334.

200 Ibid.

201 Kim Byungryull, *Dokdo nya Dakkesima nya*, 353–354.

of Gajido, Ulleungdo, and the three adjacent islands, a theory that another island existed to the right of Ulleungdo was forwarded. That island was Usando, which was recorded in old Joseon records by the Joseon government and the intellectuals of the day. The following text and two maps support such a theory. In chronological order, they begin with the book *Ten Thousand Techniques of Governance* (K. *Mangi yoram*), written in 1808 by Seo Yeong-bo, Sim Sang-gyu, and others. This book consists of two sections, the first on utilities (K. *jaeyong*) and the second on military administration (K. *gunjeong*). The second section explicitly supported the conclusions of *Yeojiji* that "Ulleungdo and Usando both belong to Usanguk and Usan is what Japanese people call Songdo."[202] What is crucial in the previous sentence is that "Ulleungdo and Usando both belong to Usanguk." This means that Usanguk consisted of Ulleungdo and Usando. The second portion of the sentence is corroborated by Japanese people calling Ulleungdo as Takeshima (Jukdo), and Dokdo as Matsushima (Songdo) until 1904. Considering that, *Ten Thousand Techniques of Governance* keenly illustrates that Usando is Dokdo.[203]

Second, the map *Haejwa jeondo*, which was compiled in 1822 but whose compiler is not known, placed Usando apart from Ulleungdo, and to the east.[204]

Third, a similar map produced at approximately the same time,

---

202 Text regarding Dokdo in *Mangi yoram* may be read in Lee Sang-Tae, *Saryo ga jeungmyeong haneun Dokdo neun Hanguk ttang*, 181. The explanation of this part in *Mangi yoram* may be found in the following: Song Byeong-Ki, *Gochyeo sseun Ulleungdo wa Dokdo*, 74–75; Shin Yong-Ha, *Hanguk gwa Ilbon ui Dokdo yeongyugwon nonjaeng*, 51.

203 Shimojō commented that the section in *Mangi yoram* was influenced by *Dongguk munheon bigo*. As discussed above in Chapter 3, Shimojō explained that *Dongguk munheon bigo* made a hero of An Yong-bok and made the mistake of separating Ulleungdo from Usando. Shimojō thus suggested that the contents of *Mangi yoram* are incorrect. Shimojō Masao, "Zoku Takeshima mondai kō (ge)" [The Takeshima issue, continued, part 2], *Gendai Koria* 372 (June 1997), 44–50. Park Byoung-sup presented counterarguments against Shimojō in Park Byoungsup, "Simojo Masao (下條正男) ui nonseol eul bunseok handa (2)," 120–131. Park suggested that Shimojō made his arguments arbitrarily.

204 This map may be found in Lee Sang-Tae, *Saryo ga jeungmyeong haneun Dokdo neun Hanguk ttang*, 49; Li Jin-mieung, *Dokdo: Jirisang ui jaebalgyeon*, 278.

Haedong yeojido, is a reproduction of *Paldo bundo*, which is a part of Jeong Sang-gi's map. In *Haedong yeojido*, Ulleungdo is located quite far from the mainland, with Usando east of Ulleungdo.[205]

Fourth is *Oju Yeonmun jangjeon sango*, which Yi Gyu-gyeong, whose pen name was Oju, composed in the 1830s and the 1840s. Yi wrote that in the East Sea are Ulleungdo and Usando. Usan was very small and was not shown in some cases. He recorded in great detail An Yong-bok's trips to Japan and the affirmation that An received from the Japanese that Ulleungdo and Usando both are Joseon territories.[206]

Fifth is *Paldo jeondo*, a map believed to have been compiled in the 1840s, but the compiler is not known. This map was also known as *Dori dopyo*, because it recorded the distance and the route to Hanyang, the capital, from each county in Joseon. This map also located Ulleungdo quite far from the mainland and showed a much smaller Usando to the right of Ulleungdo.[207]

And sixth is the map *Joseon jeondo* compiled in 1846 by Joseon's first Catholic priest, Kim Tae-gon, for the French priests smuggled into Joseon amid the persecution of Catholics. This map was based on *Haejwa jeondo* and was drawn on traditional Korean *hanji* paper. Father Kim sent this map to the French priests via Chinese fishermen in Hwanghae-do. Upon his return, he was arrested by the Joseon government and put to death.

The map probably suffered damage during its transit to the French priests or diplomats. This prompted the French to redraw the map on Western paper. The replica was then taken to France by the French ambassador Charles de Montigny. This map is known in Korea as *Joseon*

---

205 This map may be found in Lee Sang-Tae, *Saryo ga jeungmyeong haneun Dokdo neun Hanguk ttang*, 53.

206 The original text may be found in Shin Yong-Ha et al., *Dokdo yeongyugwon jaryo ui tamgu*, vol. 1, 306.

207 This map may be found in Lee Sang-Tae, *Saryo ga jeungmyeong haneun Dokdo neun Hanguk ttang*, 58.

jeondo. On the bottom of the map, the French title *Carte de la Corée* was written by Father Kim. A French geographer, Conrad Malte-Brun, reduced the size of the map and published it in the transactions of the *Geographical Society of Paris* (F. *Société de Géographie*) in 1855. In both Father Kim's map and Malte-Brun's map, Ulleungdo is located a considerable distance from the mainland. Usando is drawn much smaller and to the east of Ulleungdo. And Usan is transcribed in French as "Ousan" on the maps.[208]

In the 1860s, Kim Jeong-ho, who had compiled *Daedong yeojido*, also compiled *Daedong yeoji nojeong jeondo*. This map, now in the archives of the National Diet Library in Japan, clearly depicts Usando with its peaks.

---

208 Li Jin-mieung, *Dokdo: Jirisang ui jaebalgyeon*, 280–281; Lee Sang-Tae, *Saryo ga jeungmyeong haneun Dokdo neun Hanguk ttang*, 59.

2 Maps Produced before the Meiji Restoration Acknowledge Ulleungdo and Usando as Joseon Territories

Japanese Maps Produced in the 1700s

Before the knowledge of Ulleungdo and Dokdo became fixed in the minds of Joseon people, what was the common understanding in Japan? To state the conclusion first, all Japanese maps produced for the Japanese acknowledged the islands as Joseon territories.

First, the map *Sangoku tsūran yochi rotei zenzu* compiled by the Japanese scholar Hayashi Shihei (1738–1793) is arguably the most famous example of such images. Hayashi compiled the map as an appendix to his *Sangoku tsūran zusetsu*, which was printed in 1785. Hayashi colored each country to help illustrate national borders. In this map Joseon was colored brown and Japan green. Upon drawing Takeshima and Matsushima in their known locations, both were colored brown. Furthermore, Hayashi labeled the islands "possessed by Joseon."[209]

Korean scholars argue that this map clearly represents Takeshima, or Ulleungdo, and Matsushima, or Dokdo, as Joseon territory. In response, Shimojō responded that Hayashi's comment "possessed by Joseon" is

---

[209] Li Jin-mieung, *Dokdo: Jirisang ui jaebalgyeon*, 256; Lee Sang-Tae, *Saryo ga jeungmyeong haneun Dokdo neun Hanguk ttang*, 108–109.

merely a note and is not represented in the main text.[210] The Takeshima Issue Research Institute, then led by Shimojō, incorrectly evaluated the image in its *Final Report* presented in March 2007 as "a map irrelevant to the territorial rights issue." However, according to Hosaka, who thoroughly examined this map in comparison with other Japanese maps from the same period, the Takeshima Issue Research Institute's "report is a completely misleading opinion resulting from poor research. Hayashi's map affirmed the Korean territorial right over Dokdo more clearly than ever."[211]

Second, in *Dai Nihonzu*, another map appended to the *Sangoku tsūran zusetsu*, Hayashi again colored Joseon brown and Japan green. In this map, too, Takeshima and Matsushima were colored brown in their known locations.[212]

Third, a map titled *Sō ezu*, which was produced by a Japanese geographer in the second half of the 1700s may be cited. On this map, Japan was colored red and Joseon brown. Takeshima and Matsushima were colored brown in their known locations. Similarly, the author noted "Joseon territory" next to the islands.[213]

The three maps introduced here were compiled during the Edo period. Koreans argued that this fact is evidence that the Edo Shogunate and Japanese people understood that Takeshima and Matsushima were Joseon territories.

---

210 The most important interpretations of the map by Korean academics include Shin Yong-Ha, *Dokdo ui minjok yeongtosa yeongu*, 37. Shimojō's interpretation can be read in Shimojō, "Jeunggeo reul deureo siljeung hara," 235. This paper also appeared in Kim Byeong-yeol's *Dokdo nya Dakkesima nya*, 330–350. Shimojō's comment regarding the map is found on page 350.

211 Hosaka, *Uri yeoksa Dokdo*, 303–304.

212 Shin Yong-Ha, *Hanguk gwa Ilbon ui Dokdo yeongyugwon nonjaeng*, 193; Shin Yong-Ha, *Dokdo ui minjok yeongtosa yeongu*, 231.

213 Ibid., 37; Song Byeong-Ki, *Gochyeo sseun Ulleungdo wa Dokdo*, 76–77.

The Korean-Japanese Controversy over Nakakubo Sekisui's *Kaisei Nihon yochi rotei zenzu*

In response to this Korean assertion, today's Japanese government submits Nakakubo Sekisui's map *Kaisei Nihon yochi rotei zenzu*, compiled in 1799, as evidence showing that the Japanese have long acknowledged that the island of Dokdo is their territory.[214] This map is regarded as one of Japan's most representative maps due to its inclusion of longitude and latitude lines. It documents Matsushima in its proper location.

How does one interpret this? First, Hosaka states:

> In his map, Nakakubo Sekisui drew Ulleungdo and Dokdo together northwest of Oki Island. As stated before, at the time, the Edo Shogunate had fully acknowledged Ulleungdo as Joseon territory. Therefore, this map, in which Dokdo is drawn along with Ulleungdo, is not necessarily evidence that shows Japan acknowledging Dokdo as its territory. Rather, the fact that Dokdo was paired with Ulleungdo must be understood as an attempt to stress it as being Joseon territory. Also, to show that Ulleungdo and Dokdo are excluded from Japanese territory, longitude and latitude lines were not drawn near Ulleungdo and Dokdo. Furthermore, applying the same logic, the longitude and latitude lines are not drawn near the entire southern part of the Korean Peninsula.[215]

Second, Choi Seo-myeon of Korea stated at a press conference on April 21, 2005, that "there is not a single map from the Edo Shogunate that acknowledged Dokdo as part of Japan." He continued, arguing that "Kaisei Nihon yochi rotei zenzu" "cannot be used as evidence regarding

---

214 This map was mentioned in *Japanese Government Opinion 4*, which was prepared by the Ministry of Foreign Affairs. See Shin Yong-Ha et al., *Dokdo yeongyugwon jaryo ui tamgu*, vol. 4, 426–427.

215 Hosaka Yūji, *Ilbon gojido edo Dokdo eopda* [There is no Dokdo even on ancient Japanese maps] (Seoul: Jaeum gwa moeum, 2005), 28–29.

territorial rights. In addition, the size and the location of Dokdo are wrong. This map included Korea's Busan. Does that make Busan a part of Japanese territory?"

The Korean-Japanese Controversy over the Execution of Yauemon

The Edo Shogunate executed Yauemon, captain of a ship from Hamada Bay in Iwami Province (also called Hamada domain), for illegal logging activity on Ulleungdo in 1837.[216] Regarding this event, the Korean government and the Japanese government offer completely opposite interpretations regarding Yauemon's execution.

The Korean government viewed the execution of Yauemon as the Edo Shogunate's acceptance of Ulleungdo as Joseon territory. The representatives of the Republic of Korea in Japan on September 25, 1954, evaluated this in *Korean Government Opinion 2*. The Korean government stated that "the [Edo Shogunate kept its promise with the Joseon government] by executing Yauemon and also kept the promise to respect that the two islands belong to Joseon."[217] Korean scholars offered the same evaluation.[218]

The opinions of the Japanese government and Japanese scholars are completely opposite to the Korean view. To them, the execution of Yauemon is evidence supporting the argument that Matsushima is Japanese territory. For instance, on September 20, 1956, the Ministry of Foreign Affairs delivered *Japanese Government Opinion 3* to the

---

216 The details of this event were recorded in Kitazawa Shōsei's *The Historical Truth of Takeshima* (Tokyo: Ministry of Foreign Affairs, 1881). The Japanese transcript and Korean translation may be found in Shin Yong-Ha et al., *Dokdo yeongyugwon jaryo ui tamgu*, vol. 4, 109–115 and 116–119. Hosaka renders his name as "Hachiemon" rather than "Yauemon."

217 *Korean Government Opinion 2* may be found in Shin Yong-Ha et al., *Dokdo yeongyugwon jaryo ui tamgu*, vol. 4, 257–258.

218 Lee Han-key, *Hanguk ui yeongto*, 248; Shin Yong-Ha, *Dokdo ui minjok yeongtosa yeongu*, 283–284.

representatives of the Republic of Korea in Japan, in which they argued that (1) Yauemon held only a passage license to Matsushima, not one for a trip all the way to Ulleungdo, and that (2) this shows that Yauemon would not have been punished if he had traveled only to Matsushima. In other words, the Japanese government argues that had Yauemon only gone to Matsushima, he would not have been executed. However, he traveled all the way to Takeshima, and thus he had to be punished.[219] Yet, in *Japanese Government Opinion 4*, sent to the representatives of the Republic of Korea on February 5, 1963, the Ministry of Foreign Affairs stressed that the verdict issued regarding Yauemon stated that "there was a loophole for going to Takeshima with only a passage license allowing travel to Matsushima." "This record shows that going to Matsushima was not a problem but going to Takeshima was."[220]

However, it is difficult to find evidence that Yauemon only applied for a passage license to Matsushima. Korean researchers collectively note that it is common sense to consider that there was little or no economic incentive to be gained from traveling only to Matsushima.[221] Moreover, as indicated in Chapter 3, the Edo Shogunate already acknowledged Takeshima and Matsushima as Joseon territory, thus the passage license was only issued as a type of passport. Again, as *Korean Government Opinion 2* indicates, "The passage license was given only to those who were permitted to trade internationally. Clearly, this is the case, and this is the interpretation of Japanese precedents."[222]

What must be added is the map that Yauemon drew during his trial. Titled "Takeshima hōkakuzu," the Japanese islands and Okishima were

219 *Japanese Government Opinion 2* may be read in Shin Yong-Ha et al., *Dokdo yeongyugwon jaryo ui tamgu*, vol. 4, 335.

220 *Japanese Government Opinion 4* may be read in Shin Yong-Ha et al., *Dokdo yeongyugwon jaryo ui tamgu*, vol. 4, 463–464.

221 Yang Tae-jin, *Hanguk dongnip ui sangjing Dokdo*, 92–93.

222 Shin Yong-Ha et al., *Dokdo yeongyugwon jaryo ui tamgu*, vol. 4, 258.

colored yellow. On the other hand, Joseon, Takeshima, and Matsushima were all shaded red. Yauemon's understanding was that Takeshima and Matsushima were Joseon islands.[223]

Japanese Maps Produced in the 1800s

The Korean argument that Japanese did not regard Dokdo as Japanese territory is supported by Japanese maps produced in the nineteenth century as well. These maps did not include the small island. The most famous examples are (1) Takashiba Eisanyu's *Kaei shinzō Dai Nihon-koku gun yochi zenzu* compiled in 1849, (2) Nakajima Akira's *Kaitei Dai Nihonzu* produced in 1853, (3) Kikuya Kōsaburō's *Kōsei Dai Nihon yochi zenzu* completed between the late 1850s and the early 1860s, and (4) *Dai Nihon yochi zenzu*, compiled at an unknown date during the Edo Shogunate.[224] Again, these images show that Japanese did not consider this small rock island to be Japanese territory.

The above list is not an exhaustive roster of maps depicting the geography of Japan in detail while failing to include Matsushima.[225] The fact that Oki Island was drawn in the maps but not Matsushima deserves attention for the following reason.

In *Takeshima zusetsu* written by Hokugan Tsuan between 1751 and 1763, Matsushima was introduced as "Matsushima of Oki Province." The title originated from local tales at the time. Also, in *Chōsei Takeshima ki*, published in 1801 by Yada Takamasa, it is written that "Japanese people used Matsushima as a rest point in the voyage from Oki Island to Ulleungdo, and that is the farthest western border of our country."

---

223 Hosaka, *Uri yeoksa Dokdo*, 282–283.

224 Hosaka, *Ilbon gojido edo Dokdo eopda*, 22–24.

225 Those maps and their explanations may be found in Hosaka, Ibid., 24–26.

The Ministry of Foreign Affairs presented these records in *Japanese Government Opinion 4* sent on February 5, 1963, as evidence in arguing that Matsushima or Dokdo is a Japanese island. Kawakami Kenzō also took the same position.[226]

However, the fact that Japanese people drew Okishima but did not include Matsushima in late Edo period maps undermines the assertions of the Ministry of Foreign Affairs in *Japanese Government Opinion 4*. This implicitly reveals that the local tales *Takeshima zusetsu* and *Chōsei Takeshima ki* are not based upon what was accepted by the majority of Japanese in the 1800s. Furthermore, as the authors of both books admitted, the books are merely collections of multiple local stories.

Kajimura suggested that the way in which these books were written shows that Matsushima is not included as part of Japan. In contrast, in *Oki-kuni chishiryaku*, written by Shimizu Seitarō, both Oki Island and Matsushima are mentioned. Yet, in a map from this period, *Nihon yochi rotei zu*, Matsushima is placed among the many islands that belong to Oki Island. Combining these, the conclusion may be drawn that the Matsushima of the people of Shimane Prefecture is not likely to be today's Dokdo (Takeshima in Japanese).[227]

---

226 *Takeshima zusetsu* and *Chōsei Takeshima ki* may be found in Shin Yong-Ha et al., *Dokdo yeongyug-won jaryo ui tamgu*, vol. 4, 443. The name of the author of *Takeshima zusetsu* is recorded in English as Hokugan Tsuan. However, other texts identify him as Kitakuni Michian. See Kawakami, *Jukdo ui yeoksa jirihakjeok yeongu*, 53–54.

227 Yoon So-young, "Ilbon Meiji sidae munheon e natanan Ulleungdo wa Dokdo insik" [Japanese perception of Ulleungdo and Dokdo shown in the Japanese literature of the Meiji period], *Dokdo yeongu (The Journal Of Dokdo)* 1 (December 2005), 119 footnote 11 and 124–125.

3 The Meiji Government Inspects Takeshima and Matsushima

The Conclusions of "Chōsen-koku Shimatsu Naitansho"

Unlike the Edo Shogunate's admission that Takeshima and Matsushima were Joseon territory, its successor, the Meiji government, reoriented its perception of the islands with an aggressive ambition. As will be seen below, the evolving context was directly reflected by the revolutionary shift in Japan.

Western empires began their invasions of East Asia, and exemplary was the opening of Japan in 1853 by the United States through gunboat diplomacy. The Meiji Restoration, led by numerous elite figures, ended the Edo Shogunate in 1868. A new political order was established, and centralized power revolving with the emperor at the center was established. However, political and economic anxiety remained a legacy of the restoration.

In the Meiji government were men who dreamed of continental expansion and the conquest of "Samhan." (At the time, Japanese referred to the entire Korean Peninsula as "Chōsen" [K. *Joseon*], as "Sankan" [K. *Samhan*], and as "Kankoku" [K. *Hanguk*]). The debate over the "*seikanron*" (K. *jeonghannon*), which was an argument in Japan for conquering Korea, reached its peak between 1870 and 1873. However,

Japanese leaders, such as Itō Hirobumi, were well aware of Western politics and suppressed the *seikanron* group, arguing that strengthening domestic politics must come before overseas expansion.

In response, in February 1877, Saigō Takamori, the leader of the *seikanron* group, led a revolt that continued for two months and ended in Saigō's defeat and suicide. The revolt is known as the Seinan War or as the Revolt of Seinan. Using this opportunity, the Meiji government began mandatory military service and the socialized worship of the emperor as the "commander-in-chief of the Japanese imperial army and navy." When the *seikanron* was at its peak, the Meiji government ordered the Ministry of Foreign Affairs to carefully examine the domestic situation in Joseon. In December 1869, Japan sent Sada Hakubo, Moriyama Shigeru, and Saitō Sakae to Busan as inspectors.

Among the many items which the inspectors were ordered to undertake was a request to the Dajōkan made to include the "inspect[ion of related] facts of Joseon's territorial rights over Takeshima and Matsushima." The Dajōkan was not the name of a specific government post. Rather, it was a name for what is known today as the office of the prime minister. The person in charge of the Dajōkan was the *dajō daijin*, which was equivalent to today's prime minister. The dajō daijin accepted the request and ordered an examination into the process by which the two islands became Joseon territories. It is important to note that both the Ministry of Foreign Affairs and the Dajōkan acknowledged Takeshima and Matsushima as "part of Joseon territory."

The inspectors who received this order concluded their investigation and filed a report in 1870 called *Joseon-koku kosei Shimatsu naitansho*. The last section of this report was titled "Facts of How Takeshima and Matsushima Came to be Part of Joseon." The following is an excerpt.

Matsushima is a neighboring island of Takeshima, and there are no written documents on Matsushima. In the case of Takeshima, there is a document that shows Japan renting the island for a brief period. At the time, it was an unpopulated island. Bamboo, reed, and ginseng grow naturally on the island. It is also known to be abundant in seafood.[228]

To reiterate, this document illustrates that Japan's Ministry of Foreign Affairs and the Dajōkan were well aware that Takeshima and Matsushima were Joseon islands.

Some Japanese scholars do not accept this interpretation. For instance, the chief librarian at the National Diet Library of Japan, Tsukamoto Takashi, argued that in the early Meiji period many Western maps were introduced, which caused confusion in the naming of islands. That was why the inspectors were sent to check the existence of Takeshima and Matsushima. However, the result of the inspection was that "Matsushima is a neighboring island of Takeshima," but "there are no documents on Matsushima." In other words, Tsukamoto stressed that the inspectors failed to grasp any conceptual understanding of Matsushima. Here, the intended conclusion of Tsukamoto is that Matsushima is an adjacent island of Ulleungdo but not Dokdo.[229]

However, there are Japanese scholars, such as Hori Kazuo, who agree that the Ministry of Foreign Affairs acknowledged Matsushima as Joseon territory. Hori added that "this report . . . was understood as Matsushima [being] transferred to Joseon during the 'Takeshima Incident [J. *Takeshima ikken*].'"[230] This report included an additional section covering the recommendation of the inspectors to exercise military force

228 Kim Byungryull, *Dokdo nya Dakkesima nya*, 249; Shin Yong-Ha, *Dokdo ui minjok yeongtosa yeongu*, 157; Kang Mangil, "Oeguk ui munheonsang e natanan Dokdo" [Dokdo in foreign literature], in *Dokdo yeongu* (Seoul: Mungwangsa, 1985), 297–331.

229 Kim Young-soo, "Geundae Dokdo wa Ulleungdo myeongching munje reul dulleossan nonjaeng gwa geu uimi" [Modern disputes over the issue of naming of Dokdo and Ulleungdo, and its significance], in *Dokdo wa Han-Il gwangye: Beopyeoksajeok jeopgeun*, ed. Northeast Asian History Foundation (Seoul: Northeast Asian History Foundation, 2009), 173. Kim, who is a researcher at the Northeast Asian History Foundation Dokdo Research Institute, analyzed Tsukamoto's 1994 paper.

230 Ibid., 172.

or an intervention targeting the Daewongun, the ruling regent of King Gojong. Sada Hakubo, a member of the inspection team, suggested that "if [Japan] occupies Joseon, a land full of gold, rice, and barley, then there will be great benefits and no loss," which ultimately supports the *seikanron* argument.[231] These Japanese diplomatic documents clearly express the Meiji government's desire to occupy Joseon.

The Decisions by Japan's Home Ministry and the Dajōkan

Official documents held by Japan's Ministry of Foreign Affairs reiterate that Takeshima and Matsushima are Joseon territories. This is clearer in these documents than in documents from the Home Ministry. In 1876, the Home Ministry ordered a geographical survey of all Japan on a cartographic mission.

On October 16, 1876, Shimane Prefecture asked the Home Ministry if it should include Takeshima and Matsushima as part of Shimane Prefecture. The Home Ministry thought it would be permissible to include the two islands only if it was deemed appropriate by the residents. Ultimately, Shimane Prefecture eventually submitted *Report on an Island Other than Takeshima in the Sea of Japan* (J. *Nihon kai-nai Takeshima-gai ichidō chiseki ni hensan hōshi*). In this text is the phrase "Takeshima-gai ichidō," that is, "an island other than Takeshima," which illustrates that Shimane Prefecture conceived the "other island" to be an island adjacent to Takeshima. The Korean government and Korean scholars interpret "an island other than Takeshima" to mean Matsushima in Japanese and Dokdo in Korean.[232]

At the same time, over a five-month period, the Home Ministry

---

231 Shin Yong-Ha, *Dokdo ui minjok yeongtosa yeongu*, 160–162.

232 For example, Shin Yong-Ha, ibid., 164.

investigated all of the records regarding the "Takeshima Incident" and diplomatic exchanges from the end of the seventeenth century. As a result, the Home Ministry concluded that the Takeshima and Matsushima problems had already been solved in 1699 and were determined to be "not related to our country." It was then decided to remove Takeshima and Matsushima from maps and geographical surveys.

Despite the Home Ministry's decision, the Home Minister asked the Dajōkan on March 17, 1877, to consider the issue under the premise that "declaring or disposing of national land is too important a task." The Home Ministry included its report *Gazetteer of an Island Other than Takeshima in the Sea of Japan,* explicitly stating that the "other island" is Matsushima. In response, the Dajōkan, upon completing an investigation, concluded that "Takeshima and the other island" have nothing to do with Japan. This conclusion was relayed to the Home Ministry on March 29, 1877. The message was delivered to Shimane Prefecture on April 9, 1877.[233]

Again, these documents prove that the Meiji government officially acknowledged that Takeshima and Matsushima were not its possessions. If these islands were not Japanese islands, then they must be Joseon islands. Takeshima was already determined to be a Joseon island by the Edo Shogunate, and Matsushima was acknowledged to be a Joseon island by the Meiji government. Shimane Prefecture, the Home Ministry, and the Dajōkan all admitted this fact in their official records and documents.

Hori Kazuo of Kyoto University made this discovery. He began his research with Kawakami's book because much of the Japanese argument and research originates from that text. Hori concluded that Kawakami's research was too vague and not realistic. However, he refrained from

233 Shin Yong-Ha, ibid., 38–39; Lee Sang-Tae, *Saryo ga jeungmyeong haneun Dokdo neun Hanguk ttang*, 212–213.

academic criticism of Kawakami's book, knowing that Kawakami had been ordered by the Ministry of Foreign Affairs of the Japanese government to conduct the research. Hori subsequently published the paper "Japan's 1905 Incorporation of Takeshima."[234] Due to this paper, Hori was criticized, threatened, and ignored by many Japanese people.

The Counterarguments by Japanese Scholars and the Korean Rebuttals

Hori Kazuo surely is one of the most exceptional scholars in Japanese academia. Scholars with completely opposing views to him interpreted the abovementioned documents favoring Japan.

First, Shimojō focused on the fact that Iso Takeshima (Ulleungdo) and Matsushima are drawn on the map *Iso Takeshima ryakuzu* presented by the Dajōkan. He suggested further that, after analyzing the map, there is no mention of Dokdo (Takeshima). He therefore concluded that the two islands represent two Ulleungdos.[235]

Korean scholars immediately countered the vague claim. Park Hyun-jin considered *Iso Takeshima ryakuzu* as merely a sketch of the island, not an official map as its name suggested. This map, Park noted, has a compass, but it cannot be considered a regular map.[236]

---

234 This paper is introduced in detail in Kim Young-Koo's book, *Hanguk gwa bada ui gukjebeop* (Seoul: Korea Institute for Maritime Strategy, Hyoseong Chulpansa; 1999)), 317–318. Hori Kazuo's article was published as "1905-nen Nihon no Takeshima ryōdo hennyū," *Chōsenshi kenkyūkai ronbunshū* 24 (1987).

235 Shimojō's 2007 paper is analyzed in Kim Young-soo, "Geundae Dokdo wa Ulleungdo myeongching munje reul dulleossan nonjaeng gwa geu uimi," 176; Kim Hwa-kyong, "Kkeut eomneun wijeung ui yeonsok: Simane-hyeon Jukdo Munje Yeonguhoe 'choejong bogoseo' ui munjejeom" [Continuation of the endless perjury: Points of contention in the Shimane Prefecture "Final Report" of the Takeshima Issue Research Group], *Dokdo yeongu* 3 (December 2007), 5 footnote 8, and 33–34.

236 Park Hyun-jin, "Yeongto, haeyang gyeonggye bunjaeng gwa jido, haedo ui jeunggeo jiwi, gachi: Dokdo gwallyeon jido, haedo ui beop, jeongchaek, oegyo reul jungsim euro," 69.

Second, Funasugi Rikinobu, of the Shimane University Department of Geography, wrote, "On the *Takeshima-gai ichidō* map it is written that the island other than Takeshima is not Japanese territory. [But] it is not written that Matsushima, to which this [comment] refers, that is, today's Takeshima, is Korean territory." Funasugi continued, "The Dajōkan decided that Takeshima and Matsushima are not Japanese territories. It is wrong to interpret [that] the Meiji government acknowledged what is known today as Takeshima in Japan or Dokdo in Korea." Funasugi's final remarks were that "in order for Takeshima to be proven as Joseon territory, proper evidence supporting an actual ruling and actual management of the island by Joseon must be presented."[237]

Korean scholars have refused to accept such claims. For example, Kim Young-soo commented that the Japanese scholars mentioned above "argued that there are no accurate records on Matsushima once the Dajōkan documents were proven to be less than helpful for the Japanese government. This, therefore, discredits their own government's records."[238]

It should be noted here that Shimojō and Funasugi are leaders of the Takeshima Issue Research Group. As will be seen below, on March 16, 2005, the Shimane Prefectural Assembly declared February 22 as "Takeshima Day" so as to celebrate February 22, 1905, the day on which Takeshima was incorporated into Japanese territory. The Takeshima Issue Research Group was founded on June 6, 2005, led by Shimojō as its president. The institute has made great strides in developing a suitable logic to support Dokdo (Takeshima) as a Japanese island.

---

237 Naitō Seichū, "Jukdo munje boyu (竹島問題補遺): Shimane-hyeon Jukdo Munje Yeonguhoe choejong bogoseo bipan" [The Takeshima issue on hold: Criticism of final report by the Shimane Prefecture Takeshima Issue Research Group], *Dokdo yeongu* 3 (December 2007), 63–64; Kim Young-soo, "Geundae Dokdo wa Ulleungdo myeongching munje reul dulleossan nonjaeng gwa geu uimi," 177.

238 Kim Young-soo, "Geundae Dokdo wa Ulleungdo myeongching munje reul dulleossan nonjaeng gwa geu uimi," 180.

Shimojō, who published multiple articles on Takeshima and Japanese sovereignty over the island since the late 1990s, based his book *Takeshima ha Nichi-Kan dochira no mono ka* (Korea or Japan, to which does Takeshima belong?) upon this research. Korean scholars were extremely critical of the book, considering it as nothing more than a coached collage of snapshots that selected examples and evidence when the needs of the Japanese government arose. The *Takeshima Research Report: Final Report* published in March 2007 by the Takeshima Issue Research Group under Shimojō's supervision used records from the *Annals of the Joseon Dynasty* as evidence. The report lacks objective credibility and is little more than personal accounts. Korean scholars have also pointed out many misinterpretations and distorted information in the final report. Naitō Seichū, from Japan, also criticized many aspects of the final report. Some of these criticisms have been touched upon in previous sections and will be referenced again below.

The Korean-Japanese Controversy over Maps from Japan's Army and Navy

How did the Japanese army and navy treat Matsushima? First, the map *Chōsen zenzu* (E. *Map of Chōsen*), compiled by the Office of the Chief of Staff of the Department of the Army in 1875, identified Matsushima as Joseon territory. This map included Matsushima as part of Joseon territory inside the border, despite the actual location of being outside the eastern borders of Joseon.[239]

Next, let us examine the maps from the Department of the Navy. The Japanese navy composed the map *Chōsen Tōkaigan zu* (E. *Map of the*

---

[239] This map may be found in Lee Sang-Tae, *Saryo ga jeungmyeong haneun Dokdo neun Hanguk ttang*, 114.

Eastern Coast of Chōsen) in 1876 based upon Russian and British maps. The Department of the Navy not only included Matsushima as part of Joseon territory, but also drew the island within Russian specifications. If the navy considered this island to be Japanese, it would have placed the island in the sea northwest of Honshu island and not in the East Sea (K. *Donghae*) of Joseon.[240]

The Hydrographic Bureau in the Japanese navy published the book *Kanei suiroshi* (E. *World Waterways*) in 1883. In volume 2, chapter 4, "Chōsen tōgan" (E. *Eastern Coast of Chōsen*), an island known today as Dokdo in Korea and as Takeshima in Japan, was called "Rianko amu" and was described in detail along with Ulleungdo.[241] This provides evidence that Japan acknowledged Ulleungdo and Rianko amu as Joseon territory.

What exactly is "Rianko amu"? On January 27, 1849, the *Liancourt*, a French whaling ship, spotted a large rock approximately southwest of Ulleugdo. During this time, many Western countries, such as the United States, France, and Russia, were heavily involved in whaling. Jean Lopez, captain of the *Liancourt*, noted that "this rock appears on no maps or [in any] books." Thus, he named the rock after his ship, "Rochers Liancourt," and this place name was translated into English as "Liancourt Rocks." In 1851, the Hydrographic Bureau of the French navy published the *Map of the Pacific Ocean* with Liancourt Rocks in this now known position. Since that time the island appeared in Western waterways as Liancourt Rocks. Japanese people in turn called this feature "Rianko amu" or "Ryangko-tou." This island is known today as Dokdo in Korea or Takeshima in Japan.[242]

In 1854, five years after the *Liancourt* found this rock, the Russian

---

240 Shin Yong-Ha, *Dokdo ui minjok yeongtosa yeongu*, 39–40.

241 Ibid., 214.

242 Li Jin-mieung, *Dokdo: Jirisang ui jaebalgyeon*, 59–65.

warship *Pallada*, led by Vice Admiral Yevfimy Vasilievich Putiatin (1803–1883), located the rock, as well. He named Dongdo and Seodo in Russian as Menalai and Olivutsa, respectively. Dokdo, as a whole, was accordingly named the Menalai and Olivutsa Rocks. Menalai was a name of the *Pallada* during its voyages in the Black Sea Fleet and the *Olivutsa* was a name of one of the scout boats that belonged to the *Pallada*.

In 1855, one year prior to the *Pallada*'s rediscovery of Dokdo, a vessel from the British Royal Navy fleet dispatched to China, the HMS *Hornet*, led by Commander Charles C. Farsyth, measured the rock and named them the Hornet Rocks. All of the Westerners who came across Dokdo saw it not as an island, only as a rock.

"Liancourt Rocks" was the most popular name for the rocks among its many western names. The Japanese pronounced it as "Riankuru Rokkusu," hence the nickname, "Ryangko-tou." This fact is shown in *Dai Nihon-koku enkai ryakuzu* (E. *Map of the Coast of Great Japan*), which was composed in 1867 by the Japanese naval officer Katsu Kaishū, and in *Dai Nihon shishin zenzu* (E. *Complete Map of Great Japan of the Four Gods*), which Hashimoto Gyokuran compiled in 1870.[243]

The name of the Hydrographic Bureau of the Japanese navy was soon changed to the Department of Hydrographics, and this department issued *Chōsen Tōkai gando* again in 1887. In this map, Ulleungdo and "Rianko amu" were marked as Joseon territory. Later, further editions of the maps were reprinted, and until 1905 the map marked the islands as Joseon territory.[244]

In 1894, the Department of Hydrographics composed *Chōsen suiroshi*. Ulleungdo and the small rock were marked as Joseon territory and

243 Ōnishi, *Dokdo*, 51–52; Song Byeong-Ki, *Gochyeo sseun Ulleungdo wa Dokdo*, 93 footnote 7.

244 The 1887 version of this map was discovered by Lee Jong-hak, a Korean scholar of Dokdo. Shin Yong-Ha, *Hanguk gwa Ilbon ui Dokdo yeongyugwon nonjaeng*, 144 footnote 47.

therefore not included in *Nihon suiroshi*. The Department of Hydro-graphics maintained this stance through 1899, which provides further evidence that the Japanese navy officially acknowledged this rock to be Joseon territory.[245] In this context, in 1907, Shimane Prefecture formed a joint official-civilian inspection, which reported that it is extremely regretful that the Rianko amu are included in the map of Joseon.

On September 9, 1953, the representatives of the Republic of Korea in Japan stressed in *Korean Government Opinion 1* that, based on what is drawn in *Chōsen suiroshi*, it was understood by the Meiji govern-ment that Dokdo is Joseon territory.[246] The Japanese side countered by arguing in *Japanese Government Opinion 2*, dated February 10, 1954, that *Chōsen suiroshi* is merely a waterway navigation reference aide, not a political map with definitions of borders. "A hydrographic directory is compiled for the convenience of its users and has nothing to do with the territorial jurisdiction over the island," they wrote.[247]

In response, the Korean government and Korean scholars argued in *Korean Government Opinion 2*, issued on September 25, 1954, that even if *Chōsen suiroshi* is merely a hydrographic directory, it contains neither fiction nor inaccuracies. Rather, the directory is drawn on a factual basis and is based upon evidence.[248] In the same context, Lee Han-key stated, "The hydrographic directory made by the Japanese navy is an official document of the Japanese government, and its editor could not have composed the document under false premises."[249] Shin Yong-Ha was more detailed in his explanation. He stated that "despite the [fact that

245 Lee Sang-Tae, *Saryo ga jeungmyeong haneun Dokdo neun Hanguk ttang*, 215; Lee Han-key, *Hanguk ui yeongto*, 253–254; Shin Yong-Ha, *Hanguk gwa Ilbon ui Dokdo yeongyugwon nonjaeng*, 144–145.

246 *Korean Government Opinion 1* may be found in Shin Yong-Ha et al., *Dokdo yeongyugwon jaryo ui tamgu*, vol. 3, 432–442. Mention of the *suiroshi* is found on page 441.

247 *Japanese Government Opinion 2* may be found in Shin Yong-Ha et al., *Dokdo yeongyugwon jaryo ui tamgu*, vol. 4, pages 215–231. "*suiroshi*" is mentioned on page 262.

248 Ibid., 251–268.

249 Lee Han-key, *Hanguk ui yeongto*, 254.

the] Japanese navy was fully aware of the location of Dokdo, Dokdo was not included in *Nihon suiroshi*. Rather, it was included in *Chōsen suiroshi*."[250]

Needless to say, Japanese scholars rejected the Korean arguments. Sasaki Shigeru, for example, wrote in *Takeshima Research Report: Final Report* (2007), "Hydrographic directories were made only to secure safety of the ships on voyages, and it is not a map marking any borders." Funasugi argued similarly. In the same report he wrote, "Hydrographic directories, or *suiroshi*, are used for directions, and the Japanese navy [. . .] is not a department of the Japanese government in charge of drawing maps."[251]

Kim Young-soo argued the opposite. He concluded, "Sasaki did not reject national borders represented in the *suiroshi*." About Funasugi, Kim noted, "In 1894, during the analysis of *Chōsen suiroshi*, Funasugi denigrated Joseon's hydrographic survey results for Ulleungdo and Dokdo when arguing that they are the results of British surveys."

Park Byoungsup contributed to criticism of Funasugi. Funasugi stressed in *Chōsen suiroshi*, "Ulleungdo was surveyed at east 140 degrees, 53 minutes, and the Liancourt Rocks were surveyed at east 131 degrees, 55 minutes," and he concluded that the eastern border of Joseon is at Ulleungdo and today's Takeshima is not included. Park stated, "There is a contradiction in [Funasugi's] argument." He continued that "if the eastern border of Joseon is at 130 degrees, 35 minutes, then Ulleungdo, whose coordinates are 130 degrees, 53 minutes, should not be included within the border. Nevertheless, [Funasugi] wrote, 'The eastern border of Joseon is at Ulleungdo.'"[252]

---

250 Shin Yong-Ha, *Hanguk gwa Ilbon ui Dokdo yeongyugwon nonjaeng*, 146.

251 Kim Young-soo, "Geundae Dokdo wa Ulleungdo myeongching munje reul dulleossan nonjaeng gwa geu uimi," 145.

252 Park Byoungsup, "Simojo Masao (下條正男) ui nonseol eul bunseok handa (2)," 145.

Other than military maps, there were multiple civilian maps from Japan that did not include Matsushima, or Dokdo. There are two famous examples of this occurrence. The first is the case of *Dai Nihon zenzu* (E. *Map of Japan*), which was composed in September 1876. Two months prior to the coerced agreement of the Japan-Korea Treaty of 1876, this map was compiled and included detailed descriptions of every region in Japan. Matsushima (Dokdo) was excluded, however. The second case is the map *Dai Nihon zenzu*, compiled in September 1881. These two maps did not include Ulleungdo or Dokdo.[253]

---

253 Hosaka, *Ilbon gojido edo Dokdo eopda*, 31–33.

4 The Korean-Japanese Controversy over Director Tanabe Taichi's Remarks

Japanese Merchants Demand the Development of Matsushima

During the Meiji period, how did Japan's Ministry of Foreign Affairs understand the issues surrounding the islands? Considering that the Ministry of Foreign Affairs directly dealt with Japan's diplomatic matters, this question will be addressed through such a light in this chapter.

In 1874, Fujiwara Shigechika, a descendant of an elite family in Fukuoka Prefecture and a merchant based on Oki Island, made plans to commence logging on Takeshima and submitted a business plan titled "Request for Aid: Takeshima Development." This was not long after Oki Island had been raised to the status of prefecture. Oki Island voluntarily expressed the ambition for this plan with clear financial motives.[254]

In July 1877, the merchant Mutō Heigaku submitted "Suggestions for the Development of Matsushima" (J. *Matsushima kaitaku no gi*) to the Ministry of Foreign Affairs. He wrote that he had "come across a lump of islands to the northwest on his trips from Nagasaki to Vladivostok,

---

254 Ōnishi, *Dokdo*, 62. This book did not discuss to which department Fujiwara submitted the request.

158

Russia." Mutō continued, "The island is elevated, and there are no people on it. However, . . . the island is rich with pine trees." He suggested that this island is "Matsushima, located north of Oki," and that although he is not completely certain, "the island seems to be mineable," and he requested permission to do so. In an addendum to the report, he remarked that this island is not Takeshima, and that the Edo Shogunate gave the island to Joseon and therefore it is not Ulleungdo.[255]

Mutō's development plan became popular quickly and numerous similar plans were submitted to the Ministry of Foreign Affairs. The Japanese government's economic attaché in Vladivostok, Sewaki Toshihito, even requested that the central government quickly accept the development proposals. Around the same time, Kodama Sadayasu and Saitō Shichirōbei submitted a similar request for the development of Matsushima to the Ministry of Foreign Affairs.[256] And in 1878, Toda Keigi submitted to the Tokyo prefectural government a "Request for Development Aid for Takeshima."[257]

The Meiji government granted none of these requests for assistance. The government had a clear understanding that the island to which the requests referred was Ulleungdo and that Joseon possessed that island. However, according to Ōnishi Toshiteru, who analyzed the requests, "The Meiji bureaucrats had no knowledge of Matsushima" (today's Takeshima, that is, Dokdo).[258]

As was shown in Mutō's case, Mutō lacked a basic level of knowledge about Matsushima when he submitted his request. During that time, most Japanese people had little if any knowledge of the islands of

---

255 This was included in *Takeshima kōshō* [The historical investigation of Takeshima] written by Kitazawa Shosei, of the Meiji government's Ministry of Foreign Affairs. The original texts may be found in Shin Yong-Ha et al., *Dokdo yeongyugwon jaryo ui tamgu*, vol. 4, 132–135.

256 *Takeshima kōshō*, vol. 2 (2), ibid., 140–142.

257 *Takeshima kōshō*, vol. 2 (2), ibid., 120–131.

258 Ōnishi, *Dokdo*, 63.

Matsushima and Takeshima. The Ministry of Foreign Affairs officials were no different. Some officials knew a great deal about Takeshima, but not Matsushima.

The lack of knowledge regarding the island was displayed in other documents, such as diplomatic cables sent to Joseon. In a document relayed to Joseon on December 16, 1882, the Japanese diplomat Inoue Kaoru wrote, "Our people call Ulleungdo, a Joseon island, either Takeshima or Matsushima."[259]

Under such circumstances, the Meiji government took two actions. First, it ordered the navy officer Miura Shigesato to survey Matsushima. In September 1880, Miura moored his ship, the *Amagi Maru*, on the eastern coast of Matsushima in order to survey the island. The basic investigation became the foundation for his argument that "Matsushima is Ulleungdo and the small islands around Ulleungdo are Takeshima. These smaller islands are no more than mere rocks, which clears the doubts cast from the past immediately."[260] Kang Mangil pointed out that it seems as if the *Amagi Maru* only verified that the affiliated islands were off the coast of Ulleungdo but had no further understanding of Dokdo.[261]

Second, Kitazawa Shosei, another Japanese diplomat, was ordered to investigate Takeshima. Kitazawa studied the materials on this matter in great detail, and his studies became the basis for the three volumes of the *Takeshima kōshō*, which was issued in 1881. This book was summarized and submitted to the Ministry of Foreign Affairs on August 20, 1881.[262]

---

259 This message is included in the *Japanese Diplomatic Cables*. The original text may be read in Shin Yong-Ha et al., *Dokdo yeongyugwon jaryo ui tamgu*, vol. 3, 181.

260 Shin Yong-Ha et al., *Dokdo yeongyugwon jaryo ui tamgu*, vol. 4, 207.

261 Kang Mangil, "Oeguk ui munheonsang e natanan Dokdo," 319–320; Kim Young-soo, "Geundae Dokdo wa Ulleungdo myeongching munje reul dulleossan nonjaeng gwa geu uimi," 174–175.

262 Shin Yong-Ha et al., *Dokdo yeongyugwon jaryo ui tamgu*, vol. 4, 26–213, 185–186; Shin Yong-Ha et al., *Dokdo yeongyugwon jaryo ui tamgu*, vol. 3, 159–180.

In the report, Kitazawa noted that Matsushima is Ulleungdo, which was referred to as Takeshima, and that what was called Matsushima previously is nothing more than a rock. He concluded that Matsushima, that is, Ulleungdo, "was from ancient times a land beyond our territory."[263]

"Matsushima is Usan, which Belongs to Ulleungdo"

As seen above, numerous Japanese requested aid to develop Matsushima. In order to reach Matsushima, they had to pass through Takeshima. Tanabe Taichi commented, "Matsushima is a name of a Joseon island known as Usan, which the Japanese people just labeled [as such]." He continued, "Sending people to the island without a clear purpose is [the] same as counting another's wealth. In addition, sending our people to foreign lands is no more than trespassing."[264] For this reason, the decision was made to reject all requests to develop Matsushima.

The Korean government interpreted what Tanabe referred to as "Usan" as today's Dokdo, a Korean island off the coast of Ulleungdo. Under such circumstances, the representatives of the Republic of Korea in Japan submitted *Korean Government Opinion 3* on January 7, 1959. This report stressed Tanabe's remarks and made public the Japanese record "Matsushima no ki." In this *Opinion*, the Korean government concluded, "This . . . should serve as evidence to support an argument that territorial possession [by Korea] was already recognized in the Meiji period by the Japanese government."[265]

Needless to say, Japan's Ministry of Foreign Affairs rejected the

---

263 Shin Yong-Ha et al., *Dokdo yeongyugwon jaryo ui tamgu*, vol. 3, 209. Kim Young-soo, "Geundae Dokdo wa Ulleungdo myeongching munje reul dulleossan nonjaeng gwa geu uimi," 174.

264 *Takeshima kōshō*, vol. 2, 14; Shin Yong-Ha et al., *Dokdo yeongyugwon jaryo ui tamgu*, vol. 4, 199–200.

265 Shin Yong-Ha et al., *Dokdo yeongyugwon jaryo ui tamgu*, vol. 4, 377–378.

Korean government's interpretation. In *Japanese Government Opinion 4*, sent on July 13, 1962, the Japanese government commented, "The Korean government is twisting Tanabe's words to support their arguments and strengthen them." The Japanese continued to argue that "Tanabe's assertion that there are some who referred to Matsushima as Usando" is nothing more than a "preemptive hypothesis" and not "his own opinion."

The Ministry of Foreign Affairs argued further that the Matsushima to which Tanabe referred was "a Matsushima of uncertain identity" to the Japanese who wanted to develop the Ulleungdo area. The Ministry of Foreign Affairs also stated that "if Matsushima is truly Takeshima, then the island belongs to them (Joseon). But if the island is proven to be another island, then there is no way that the island does not belong to us (Japan)," and that Tanabe's true meanings are found near the end of his remarks.[266]

---

266 Ibid., 452.

5 The Korean-Japanese Controversy over the Confusion of the Takeshima and Matsushima Naming Convention in Japanese Texts

What should be highlighted here is that most Japanese texts, including Meiji period texts, mixed Takeshima and Matsushima. Why was there such confusion?

In *Korean Government Opinion 3* submitted by the representatives of the Republic of Korea to Japan's Ministry of Foreign Affairs on January 7, 1959, explained that "at that time, Japanese people had a limited geographical knowledge of these islands." The opinion emphasized that this was evidence countering the view that Dokdo is Japanese territory. If Japanese people acknowledged these islands, which today the Japanese side calls Takeshima and which the Korean side calls Dokdo, then the confusion would not have occurred, as the Korean government and Korean scholars pointed out.[267]

The Ministry of Foreign Affairs responded in *Japanese Government Opinion 4* filed with the representatives of the Republic of Korea on July 13, 1962. The Japanese government's response is summarized below:

---

[267] The texts of *Korean Government Opinion 3* are included in Shin Yong-Ha et al., *Dokdo yeongyugwon jaryo ui tamgu*, vol. 4, 373–388. The point about "confusion" may be found on page 380.

163

First, until the early Meiji period, the Japanese people unanimously thought that Ulleungdo was Takeshima, and that Dokdo was Matsushima.

Second, errors in European surveys of Ulleungdo resulted in faulty cartography, which ultimately led to the international confusion related to the designation of Ulleungdo and Dokdo in Japan.[268]

How were Ulleungdo and Dokdo represented on Western maps? As noted in Chapter 1, having been influenced by Chinese maps of the time, Western maps identified these two islands as Fan-ling-tao (K. *Balleungdo*) and Tchiang-chan-tao (K. *Cheonsando*), respectively. Ulleungdo was first discovered by Joseph Lepaute Dagelet, professor of astronomy at the École Militaire, aboard the ship of Commander Jean-François de Galaup, comte de La Pérouse on May 27, 1787. La Pérouse named the island after Dagelet, and drew it on the map according to its actual size and location.[269] Although he did not state on the map the country that possessed the island, there is ample information which shows that the island belonged to Joseon.

Upon discovering the island, neither La Pérouse nor Dagelet were aware that the island was the "Fan-ling-tao" that appeared in their charts. Stated differently, they did not realize that the island they had discovered was Ulleungdo. This explains why they wrote "Dagelet Island" next to these two islands. Could La Pérouse's ship have seen Dokdo, or the island that Japanese called Matsushima? Unfortunately, they were not able to discover this small island and continued their voyage north. This explains further why Matsushima was not drawn in the maps compiled in 1787.

In 1789, two years after La Pérouse's discovery of Ulleungdo, the

---

268 *Japanese Government Opinion 4* is the same as above. See pages 432–433.

269 Li Jin-mieung, *Dokdo: Jirisang ui jaebalgyeon*, 52–53.

British explorer James Colnett sailed aboard the *Argonaut* and entered the East Sea via the Korean Strait. Colnett believed that he had discovered an island and named the island after the ship upon which he sailed.

Regarding the name "Argonaut," it is necessary to review the records of Philipp Franz Jonkheer Balthasar von Siebold (1796–1866). He was a German-Dutch doctor who worked in Japan from 1823. He recorded detailed surveys of Japanese nature and geography. His records became the foundation for his periodical *Nippon* (日本), which was discontinued in 1854. However, in 1840, he published a reference map to Nippon.[270]

Here, Siebold wrote, "In 1797, a British naval officer, William Robert Broughton, led his ship the HMS *Providence* [and] found Ulleungdo on his voyage down the edge of the East Sea and named it Argonaut." Broughton never found Ulleungdo and should not be related further to the name Argonaut. Siebold was mistaken. Nonetheless, according to Siebold's description, and as a result of frequent Western voyages to the area, in some Western maps produced between 1820 and 1850, "Fan-ling-tao" and "Tchiang-chan-tao" were replaced with "Dagelet Island" and "Argonaut Island.".

Later, Argonaut Island came to be understood as unrelated to Ulleungdo. This proved Siebold's records wrong. Naturally, Argonaut disappeared from Western maps and only Dagelet Island remained. This is why in *Japanese Government Opinion 1* submitted by the Ministry of Foreign Affairs on July 13, 1953, Dagelet Island came to be known as Matsushima and is known today as Dokdo. Ulleungdo "was mistakenly indicated as Matsushima." Through this process, the small island previously called Matsushima acquired the name Takeshima.

As will be addressed in Chapter 5, this is the background in which the Meiji government, on February 22, 1905, selected the name Takeshima

---

[270] The map and its influence are discussed in detail in ibid., 110–112, 262–263; Ōnishi, *Dokdo*, 45–26.

over Matsushima when it decided to incorporate Dokdo. This is explained in *Japanese Government Opinion 4*, submitted on July 13, 1962.[271]

The Korean side countered that such an explanation by Japanese only creates further confusion and doubt. As Lee Han-key pointed out, if Ulleungdo had been called Takeshima from past times, the Europeans should have used the name Takeshima and nothing else to name the island. Also, if Dokdo was called Matsushima and had been a Japanese island since olden days, as the Japanese side argues, then Dokdo should be called Matsushima and its name should not have changed. It is difficult to understand why the indigenous name of Dokdo was taken away to label Ulleungdo. In the words of Lee Han-key, "If the Japanese blindly followed the inaccurate maps of Siebold, then the Japanese side's claim that Japan long ago 'thoroughly understood' the geography of Ulleungdo and Dokdo is a lie."[272]

---

271 Shin Yong-Ha et al., *Dokdo yeongyugwon jaryo ui tamgu*, vol. 4, 450–451.

272 Lee Han-key, *Hanguk ui yeongto*, 255–256.

Dokdo: The Joseon Government Incorporates the Island into Ulleung-gun County as "Seokdo," but Four Years and Four Months Later the Japanese Government Incorporates the Island into Shimane Prefecture as "Takeshima"

Chapter 5

1 The Joseon Government Decides to Develop Ulleungdo and Its Affiliated Islands

The Office for Extraordinary State Affairs Suggests Inspections of Ulleungdo and Its Affiliated Islands

As the previous chapter shows, examining official Meiji government records from 1874 to 1878 indicates that the Japanese took great interest in developing Takeshima and Matsushima. This period extended from the years immediately prior to through the opening of Joseon by the Meiji government's military power in 1876. It was only four to five years later that the Japanese decided to survey Matsushima during the aggressive investigation of Takeshima by the Ministry of Foreign Affairs. All of these were signals of the Japanese attempt to occupy Joseon with hidden purposes.

The Joseon government discovered the Japanese plan in its infancy. Im Han-su, a Gangwon-do province governor, noted the scheme in his report to what was then the chief executive office, the Office for Extraordinary State Affairs (K. *Tongni gimu amun*). Im Han-su detailed the frequent Japanese logging activities occurring on Ulleungdo, in which the cargo would be transported to Wonsan, in Hamgyeong-do province, and then through Busan, in Gyeongsang-do province, to be ultimately shipped to Japan. Or the lumber was sold to a third party. This report, completed in 1881, warned that "Japanese people have set their eyes and interest on this island, [and] thus, a negative effect is inevitable," in an attempt to convince the central government to take appropriate countermeasures.[273] The Office for Extraordinary State Affairs granted the request, and took the following two actions. First, a demand was formulated to halt Japanese intrusions articulated through documents sent to the Japanese embassy in Dongnae-gun county. Second, and more importantly, a plan to inspect Ulleungdo and the affiliated region was framed. Finally, a suggestion was made to the king:

> It is negligent to leave the island in the middle of the sea empty. The region must be inspected to determine whether it has the appropriate defensive qualities to be a strategic point. Appoint Fourth Deputy Commander [K. *buhogun*] Yi Gyu-won as Ulleungdo inspector [K. *Ullengdo geomchalsa*] and have him ready a report soon as possible.[274]

King Gojong granted the request and appointed Yi Gyu-won as Ulleungdo inspector on May 23, 1881. After having established diplomatic relations with Japan, King Gojong was keen to keep the Japanese intrusions into Joseon under surveillance.

Yi Gyu-won Inspects Songdo, Jukdo, and Usando

Yi Gyu-won postponed his departure to early April because he wanted the element of surprise against the logging site in catching them in the act. Once Yi Gyu-won had fully prepared for departure, King Gojong expressed great interest in Ulleungdo and assigned him five specific

273 Shin Yong-Ha et al., *Dokdo yeongyugwon jaryo ui tamgu*, vol. 2, 9.
274 Ibid., 10.

tasks: (1) inspect the Japanese trespassers; (2) calculate the distance between Songjukdo and Usando, which are located near Ulleungdo; (3) investigate the rumor that the three islands of Songdo, Jukdo, and Usando are a set called Ulleungdo and confirm the situation; (4) prepare an Ulleungdo development plan and maps, with detailed descriptions of the region's ecosystem and biology; and (5) since past inspections of the region were lacking, ensure that the highest quality and detail are achieved during the inspection.[275]

It is interesting to note King Gojong's wording, "Songdo, Jukdo, and Usando are a set called Ulleungdo." It was clear that the monarch understood that the three islands were separate landmasses and yet referred to as Ulleungdo. In other words, the king understood that Usando was the main island of Ulleungdo and Songdo and Jukdo were affiliated.

Yi Gyu-won led a convoy of 102 men and departed from Hanyang on April 7. He and his men passed through Gwangju-gun county in Gyeonggi-do province, and Wonju-gun county and Uljin-gun county in Gangwon-do province, and arrived in Pyeonghae-gun county in the same province. There his crew was divided into three teams aboard three vessels. These crews departed from Gusanpo Port on April 29 and arrived at Sohwangtogumi on the west side of Ulleungdo the next day, April 30.[276]

The crews walked to Nari-dong, in central Ulleungdo, and remained there throughout the duration of the inspection. The crews began the inspection by collecting census data. The results indicated that, as of April 1882, a total of 140 Joseon people resided on the island. Of them, 115 people were from Jeolla-do province, comprising 82 percent of the total; fourteen people, or 10 percent, were from Gangwon-do province;

---

275 Ibid., 12–14.

276 Lee Sungun, "Ulleungdo mit Dokdo tamheom sogo" [Short journals on an expedition to Ulleung-do and Dokdo], in *Dokdo* (Seoul: Daehan Gongnonsa, 1965), 124–128.

ten people, or 7 percent, were from Gyeongsang-do province; and one person was from Gyeonggi-do province.

On May 9, Yi Gyu-won piloted a small boat to inspect two nearby islands south of the main island of Ulleungdo. He saw that the islands were full of bamboo but void of people. One island was called Jukdo and the other was called Dohang, which is a word that translates literally as "neck of the island." [He only confirmed that bamboo trees grew abundantly on this island, and that there was absolutely no evidence of residence by people. The island that he called Jukdo is now called Jukseo, and Dohang is now called Gwaneumdo. The shore opposite Gwaneumdo is written in Chinese characters as "島項," that is, "Dohang," and in Korean these characters mean "neck of the island" and are pronounced in Korean as Seommok.

After his inspection of Usando, Yi Gyu-won delivered his report. "The Joseon people residing in Ulleungdo consider the islands Songdo, Jukdo, and Usando as affiliated islands. However, there exists no map to support such claims, nor is there any written documentation of the case. On clear days, one can climb up the highest hill on the islands and see a thousand miles away, but there is not a single grain of dirt besides Ulleungdo. Calling Usando as Ulleungdo is exactly like calling Tamna as Jeju."[277]

These words from Yi Gyu-won's report to King Gojong reveal that the Joseon people of Ulleungdo had the same understanding as their king, that Songdo, Jukdo, and Usando are separate islands but are conceived of as Ulleungdo. Yet, there is no recognition of the island called Dokdo today. It is thought that the people risking their lives by making a living through violating the government's no-entry law for the island were poorly educated in comparison to the larger population.

---

277 Shin Yong-Ha et al., *Dokdo yeongyugwon jaryo ui tamgu*, vol. 3, 21–53.

Japanese People Identified Ulleungdo as Matsushima

On May 10, Yi Gyu-won discovered a Japanese ship moored near Dobangcheong Port. On the shore were Japanese tents, from which approximately six or seven Japanese people greeted Yi Gyu-won. As the Korean official was not accompanied by an interpreter, Yi Gyu-won conversed with the Japanese men in writing by using Chinese characters.

Yi Gyu-won posed the question, "This island is a Joseon island, [and] so the Japanese government prohibits its people from trespassing on it. But how is it that you people are here logging?" The Japanese people answered, "We thought that this island belonged to the Japanese empire, because there was a wooden sign written in Chinese characters that read 'Matsushima' (松島) in Japanese." There was a Japanese testimonial that the sign had been erected in 1869, thus it can be extrapolated that Japanese people had begun to exploit the islands at this time. Yi Gyu-won explained that "this island is called Ulleungdo. Goryeo inherited the island from Silla, and Joseon received the island from Goryeo." He warned the Japanese loggers to "stop logging and return to your homeland immediately." The Japanese men promised to leave the island. It is estimated that at that time there was a total of seventy-eight Japanese lumberjacks.[278]

An interesting point to note is that the Japanese who trespassed on Ulleungdo had no familiarity with the names "Dokdo" or "Ulleungdo." For some time, the Japanese referred to Ulleungdo as Takeshima, and Dokdo as Matsushima, illustrating their confusion about the two islands, and also a general lack of understanding.

Yi Gyu-won and his crew left Ulleungdo on May 11 and traveled through Pyeonghae-gun county in Gangwon-do province. They arrived

---

278 Ibid., 68–71.

in Gangneung-gun county in Gangwon-do province on May 21. From there, they returned to Hanyang via Wonju-gun county in Gangwon-do province, and Gwangju-gun county in Gyeonggi-do province, arriving in Hanyang on May 27. Yi Gyu-won reported to King Gojong on June 5, and he submitted his report and a map titled *Ulleungdo oe do*. The most important content was, "The Japanese are cunning and insincere people, and they erected a wooden sign on which was written 'Songdo.' The name Songdo has been criticized by both countries. Thus, it was inevitable [that we] . . . sent an official document to the Japanese ambassador Hanabusa Yoshitaka and an official document to the Ministry of Foreign Affairs." King Gojong replied, "Deliver the message to the prime minister and to the ministers. Addressing these matters is not to be delayed. Despite the island being a small piece of our territory, we are not to abandon it." Yi Gyu-won responded, "The island is small [indeed], yet [it is the] small territory of Joseon. How is it possible even to discuss the possibility of abandoning it?"[279] This conversation was an affirmation of the determination to protect the national boundary.

King Gojong Orders the Redevelopment of Ulleungdo and Its Affiliated Islands

According to the orders of King Gojong, from June 1882 the Joseon government demanded that the Ministry of Foreign Affairs ban Japanese people from trespassing into Ulleungdo for any reason, but especially for logging. Simultaneously, the Joseon government ordered Koreans to occupy Ulleungdo for development purposes. What once had been a ban on entering Ulleungdo that had lasted several hundred

---

279 Ibid., 96–98.

years suddenly reverted to a policy focused on development. Chief State Councilor (K. *yeonguijeong*) Hong Sun-mok suggested the installation of island security. The government appointed Jeon Seok-gyu, who was living on Ulleungdo, as the first head of the island in August 1882, to be monitored by Pyeonghae-gun county, Gangwon-do province.[280]

In March 1883, King Gojong appointed Kim Ok-gyun, a leader of the reformist faction and a secretary in the Foreign Office (K. *Tongni gyoseop tongsangsamu amun*), as southeastern islands development official and concurrent whaling management supervisor (K. *dongnam jedo gaecheoksa gyeomgwanpogyeongsa*) in order to aggressively pursue development and the whaling industry of the Ulleungdo region.[281] Note that Kim Ok-gyun's extent of authority was not bounded by Ulleungdo but included the entire southeastern coastal region. Among the many islands, it is clear that he was responsible for Songdo, Jukdo, and Usando as mentioned by King Gojong on April 7, 1882.

There have been alterations to names in the years that have passed. Considering that those names are all variants of Dokdo in some way, one can fairly interpret that King Gojong's orders included the development of Dokdo, as well. This will be examined below in greater detail. King Gojong also ordered Joseon administrators to exempt Kim Ok-gyun from paying respect to elders he may encounter en route to the site, thus increasing his freedom of movement during this trip. Not only does the exemption signify King Gojong's trust in Kim Ok-gyun, but it also suggests that King Gojong's interest and passion for development and protection of the region were of high importance.

Kim Ok-gyun poured his energy into the new post he was ordered to fill. There already were families moving to Ulleungdo, seven or eight from Gangwon-do province and ten from Gyeongsang-do province.

---

280 Ibid., 114–115.
281 Ibid., 186.

Kim continued this momentum by moving other families to the island. In April 1883, he moved sixteen families, totaling fifty-four people. In that same year, he arrested and prosecuted the first head of Ulleungdo Island, Jeon Seok-gyu, for receiving payoffs for aiding the Japanese with illegal logging and grain distribution. The Joseon government later expelled Jeon Seok-gyu from the post in January 1884 and ordered the magistrate of Pyeonghae-gun county, Gangwon-do province, to take over the post and the administration of the island in addition to his existing duties.[282] Furthermore, Kim Ok-gyun deported all of the Japanese people on Ulleungdo. By September 1883, no Japanese were to be found on the island.[283] Kim's actions soon ended after a failed coup against the Joseon government. The event was known as the Gapsin Coup 1884 (K. *Gapsin Jeongbyeon*), and it resulted in his defection to Japan.

After the Joseon government expelled Jeon Seok-gyu, it was difficult to find a replacement. Further, the Gapsin Coup left domestic politics in disarray, which distracted the government's attention from Ulleungdo. Four years after the coup, in February 1888, the Joseon government finally installed a military encampment at Wolsongjin and made Pyeonghae-gun responsible for supervising Ulleungdo. Two years later, in February 1890, King Gojong personally ordered Gangwon-do province's Governor Yi Won-il to "inspect the island where foreigners illegally log trees."[284]

With Joseon at an advantage and Japan at a disadvantage, from 1891 more Japanese illegally occupied the islands despite the aggressive policies of the Joseon government for Ulleungdo and its adjacent islands. That number increased greatly especially after 1895, when

---

282 Ibid., 129, 133.

283 Shin Yong-Ha, *Dokdo ui minjok yeongtosa yeongu*, 52.

284 Shin Yong-Ha et al., *Dokdo yeongyugwon jaryo ui tamgu*, vol. 2, 137–138.

Japan won the Sino-Japanese War. The population grew to nearly 200 Japanese on Ulleungdo.[285] They logged Zelkova trees, a principle species of Ulleungdo, to near extinction and smuggled other goods off the island. In addition, they even swung swords at Ulleungdo locals who complained about their behavior.

The Joseon government was losing its influence, but it did not relegate itself to the sidelines. In 1894, as a result of the Gabo Reform (K. *Gabo Gyeongjang*), a reformist government emerged. Its focus on developing and maintaining Ulleungdo strengthened. In August 1895, King Gojong considered the recommendation from Home Minister Park Jeong-yang to raise the status of *dojang*, or island head, to a higher rank of *dogam*. Bae Gye-ju was appointed as the first *dogam* island head, and he landed on Ulleungdo in May 1897.[286]

The Joseon government actively recommended relocation to Ulleungdo. It did so by offering material incentives and subsidizing moving expenses. The response from people differed regionally. According to *The Independent*, by March 1897, there was a total of twelve *dong-ri* and 397 households, totaling 1,134 people on the island: 662 men and 472 women. Cultivated farmland totaled nearly 800 acres (4,775 *durak*).[287]

At this point, it seemed that a general understanding of Dokdo among the Joseon people of Ulleungdo had become fixed. This was evident in the testimony of Hong Jae-hyeon, an elder among the first generation of settlers that moved to Ulleungdo in 1887. After Japan lost World War II and left Joseon, Hong testified in a report composed on August 20, 1947, under the supervision of the United States Army Military Government in Korea (USAMGIK) that "Dokdo can be seen from the main island

---

285 Song Byeong-Ki, *Gochyeo sseun Ulleungdo wa Dokdo*, 131.

286 Ibid., 142.

287 Shin Yong-Ha, *Dokdo ui minjok yeongtosa yeongu*, 53.

on good days, and there have been numerous incidents in which fishing ships drifted ashore at Dokdo, thus people's attention to Dokdo has been deepened."[288]

Maps from the Korean Empire Label Usando Accurately

The attention given to Ulleungdo and its adjacent islands were essentially oriented toward national defense. This became more apparent after October 1897, when the Joseon government declared itself an empire and King Gojong became Emperor Gojong. Subsequently, the Ministry of Education (K. *Hakbu*) of the Korean Empire drafted new maps that illustrated all Korean territory in detail. The *Daehan yeojido* image completed in 1898 and the *Daehan jeondo* image completed in 1899 are examples of such maps.[289] These images showed Korean territories and the empire's administrative districts, and, more importantly, Ulleungdo and Usando. Here, Usando is drawn as a small island to the east of Ulleungdo. This Usando is the island that Koreans now call Dokdo.

The Joseon government raised the rank of the *dogam* post to the *pan-imgwan* ranks in May 1898. The Joseon government's administrative ranks were divided into eighteen, extending from senior first grade to junior ninth grade. However, among the Gabo Reforms introduced from 1894 to 1896, the eighteen ranks were reduced to eleven. Among the eleven ranks, those from seven through nine were the *pan-imgwan* ranks. In a sense, that Ulleungdo's administrative posts were elevated to *pan-imgwan* reflects the Joseon government's increased commitment to the island.

---

288 Kajimura, "Ilbon ttang jujang eun paengchang – singminjuui sosan," 621.

289 Lee Sang-Tae, *Saryo ga jeungmyeong haneun Dokdo neun Hanguk ttang*, 64.

The Korean Empire Government Investigates the Wrongdoings of Japanese vis-à-vis Ulleungdo

Despite the efforts of the Korean Empire, the Japanese continued to illegally trespass on the island for logging and smuggling. The situation became so serious that it received the attention of the Russian delegation in Hanyang. Russian diplomats filed diplomatic documents with the Joseon government, complaining about the illegal activities of the Japanese people. Upon receiving these complaints, the Korean Empire ordered the Ulleungdo *dogam* Bae Gye-ju to conduct an investigation of the matter. Bae reported the wrongdoings of Japanese people on the island in detail and stressed that the Joseon people on the island were living in fear.[290]

The Korean Empire immediately publicized the seriousness of the matter. Thus, Minister of Foreign Affairs (K. *oebu daesin*) Park Je-sun requested of the Japanese delegation based in Hanyang the following: (1) choose a date of return for the Japanese people on Ulleungdo and expedite their travel home by the set date; and, (2) conduct an investigation regarding illegal logging and smuggling activities committed on and from Ulleungdo.

The Japanese side responded that (1) if citizens of Japan have conducted illegal activities on Ulleungdo, the Korean Empire must send a request for investigation directly to the Japanese consulate that deals with Ulleungdo; (2) the Japanese government sent a patrol boat to Ulleungdo to conduct the investigation but, because of the strong winds, it was unable to dock; and (3) if trade conducted on Ulleungdo was illegal and was considered smuggling, then jurisdiction over the matter belongs to the Korean Empire.[291]

---

290 Shin Yong-Ha et al., *Dokdo yeongyugwon jaryo ui tamgu*, vol. 2, 155.
291 Ibid., 157–158.

In response, on December 15, 1899, the Korean Empire appointed Wu Yong-jeong as the head of the Ulleungdo Watch Council and sent a team of investigators to Ulleungdo, to which the Japanese government finally agreed.

Wu left Hanyang on May 25, 1900, aboard a boat bound for Busan that departed from Incheon on May 27. His team left Busan with the Japanese assistant consul Akatsuka Shōsuke and a British accountant, E. Raporte, on May 30. The crew arrived on Ulleungdo the next day and conducted an on-sight investigation from June 1 to 5. They returned to the mainland immediately afterward and submitted *Report: Ulleungdo Explained* (K. *Bogoseo: Ulleungdo sahaek*) to Home Minister Yi Geon-ha.[292]

This report recorded the "violence" and "arrogance" of the Japanese people in great detail. It criticized the illegal logging activity for being out of control and warned that the island will soon be stripped bare if such activity continues. This report also recorded that Japanese people harassed and abused Joseon women and islanders.[293]

This raises the question, what was the *dogam*, the head of the island, doing at the time? The report indicated that neither the head of the island nor his men were working to meet the standards of their positions and questioned their ability to govern the islands, let alone dissuade the Japanese.[294]

Meanwhile, the Japanese consulate in Hanyang delayed their response to the Korean Empire. They finally responded in September 1900. The essence of the response blamed the Koreans, more precisely, the *dogam*. The principal argument claimed that the *dogam* probably coaxed the islanders to provide the information in the document, or merely

---

[292] Ibid., vol. 3, 69–79.

[293] Ibid., 88–91.

[294] Ibid., 85–99.

received tacit or implied consent on desired details. Furthermore, the argument included false statements that outlined the convenience for the Joseon people to have the Japanese present on the island. Not only was this response irresponsible, it was also disrespectful and arrogant. In response, the Korean Empire sent a rebuttal to the Japanese consulate. Yet, the Japanese consulate ignored the response, providing convenient assurances to the Japanese people regarding Ulleungdo.[295]

---

295 Ibid., 113–115.

2 The Dokdo Jurisdiction Transferred to Ulleung-gun County by an Enactment of the Korean Empire

The Isle of Seokdo is Incorporated into Ulleung-gun County

The government of the Korean Empire decided to strengthen efforts to protect Ulleungdo. Therefore, on October 24, 1900, the cabinet meeting (K. *Uijeongbu hoeui*) unanimously (8–0) passed the Imperial Order 41: Changing the Name of Ulleungdo to Uldo and Amending Dogam to Gunsu. The order was enforced the same day that it was signed.[296]

Clause 1 of this imperial order changed the name of the island from Ulleungdo to Uldo and installed it as a *gun*, which was a higher level of county in Korean administration, by combining Ulleungdo and the adjacent islands. Accordingly, the *dogam* post was elevated to the *gunsu* post. With an elevation of status, the county (K. *gun*) office was placed in Taeha-dong. The office had jurisdiction over the "entire[ty of] Ulleungdo, Jukdo, and Seokdo."

Here, the focus must fall first on Jukdo and Seokdo. The "entire[ty of] Ulleungdo" is comprehensible, but to what does the usage of "Jukdo and Seokdo" refer? First is the question of what was meant by Jukdo. Lee

---

296 Ibid., vol. 2, 167–169.

Han-key explained that "Jukdo seems to be the name of an island near Ulleungdo, Jukseo."[297]

Bae Sung-joon pointed out that excluding Jukdo implies what Seokdo was supposed to be. He thus can narrow down the delineation to the two islands remaining near Ulleungdo, those being Gwaneumdo or Dokdo. He continued to argue that on the map *Ulleungdo oe do*, which Yi Gyu-won had compiled and submitted to King Gojong, Gwaneumdo was labeled as Dohang. Given that the islands take the shape of a cow lying down, Bae's assumption is probably correct. By logical inference, Bae argues that Seokdo is Dokdo.[298]

The Korean linguist Seo Jong-hak and the historian Yoo Mirim both approached this question through their respective areas of expertise and reached the same conclusion, that Seokdo is Dokdo. Yu concluded that Gwaneumdo was an island included as part of Ulleungdo and therefore cannot be considered as Seokdo.[299]

Seokdo is Dokdo

Let us examine Seokdo further. The Korean scholar who first considered Seokdo to be Dokdo was the linguist Bang Jong-hyeon. In his 1947 publication on Dokdo, he argued that the name of Dokdo is etymologically derived from rock island, which originated from the name Seokdo. He explained that there is no dirt on Dokdo, but only rocks. Rocks are

---

297 Lee Han-key, *Hanguk ui yeongto*, 250.

298 Bae Sung-joon, "Ulleungdo Dokdo myeongching byeonhwa reul tonghaeseo bon Dokdo insik eui byeoncheon" [Transition of Dokdo awareness seen through the name changes of Ulleungdo and Dokdo], *Jindan hakbo* (*The Chin-Tan Society*) 30, 68–96; Kim Young-soo, "Geundae Dokdo wa Ulleungdo myeongching munje reul dulleossan nonjaeng gwa geu uimi," 167.

299 Seo Jong-hak, "'Dokdo,' 'Seokdo' eui jimyeong pyogi e gwanhan yeongu" [Study on "Dokdo," and "Seokdo" naming], *Eomunyeongu* 36, no. 3 (2008), 18–39; Yoo Mirim, "Ilbon eui Seokdo = Dokdo-seol bujeong e daehan bipanjeok gochal" [A critical study on Japan's denial of the Seokdo = Dokdo theory], *Haesang jeongchaek yeongu* (*Ocean Policy Research*) 23, no. 1 (2008), 48–68.

called "*dok*" along the coast of Jeollanam-do province. This then leads to the derivation of the name as follows: Dolseom = Dokseom = Seokdo = Dokdo. Also, Bang pointed out that it is possible that Dokdo looks like a water jar, called "*muldok*" in Korean, whence the "*dok*" in Dokdo could have originated.[300]

On a similar note, Shin Sok-ho, who studied Dokdo as a historian, wrote as follows:

> There are too many arguments and explanations as to where and how the name of Dokdo originated. Some say that it is called Dokdo because it is a lonely island in middle of the East Sea, some that the name represents the rocky nature of the island, and some say that the name came from a regional speech of calling rocks '*dok*.' It is impossible to trace which story is true.[301]

Lee Han-key explained, "Seokdo is meant to be Dokdo. The "*dok*" from Dokdo is rock."[302] Song Byeong-Ki had the same interpretation.[303] And Shin Yong-Ha is certain that Seokdo is Dokdo. At the time, most of the Ulleung islanders were fishermen who had migrated from Jeolla-do province. In the Jeolla dialect, "*dol*" (rock) is "*dok*" and the rock island that they referred to was Dokdo. Shin states that once the Korean Empire learned of this, it called the rock island Seokdo, which indicated Dokdo.

Shin Yong-Ha provided several pieces of related circumstantial evidence.[304] His examples include: (1) in Gomak-ri, Nohwa-myeon,

300 Bang Jong-hyeon, *Dokdo ui haru* [A day of Dokdo], *Gyeongseong daehak yegwa sinmun* 13, 1947. Bang's writings were discussed in Kim Young-soo, "Geundae Dokdo wa Ulleungdo myeongching munje reul dulleossan nonjaeng gwa geu uimi," 164–165.

301 Shin Sok-ho, "Dokdo ui naeryeok," 30.

302 Lee Han-key, *Hanguk ui yeongto*, 250.

303 Song Byeong-Ki, *Gochyeo sseun Ulleungdo wa Dokdo*, 156–163.

304 Shin Yong-Ha, *Dokdo ui minjok yeongtosa yeongu*, 197–198.

Wando-gun, Jeollanam-do, are many rocky features south of Minari Island, which the people call "Dokseom" and write as "Seokdo"; (2) in the village of Chungdo-ri in Wando-gun, a rock island south of Yukdo is also called Dokseom to this day and its administrative name is Seokdo; and (3) in Sanho-ri, Hwawon-myeon, Haenam-gun, Jeollanam-do, there is an island that people call "Dokseom," but its administrative name is "Seokhodo."

Meanwhile, there are several islands that people call "Dokseom" but which were named "Dokdo." Again borrowing from Ocheon-ri, Namyang-myeon, Goheung-gun, Jeollanam-do Shin explains there is an island called Monyeodo, and to the east of this island is a rock island that is called "Dokseom" and written as "Dokdo" in Chinese characters.

Such names and labels were not limited to these islands. Village names and valley names were common subjects of interchangeable naming and labeling conventions. Again, according to Shin, there are many villages and valleys with numerous rocks called "Dokgol," which, when written in Chinese characters, would either be read as "Seokgok" or as "Dokgok."

In this sense, it can be inferred that when the government of the Korean Empire issued Imperial Order 41 in October 1900 creating a new district that included Ulleungdo and the adjacent islands, "Seokdo" must have meant "Dokdo." Furthermore, at the time, the Ulleungdo islanders called rock islands "Dokseom" and wrote that word as "Dokdo." Therefore, "Seokdo," and "Dokdo" were used interchangeably.

This type of analysis is not undertaken in order to interpret the evidence to Korea's advantage, because the people of Joseon called this island "Dokdo." This is also apparent in Japanese texts from the late Korean Empire period. As will be explored in detail below, during the Russo-Japanese War the Japanese navy sent the vessel *Niitaka Maru* to investigate Dokdo. The *Niitaka Maru* reported its findings to the Japanese government. According to the report filed by the *Niitaka Maru*,

"Liancourt Rock is written as Dokdo by Korean people, and Japanese fishermen call this island Riankoroto-amu or Ryangko-tou for short." This is the first case in which the word "Dokdo" was found in Japanese documents.[305]

An interesting point regarding this fact is that "Korean people call this island Dokdo," and yet this line of thought suggests that the island was called and pronounced a name other than Dokdo. In short, Seokdo is a written rendition in Chinese characters of rock island, which means Dokdo. It is with confidence and historical evidence that the Korean government explained that from October 1900, Dokdo was incorporated into Ulleung-gun county with Seokdo as its labeled name. The representatives of the Republic of Korea in Japan wrote in *Korean Government Opinion 1*, which was filed with the Japanese Ministry of Foreign Affairs on September 9, 1953, that "Dokdo means an island of stones or rocks…" concluding that "Dokdo is really a rocky island."[306]

The Japanese Government Remains Silent, the Rebuttal by Japanese Scholars, and the Korean Government's Rebuttal

Of the four *Japanese Government Opinions* that the Japanese government sent to the Korean government, there was not a single case that denied the abovementioned facts. The Japanese government did not dare to deny the fact that Seokdo, which was incorporated into Ulleung-gun county, was Dokdo.

Kajimura even pointed out that Seokdo was Dokdo when he wrote that "according to Korean Empire Imperial Order 41, clause 2 . . . it is

---

305 Shin Yong-Ha, *Dokdo ui minjok yeongtosa yeongu*, 1996, 44; Shin Yong-Ha et al., *Dokdo yeongyugwon jaryo ui tamgu*, vol. 2, 252–253; Kim Young-soo, "Geundae Dokdo wa Ulleungdo myeongching munje reul dulleossan nonjaeng gwa geu uimi," 162.

306 Shin Yong-Ha et al., *Dokdo yeongyugwon jaryo ui tamgu*, vol. 3, 433–442.

most logical and natural to understand that 'Jukdo' refers to an adjacent island next to Ulleungdo while 'Seokdo' does not refer to another adjacent island named Gwaneumdo, but rather to Takeshima, or Dokdo."[307]

However, Japan's Takeshima Issue Research Group, which was founded in 2005, argued that Seokdo is not Dokdo. Shimojō Masao turned his attention to Imperial Order 41, which did not address the coordinate location of Seokdo. He subsequently argued that Seokdo was Gwaneumdo, which was also called Dohang. Shimojō referenced *Hanguk susanji* (E. *The Encyclopedia of Korean Waterways*), published by the Korean Empire's Department of Agriculture and Commerce (K. *Nongsanggongbu*), and noted that Seohangdo was among the many adjacent islands of Ulleungdo, and that when read in a certain way the pronunciation resembles "sokōtō," which shows that "Seokdo" means "Seohangdo." However, the original Japanese version of the *Encyclopedia of Korean Waterways*, which was published by Japan's Department of Waterways (J. *Suirobu*), identified Seohangdo as "Somoku Somu." "Somoku Somu" is the written version of "Seommok-seom," which is the colloquial Joseon pronunciation. Seommok-seom is the same Seommok-seom drawn on the map that Yi Gyuwon compiled and presented to King Gojong. Seommok-seom written in Chinese characters is 島項.

Tsukamoto Takashi also disregarded the Korean government's interpretation that Seokdo is Dokdo. He went even further by stating, "Even if Seokdo upon the Imperial Order does represent Dokdo, just because Uldo-gun was elevated as an area under Joseon jurisdiction is not sufficient reason for Dokdo to become Korean territory." In other words, neither the government of the Korean Empire nor the new Republic of Korea indicated action to occupy the island. Therefore, Dokdo cannot be Korean territory.

---

[307] Kajimura, "Ilbon ttang jujang eun paengchang – singminjuui sosan," 621–622.

However, Ōnishi Toshiteru accepted that Seokdo is Dokdo. He concluded that since Imperial Order 41 dictated that the jurisdiction of Ulleung-gun county extends to "the entire Ulleungdo Island, Jukdo, and Seokdo," Gwaneumdo and other islands next to Ulleungdo must be included in the phrase "the entire Ulleungdo Island." If other islands located far from Ulleungdo were named independently, then Seokdo is Dokdo. Naitō Seichū had the same interpretation, arguing it would be a logical conclusion.[308]

308 Park Byoungsup, and Naitō Seichū, *Dokdo=Dakesima nonjaeng: Yeoksa jaryo reul tonghan gochal* (Seoul: Bogosa, 2008), 141–143; Park Byoungsup, "Simojo Masao (下條正男) ui nonseol eul bunseok handa (2)," 118, 131–136; Kim Young-soo, "Geundae Dokdo wa Ulleungdo myeongching munje reul dulleossan nonjaeng gwa geu uimi," 169–170.

3 The Government of the Empire of Japan "Incorporates" Dokdo into Shimane Prefecture

Are the 1904 Treaties Forced on the Korean Empire by Japanese Forces Linked to the Illegal Occupation of Dokdo? The Korean-Japanese Controversy

To this point, we have discussed and examined the government of the Korean Empire's interpretations of Imperial Order 41, which was issued on October 25, 1900. We are able to see that Seokdo, which was referred to in Imperial Order 41, is today's Dokdo. Through these interpretations, we have learned that the Korean Empire began to extend its territorial rights over the island under the conviction that Seokdo is Joseon territory. Nevertheless, Japan "incorporated" this island into its territory.

Imperial Japan realized that in order to make the Korean Empire its colony it must drive Russia from the Korean Peninsula. It was in this situation that Japan began a war with Russia on February 8, 1904. Japan immediately occupied Hanyang and forced the government of the Korean Empire to sign the Japan-Korea Treaty of 1904 on February 23. This treaty legitimized Japanese interference in Korea's political, military, economic, and diplomatic affairs, and specifically allowed Japan to use Korean territory in any way that it wished.

In May 1904, after the coerced signing of the treaty, Japan forced the

Korean Empire government to announce a so-called imperial order under duress. This document invalidated all treaties and agreements that the Korean Empire had made with Russia and replaced them with the legitimization of Japan's ultimate authority. In this document, Japan included a clause allowing it to use Ulleungdo as a strategic base.[309]

Three months later, on August 22, Korea bowed to Japanese pressure and signed the first Japan-Korea Treaty of 1904. The requirements of this treaty were that (1) the government of the Korean Empire must install a Japanese economic advisor and a Japanese diplomatic advisor and (2) the government of the Korean Empire must consult with Japanese advisers on diplomatic matters and decision-making processes. Clearly, the purpose of these clauses was to strip the Korean Empire of its economic and diplomatic rights.

Indeed, as a result of the treaty, Japan began advisory politics (K. *gomun jeongchi*) in Korea. At the time, the war seemed to be tilting in favor of Japan, which made the Japanese more empowered and brutal on the Korean Peninsula once they realized that they had driven the Russians out. This was just one of the preliminary actions taken by Japan to incorporate Dokdo as part of Japan.

The Representatives of the Republic of Korea in Japan criticized this point in *Korean Government Opinion 1* sent to the Ministry of Foreign Affairs of Japan on September 9, 1953. The Opinion pointed out that, through the treaty of February 8, 1904, Japan coerced Korea to allow its territory to be used in the war against Russia. The treaty of August 22, 1904, forced Korea to install Japanese advisors, which contributed to the incorporation of Dokdo into Japanese territory.[310]

The Japanese government began their rebuttal of this Korean *Opinion*. On February 10, 1954, Japan's Ministry of Foreign Affairs argued in

---

309 Song Byeong-Ki, *Gochyeo sseun Ulleungdo wa Dokdo*, 179.

310 Shin Yong-Ha et al., *Dokdo yeongyugwon jaryo ui tamgu*, vol. 3, 437–438.

Japanese Government Opinion 2 that the abovementioned clauses are not related to the incorporation of Dokdo. For instance, they argued that all that the August 1904 Japan-Korea Treaty accomplished was allowing the Japanese government to "temporarily" protect the territories of the Korean Empire. Also, the Japanese government argued that the August 1904 treaty did not force the Korean Empire to install Japanese advisors, which is why the Korean Empire hired an American named Stevenson as diplomatic advisor.[311]

The Japanese were correct that the August 1904 treaty did not force the Korean Empire to employ a Japanese advisor, contrary to how this issue was presented in *Korean Government Opinion 1*. As the *Japanese Government Opinion 2* suggested, the first Japan-Korea Treaty of 1904 "suggested" a foreign advisor.

However, the same type of minor error was made in *Japanese Government Opinion 2* as well. The foreign advisor whom the Korean Empire selected was not "Stevenson," but "Stevens." What is more important here is that the accusations made in *Japanese Government Opinion 2* go beyond the essence of the issue at stake here. The *Japanese Government Opinion 2* criticized the mistake made by the Korean side while failing to mention how pro-Japan Stevens was. He not only systematically ignored and disrespected the Korean Empire and its people but also protected and promoted the rights and interests of Japan above all. Stevens publicly stated on multiple occasions that the "uncivilized nation" of Korea must be ruled by the "civilized nation" of Japan and that it is proper. He was conspicuous in promoting Japan's imperial expansion and its invasion of Korea. This is the reason why two Koreans residing overseas at the time, Jang In-hwan and Jeon Myeong-un, assassinated Stevens when he arrived in San Francisco in March 1908. In this regard, it would have

---

311 Shin Yong-Ha et al., *Dokdo yeongyugwon jaryo ui tamgu*, vol. 4, 224.

been better for *Japanese Government Opinion 2* to omit any discussion of Stevens.

The Japanese Department of the Navy Uses Nakai Yōsaburō to Shroud Japanese Actions

It is not necessary to mention again that the two forced treaties of 1904 were the frontrunners and preliminary texts for plots to seize Dokdo from Korea. As explained below, the driving force was the Department of the Navy of Japan.

The Japanese navy installed two watchtowers with radio communications on Ulleungdo in August 1904 to scout for Russian fleet activity. For the same purpose, the Japanese government sent inspectors to Dokdo to construct a watchtower there as well. The warship *Tsushima* was deployed, and it arrived at Dokdo on November 20, 1904, to land two navy officers. The officers inspected the island for approximately three hours and returned to Japan that afternoon. The captain of the ship submitted an official report on January 5, 1905, in which he suggested two locations in Dokdo for potential watchtowers—one on Seodo and the other on Dongdo.[312]

While the Japanese were preparing for war with Russia, a fisherman named Nakai Yōsaburō, from Saigō-chō, Suki District, Shimane Prefecture, was requesting that the Japanese government award him exclusive rights to seal-hunting grounds from the Korean government. It should be mentioned here that Nakai understood that Dokdo was a territory belonging to the Korean Empire. Such a perception is conveyed well in his "Business Administration" (J. *Jigyō keiei gaiyō*), which he composed

---

312 Shin Yong-Ha et al., *Dokdo yeongyugwon jaryo ui tamgu*, vol. 2, 256–261.

in 1911. Nakai wrote that he wanted to "discuss the matter with Korean officials as this island is an attachment to Ulleungdo and belongs to Korea."[313]

Nakai graduated from primary school in his hometown and later graduated from a private school in Tokyo. Subsequently, he continued his education in Vladivostok and Joseon as he worked in the fishing industry, and he maintained close contacts with Japanese government officials. This implicitly reveals his ability to understand that Dokdo was a Korean territory.[314] Nakai's acceptance that Dokdo was Korean territory is also shown in the records of a Japanese scholar, Okuhara Hekiun. In his *Takeshima oyobi Utsuryōtō*, written in 1907, Okuhara recalled that Nakai mentioned that Dokdo is "Joseon territory."[315]

Upon receiving Nakai's request, Maki Bokushin, a government official in the Department of Agriculture, notified the Department of the Navy. Kimotsuki Kaneyuki, an official from the Japanese navy, called Nakai and requested that he "submit documents requesting access to the island upon its official incorporation into Japanese territory in lieu of asking the government of [the] Korean Empire, as the island is not possessed by anyone." The Department of the Navy was well aware that the island was part of the territory of the Korean Empire. Nevertheless, it attempted to install naval watchtowers on shore while it had considerable influence over Korea during the Russo-Japanese War.

It was only natural for Nakai to think that it would be easier and more beneficial for him to do as instructed by the Department of the Navy. Therefore, on September 29, 1904, Nakai submitted a request to the heads of the Ministry of Foreign Affairs, the Home Ministry, and the

---

313 Ibid., 262–263.
314 Ibid., 224–230.
315 Ibid., 266–270.

Ministry of Agriculture[316] to incorporate Ryangko-tou into Japanese territory and after the completion of that act, to grant him exclusive rights to the fishing grounds around the island. Again, Ryangko-tou is mentioned in the request as Dokdo.

To be noted here is that Nakai submitted the request to the Minister of Foreign Affairs, as well. If Nakai was certain that Dokdo was not a territory of the Korean Empire and was unoccupied land as Japanese officials had instructed him, he did not have to go through the trouble of submitting the document to the Ministry of Foreign Affairs, but only to the Ministry of Agriculture and the Home Ministry. Thus, his actions suggest that he worried about potential conflict with the government of the Korean Empire given his perception of Korean possession.

The Cabinet, the Ministry of Agriculture, and the Home Ministry Act to Incorporate "Ryangko-tou" into Japanese Territory

As soon as Nakai's request was submitted, the Ministry of Agriculture and the Home Ministry began reviewing the document. Less than three months after the request was submitted, on January 10, 1905, the Home Ministry sent a request for reviewing the "Matter of Incorporation of an Uninhabited Island" to the cabinet. The content of the review regarded the matter of incorporating Ryangko-tou into Japanese territory. Specifically, the island was not inhabited, and the island was renamed as Takeshima and placed under the administration of Oki Island in Shimane Prefecture.

The Cabinet approved the request made by the Home Ministry on January 28, 1905. The following is the notice of approval.

---

316 Ibid., 272–276.

Upon reviewing the request made by the Minister of the Home Ministry, this uninhabited island[,] located latitude north 37 degrees 9 minutes and 30 seconds, longitude east 131 degrees 55 minutes, 85 nautical miles north of Oki Island[,] shows no evidence of being possessed by anyone. [. . .] Two years ago, a Japanese man, Nakai Yōsaburō, built [a] fishing base there, moved his supplies [there], and began hunting for seals. He is the same man who submitted the request to incorporate the island as part of Japan, and the request to grant him exclusive rights to the fishing grounds. May this be an opportunity to decide the name of the island as Takeshima (竹島) and allow it to be incorporated [in]to Shimane Prefecture.

Nakai Yōsaburō's move to the island for fishing, by international law, clearly meets the standards of legal occupation of the territory, which thereby makes it our territory. It is without doubt that incorporating this uninhabited island into Shimane Prefecture does not violate any provisions or laws. Therefore, the request has been approved, and the cabinet acknowledges the resolution.[317]

The Home Ministry delivered the decision made by the cabinet to the governor of Shimane Prefecture via "Minister of the Home Ministry Order 87" on February 15. In accordance with the order, the governor of Shimane Prefecture declared the island located latitude north 37 degrees 9 minutes and 30 seconds, longitude east 131 degrees 55 minutes, 85 nautical miles north of Oki Island as Takeshima and extended the territorial jurisdiction to cover Takeshima via "Shimane Prefecture Notification 40."[318]

The notification was published in *Kenpō* (縣報) and the *Sanin Shimbun* newspaper in Shimane Prefecture, which contained excerpts, as follows:

317 Ibid., 277–278, 280–281.
318 Ibid., 283–287.

Okishima's New Island

The new island, Takeshima, is located latitude north 37 degrees 9 minutes and 30 seconds, longitude east 131 degrees 55 minutes, 85 nautical miles north of Oki Island, and from now on, the governor of Oki Island has full authority over the island. This island is composed of two main islands and numerous adjacent islands, and it is an island in which boats can dock. Grass lives on the island but no trees.[319]

This article is the first and only newspaper article that delivered the news of Japan "incorporating" Dokdo into Japanese territory.[320] From this point on, the island over which the Korean Empire claimed legal possession by calling it Seokdo was incorporated into Japan as Takeshima. Exclusive seal hunting rights were granted to Nakai, who killed game there for twenty-two years. It is known that in the six years after 1905 Nakai caught over 14,000 seals, which almost led to the complete elimination of seals from that area. In 1933, approximately ten seals were caught annually.

The Korean-Japanese Controversy over Nakai's Exclusive Rights

Despite the context in which Nakai received the exclusive hunting rights to the island, the Japanese government willfully misinterpreted the experience as evidence supporting Japanese development of the island. In *Japanese Government Opinion 1*, which the Ministry of Foreign Affairs submitted to the representatives of the Republic of Korea in Japan on July 13, 1953, the government of Japan explained, "From

---

319 Lee Sang-Tae, "Ilbon ui Dokdo bulbeop gangjeom e gwanhan yeongu" [A study on Japan's illegal occupation of Dokdo], in *Dokdo yeongyugwon yeongu nonjip* [Dokdo territorial right research collection], ed. Dokdo Institute (Seoul: Dokdo Research Conservation Association, 2002), 72.
320 Ibid.

the perspective of international law, if [a government] seeks to affirm its right to a territory, that government's intention to make the land its territory and the exercise of effective administration are necessary." In a sense, *Japanese Government Opinion 1* is farfetched as it argues that "ever since the Japanese person Nakai received official permission from the Japanese government to build fishing huts and hunt for seals on the island, the island has been effectively administered by Japanese people until the outbreak of the previous war."[321]

What does "the outbreak of the previous war" in this quotation represent? The phrase means that the Japanese government effectively administered the island until the Pearl Harbor attack that led to the outbreak of war in the Pacific theater. Until this time, there were three other Japanese persons who received rights to hunt seals on the island. However, as will be seen below, the wartime situation left the island under the control of the military government. With reason, the Korean government argued against the Japanese claim. The representatives of the Republic of Korea in Japan on September 9, 1953, stressed in *Korean Government Opinion 1* that Nakai had recognized in his business proposal that the island belonged to Korea.[322]

This island was incorporated into Goka-mura, of Oki Island, in 1939, following the decision of the Goka-mura council. One year after the decision was made on August 17, 1940, the jurisdiction of the island was again transferred to the navy headquarters located in Kure. From this point on, the Kure naval headquarters issued licenses to hunt seals on the island. The Japanese government stressed this point in *Japanese Government Opinion 2* delivered on February 10, 1954, as evidence that Japanese people have been exercising administrative jurisdiction over

---

321 Shin Yong-Ha et al., *Dokdo yeongyugwon jaryo ui tamgu*, vol. 3, 416–421.

322 Ibid., vol. 3, 433–442.

the island continuously.[323]

The Korean government refuted the argument. On September 25, 1954, the representatives of the Republic of Korea in Japan argued in *Korean Government Opinion 2* that seal hunting is nothing more than an act of Japanese invasion of the peninsula and that it bears no relevance to the "continuous exercise of territorial rights" in terms of international law. *Korean Government Opinion 2* offered a Japanese document that admitted that the island belongs to Joseon. Furthermore, Tabuchi Tomohiko, a Japanese scholar, wrote in his 1906 book *Korea's New Geography* (J. *Kankoku shin chiri*) that the island which Japanese people call Takeshima is Ryangko-tou, an island that belongs to Korea. Also, another Japanese scholar, Hibata Sekko, wrote in 1930 that "Takeshima and Ulleungdo are the farthest territories that belong to Joseon in the Sea of Japan [author's note: called the East Sea by Koreans]," which shows that even Japanese people were aware that Takeshima is the Dokdo that belonged to Joseon. *Korean Government Opinion 2* concluded with the following remarks, "In conclusion, we repeat that the Korean government is confident that Dokdo is entirely a Korean territory."[324]

---

323 Shin Yong-Ha et al., *Dokdo yeongyugwon jaryo ui tamgu*, vol. 4, 299.
324 Ibid., vol. 4, 267–268.

4 The Korean-Japanese Controversy Regarding the Decisions Made by the Japanese Government

How can one interpret the decisions made by Shimane Prefecture? We must approach the interpretation of these decisions from three directions. First is the question of whether the decision made by the Japanese cabinet is legitimate. Second is the issue of whether territorial "incorporation" undertakes sufficient measures and follow procedures. And third is the problem of whether that territorial "incorporation" follows international law and meets its standards.[325]

Was the Decision Made by the Japanese Cabinet Legitimate?

First, in order for the decision made by the Japanese cabinet to be legitimate, the island could not have been possessed by anyone as stated in the cabinet decision notification document. In terms of international law,

---

[325] Many scholars, including Song Byeong-Ki, Shin Yong-Ha, Kim Myungki, Kim Byungryull, Kim Young-Koo, Lee Sang Myeon, and Lee Han-key, have discussed these three problems. Among the most representative works are Shin Yong-Ha, *Dokdo ui minjok yeongtosa yeongu*, 216–231; Song Byeong-Ki, *Gochyeo sseun Ulleungdo wa Dokdo*, 247–280; and Kim Byungryull, *Dokdo nya Dakkesima nya*, chapter 7.

the island must have been vacant and not administered by anyone in order for the doctrine of prior occupation of *terra nullius* to be fulfilled.

However, as treated in previous chapters, Ryangko-tou was an uninhabited island and was possessed by the Korean Empire. An uninhabited island and *terra nullius* are two intrinsically different terms. Historical Korean kingdoms, including the Korean Empire, called this island Usando and considered it an island associated with Ulleungdo. The island belonged to the Korean Peninsula and to the Korean people. On October 25, 1900, the government of the Korean Empire took an additional measure to reaffirm that the island belonged to Korea by naming it Seokdo through Imperial Order 41.

In this sense, it was wrong from the outset for Japan to consider incorporating the territory of another nation into its own territory. As Song Byeong-Ki pointed out, differing from reaffirmation of the Korean Empire's Imperial Order 41 that the island belonged to the Korean Empire, the decision made by the Japanese cabinet was the "incorporation" of new territory that had never belonged to Japan before.[326]

Second, is the argument that Nakai moved to the island to hunt accurate? Nakai did indeed hunt seals between 1903 and 1904. However, as Nakai himself admitted, he hunted only for about a month in 1903 and for four months during 1904 (between April and August, when seals appear near the island). He may have built a hut during the hunting season, but the hut was no more than a rain cover made of sticks. Considering that he brought seven fishermen with him on a small boat, it is logical and rational to think that he did not build a fully functioning house on the island. Therefore, it is also logical to conclude that Nakai did not move to the island permanently.

Third, as has been noted multiple times, many Korean kings believed

---

326 Song Byeong-Ki, *Gochyeo sseun Ulleungdo wa Dokdo*, 186.

that Dokdo was a Korean island, whereas Japanese rulers did not. The mere fact that the Japanese government incorporated the island with a new name, Takeshima, shows that Japanese people had no understanding that the island belonged to Japan.[327]

Fourth, the final item that should be pointed out is "prior occupation" as a means of acquiring territory. Not only is this imperialistic, but it is also invasive in nature. In the past, Western colonizers based their logic of imperialism on that term in order to conquer and rule much of the territory in Africa and in Asia. Lee Han-key's criticism that "from the beginning, modern international law is closely related to modern colonialism" highlights the essence of the issue here.[328]

Did the "Incorporation" Notification Follow Appropriate Procedures?

According to the February 1905 notification, the incorporation of the island required its publication to be disseminated throughout Japan to government offices, government ministries, lower-ranking offices, and, when necessary, to prefectural offices by official notices in *Kanpō*, or government gazetteers. However, notification of this territorial addition made in Shimane Prefectural Notice No. 40, an important matter, was not even published officially in *Kanpō*. As Japanese scholars argue, if it is customary for telegrams to be officially published in the *Kanpō*, the notification of the island's addition should have been published as well.

That is not all. The executive order regarding the renaming of the island as Takeshima and its incorporation was not published, either. To counter the above arguments, Japanese scholars offered the following

---

327 Ibid., 187.

328 Lee Han-key, *Hanguk ui yeongto*, 279.

comment: in July 1898 the Japanese government decided to incorporate Minamitori Island, which is 660 nautical miles southeast of Ogasawara Island, and issued a notification via Tokyo Prefectural Notice No. 58. Yet, this notification was not published elsewhere. In response, Song Byeong-Ki stated, "If a territorial addition is not published, there is no purpose for the *Kanpō*." He continued, "Furthermore, Ryangko-tou, unlike Minamitori Island, was perceived as being possessed by another nation. Therefore, it cannot be compared to or analyzed at the same level as Ryangko-tou."[329]

In a nutshell, Shimane Prefecture's notification of the issue completely ignored and or avoided standard procedures in favor of a secretive method. That is why Korean historians criticized the Japanese government with such harsh words. Choe Nam-seon called the Japanese government "cunning and deceiving." Yi Pyong-do argued, "That is nothing more than cunning theft." Shin Sok-ho added, "If not theft, then it is fraud."[330]

Were the Conditions of International Law Satisfied?

As observed in the previous section, the incorporation of the island as Japanese territory did not satisfy the standard domestic conditions in Japan. In addition, it did not satisfy international legal procedures. Furthermore, the Japanese government did not follow official international procedures when "incorporating" the island. This naturally led to the discussion of whether this incorporation abided by modern

---

329 Song Byeong-Ki, *Gochyeo sseun Ulleungdo wa Dokdo*, 195.

330 Choe Nam-seon, "Dokdo neun eomyeonhan Hanguk yeongto," in *Dokdo*, ed. Daehan Gongnonsa (Seoul: Daehan Gongnonsa, 1965), 151; Yi Pyong-do, "Dokdo ui myeongching e daehan sajeok gochal," *Dokdo*, ed. Daehan Gongnonsa (Seoul: Daehan Gongnonsa, 1965), 69; Shin Sok-ho, "Dokdo ui naeryeok," 37.

international laws on territorial acquisition.

The Japanese government publicly announced that incorporation did satisfy all requirements. In *Japanese Government Opinion 1*, submitted to the representatives of the Republic of Korea in Japan on July 13, 1953, the Ministry of Foreign Affairs wrote, "There is not the slightest doubt from the perspective of international law [regarding the issue of incorporation]." This document argued that the will of the Japanese government to incorporate the island was sufficient and no questions were asked regarding the addition of the island to Japanese territory from the time of its incorporation until the end of World War II.[331] The Korean government responded fiercely. On September 9, 1953, the representatives of the Republic of Korea wrote in *Korean Government Opinion 1* that Shimane Prefecture's "notice was stealthily made."[332]

Both governments continued the controversy by exchanging government opinions. On September 20, 1956, through *Japanese Government Opinion 3*, Japan highlighted the cases of the Island of Palmas and Clipperton Island in order to argue that precedence has already been established such that notification of territorial acquisition to foreign states is not a necessary or an absolute condition that must be satisfied.

The Island of Palmas case was a dispute between the United States and the Netherlands regarding the issue of territorial rights of the Palmas Island in the Philippines. Judge Max Huber of the Permanent Court of Arbitration ruled in favor of the Netherlands in 1928. The Island of Clipperton case was a dispute between France and Mexico on the issue of the territorial right to the uninhabited island of Clipperton. King Victor Emmanuel III of Italy, who was responsible for ruling over the arbitration, ruled in favor of France.[333]

---

331 Shin Yong-Ha et al., *Dokdo yeongyugwon jaryo ui tamgu*, vol. 3, 430.

332 Ibid., 437.

333 Kim Byungryull, *Dokdo nya Dakkesima nya*, 226–232; Lee Han-key, *Hanguk ui yeongto*, 226–232;

In *Japanese Government Opinion 3*, the Japanese government also pointed out prior occupancy of Guana Island by the United States. When the United States occupied this uninhabited island in the Virgin Islands, it did not notify any foreign states. However, in 1890, the United States Supreme Court ruled in favor of making the territorial addition of this island as part of the United States. Under such conditions, *Japanese Government Opinion 3* argued that the measures taken by Shimane Prefecture were based on a decision taken by the Japanese cabinet, which is a national organization. Thus the decisions are to be considered as having been made by the Government of Japan. Furthermore, there is no international law requiring how international notification of territorial acquisition is to be made, which would lead to the conclusion that there was nothing improper with the actions of Shimane Prefecture.[334]

The Korean government remained firm. *Korean Government Opinion 3* concluded, "The notification was stealthily made, therefore, no one, foreigners and citizens of Japan alike, was aware of the addition." This document added that "there is no known case in which a foreign territory is secretly incorporated through notification of a local government."[335] The Korean side offered its own versions of the interpretations of the Palmas Island and the Clipperton cases. In *Korean Government Opinion 3*, the Korean government stated that both cases are completely different from Japan's stealthy "territorial addition." In the case of Palmas Island, because it was not an inhabited island but rather an island where its owner lived, stealthy territorial addition is not possible.

Lee Han-key criticized the use of the Clipperton Island case by Japan. The French government notified the Hawaiian government, and this

Sean Fern, "Tokdo or Takeshima?: The International Law of Territorial Acquisition in the Japan-Korea Island Dispute," *Stanford Journal of East Asian Affairs* 5, no. 1 (Winter 2005), 82–84.

334 Shin Yong-Ha et al., *Dokdo yeongyugwon jaryo ui tamgu*, vol. 4, 357.

335 Ibid., 382–383.

notification was published in *The Polynesian*, a newspaper based in Honolulu, on December 8, 1858.[336] Yi also criticized the misuse of the Guana Island case. It was only after the United States Supreme Court confirmed that no one possessed the island that the American government incorporated the island as part of American territory, which did not require notification.[337]

With such bases of critique, *Korean Government Opinion 3* stated that the Japanese attitude would be fruitless, as it "showed a lack of proper understanding of international law by forcefully attempting to use only parts of international precedents." This diplomatic document pointed out and directed Japan's attention to the "1888 declaration of the International Law Association which requires foreign notification prior to occupancy," with which the Japanese government had neglected to abide.[338]

The Japanese government countered the argument. In *Japanese Government Opinion 4*, delivered on July 13, 1962, it argued that the 1888 declaration was not actually selected by the International Law Association, but rather by the Institute of International Law, which thus rendered the contents of the declaration not a necessary condition to fulfill.[339]

The Japanese criticism of the confusion of "Association" with "Institute" is inconsequential and is irrelevant to the core issue at stake. What is more important to understand here is the fact that when the Japanese government added Dokdo to the territory of Japan and did not notify international society, it was before the time that decisions made on Palmas Island and Clipperton Island became key cases in territorial dispute cases. This shows that the Japanese government had no intention

---

336 Lee Han-key, *Hanguk ui yeongto*, 283.

337 Ibid., 284.

338 Ibid.

339 Ibid., 456.

to notify any country of the territorial addition from the very beginning. As will be shown in the next section, the Japanese government was cautious and wary when notifying other institutions of its decision, which eventually led to its secretive methods of decision-making. This indicates that the Japanese government itself realized that the "territorial incorporation" of Dokdo was an extremely hostile act.

The Japanese government should not have used the Palmas and the Clipperton cases to legitimize its decisions. Rather, the government should have considered the case of East Greenland concerning the territorial rights dispute between Norway and Denmark, and the ruling of the Permanent Court of International Justice. The Permanent Court ruled in favor of Denmark, stating that the Norwegian government did not abide by any existing international law concerning prior occupation and notification.[340] Similarly, even though the government of the Korean Empire declared possession of Dokdo and even gave the island a name, the fact that the Japanese government proclaimed prior occupation on February 22, 1905, does not prove its legality and therefore illegitimately nullifies the decision made by the Korean Empire.

Upon analyzing the Korean-Japanese controversy, the Korean international law expert Kim Myungki concluded that the notification by Shimane Prefecture does not satisfy international standards. According to Kim, the government of Shimane Prefecture is not a national government, nor is it a local government that can speak on behalf of the nation. Therefore, the notification of the prefecture is not a national declaration, rather a mere local notification. In sum, Kim concluded, "Shimane Prefectural Notice No. 40 is not an adequate form of notification in terms of international laws."[341]

---

340 Seonwoo Yeong-jun, "Dokdo yeongtogwon ui yeongu: Dokdo yeongto jugwon jedohwa gwajeong ui bunseok" [A study of territorial title to Dokdo: An analysis of institutionalization process of territorial sovereignty of Dokdo] (PhD diss., Sungkyunkwan University, 2006), 153.

341 Kim Myungki, *Dokdo wa gukjebeop* [Dokdo and international law] (Seoul: Hwahaksa, 1987), 37–48.

Why Did the Japanese Government Stealthily Handle the Incorporation of Dokdo?

The Korean international law expert Chung In Seop argued that the action of incorporation of Dokdo by Shimane Prefecture cannot be legitimized when the politics behind the Russo-Japanese War and Japan's invasion of Joseon are considered.[342] It is in such a context that this section seeks to examine possible reasons why the Japanese government treated the incorporation of Dokdo so secretively.

First, the Japanese government was worried about the potential uprising of the Korean people and their government. The government of the Korean Empire reaffirmed that the island belonged to the Korean government in 1900 through Imperial Order 41, and if the government found that the Japanese government had "incorporated" the island into Japanese territory, it would not sit by idly.

Second, the Japanese government was worried about the resistance of surrounding powers. Imperial Japan was in the midst of fighting Russia, a struggle that the other foreign powers supported. The Japanese government must have thought that incorporating this island and asking for the consent of others would only cause undue trouble in this context. In fact, when Nakai submitted the request to the Ministry of Foreign Affairs, a ministry official worried that "at this time, by gaining a barren rock that is doubted to belong to Korea, foreigners may realize that we have an ambition to merge Korea with Japan, and this can be detrimental to our plans."[343]

Third, Japan acted in secret toward Russia more effectively. That is, Japan seemed to have incorporated this island in preparation for the

---

342 Chung In Seop, "Ilbon ui Dokdo yeongyugwon jujang ui nolli gujo" [The logical structure of Japan's argument on Dokdo territorial rights], in *Dokdo yeongyu ui yeoksa wa gukje gwangye*, ed. Dokdo Institute (Seoul: Dokdo Research Conservation Association, 1997), 188.

343 Shin Yong-Ha et al., *Dokdo yeongyugwon jaryo ui tamgu*, vol. 2, 263.

naval battle in the East Sea against the Russian fleet in 1905. This was probably why Japan was not able to publicly announce the inclusion.[344]

The fact that Japan attempted to use Dokdo as a strategic point can be traced to the island survey that the Department of the Navy conducted in November 1904. The Japanese ship assigned the investigation, the *Tsushima Maru*, reported that it was possible to install a watchtower on the island, thus, the processes of doing so continued. It was due to very poor weather conditions that construction began on August 16, 1905, after the sea battle against Russia had concluded.

Furthermore, the fact that Japan sought Dokdo as a strategic point can be seen in the actions of Tōgō Heihachirō, commander-in-chief of the Combined Fleet of Japan. Two days before Tōgō authorized the preparation for action for the battle against the Russian Second Pacific Fleet (the Baltic Fleet) on February 20, 1905, Shimane Prefecture published its notice of the incorporation of Dokdo as part of Shimane Prefecture territory. Moreover, Tōgō maintained close contact with the Japanese cabinet while he stayed in Tokyo from January 10 to 21. January 10 was the date on which the cabinet requested the addition of the island; January 21 was when Tōgō ordered all fleet assets to rendezvous in the East Sea; and January 28 was when the cabinet decided upon "incorporation" of the island into Japanese territory.

After examining this series of events in detail, one may see that they are interconnected. This conclusion was supported by a high governmental official within the Japanese Ministry of Foreign Affairs during that time. After Nakai submitted the request and contacted officials in the Home Ministry and the Ministry of Foreign Affairs, the Foreign Ministry's director of administration, Yamaza Enjirō, stated, "The current situation calls for the addition of that island to our territory. It would be very

---

344 Song Byeong-Ki, *Gochyeo sseun Ulleungdo wa Dokdo*, 196–198.

nice if we can build watchtowers and install radio communication for the purpose of keeping our eyes on the enemy fleet."[345] This indicates that the incorporation was directly related to the Japanese war strategy against Russia.[346]

On May 27, 1905, Tōgō almost destroyed Russia's Baltic Fleet in the waters northeast of Tsushima. After this battle, he ordered all fleet assets to assemble at Ulleungdo and attack what remained of the Baltic Fleet. This attack was extremely successful. In the morning of May 28, Russian admirals Nikolai Ivanovich Nebogatov and Zinovy Petrovich Rozhestvensky surrendered near Dokdo and Ulleungdo, respectively. This further illustrates that both Ulleungdo and Dokdo were used during the Russo-Japanese War as Japan's strategic points. To reiterate, the incorporation of Dokdo into Japanese territory was carefully planned within the wartime atmosphere.

This interpretation is accepted by North Korea, too. For instance, the North Korean historian Hwang Myeong-cheol concluded that the incorporation of Dokdo by Japan is "definitely a serious crime that neither the people of the republic nor international society acknowledges [as such]."[347] Due to the stealthy nature of Dokdo's incorporation by the Japanese government, the people of Japan were left unaware. Hakubunkan, one of the largest publishers in Tokyo, labeled the island as Joseon territory in the map that it included in *Japan-Russia War Diaries*, which was published on June 20, 1905.

---

345 Shin Yong-Ha et al., *Dokdo yeongyugwon jaryo ui tamgu*, vol. 2, 265.

346 Lee Sang-Tae, "Ilbon ui Dokdo bulbeop gangjeom e gwanhan yeongu," 79–80.

347 Hwang Myong Chol, "1905 nyeon Dokdo-ui Simane hyeon pyeonip eun Ilje ui Joseon gangjeom jeongchaek gwa yeongto yamang ui beomjoejeok sanmul" [Shimane Prefecture's 1905 incorporation of Dokdo is a product of Japan's colonial practices and territorial ambition], *Dokdo yeongu* 2 (December 2006), 37.

5 The Japanese Government Notifies Ulleung-gun County of Its Incorporation After Stripping Korea of Diplomatic Rights Despite Not Acknowledging Incorporation by the Government of the Korean Empire

A Shimane Prefecture Government Officer Orally Notifies the Ulleung-gun County Magistrate

Upon concluding the incorporation in secret, the Japanese government promoted the colonization of Korea more overtly. In September 1905, a treaty ending the Russo-Japanese War was signed by both parties in Portsmouth, New Hampshire. This became a platform for the Japanese government to convince the West of its established control over Korea. In November, Japan forced the Korean Empire into the Japan-Korea Agreement of November 1905. The agreement was composed of five articles, and each article stripped Korea of diplomatic rights. The Ministry of Foreign Affairs of the Korean Empire was closed between December 1905 and January 1906, and all Korean diplomats were summoned home. This was the moment when Korea became a dependent state of Japan.

Once Korea was stripped of all diplomatic rights, Japan finally notified Korean authorities of the incorporation of Dokdo. The notification was not made to the central government, but rather to a local government, and not in written format, but orally. This occurred on March 28, 1906, when the Shimane Prefecture officials Kaminishi Yoshitarō and Azuma Fumisuke led a team of forty-five inspectors to Dokdo and Ulleungdo.

When the group reached Ulleungdo and met Ulleung-gun county magistrate Sim Heung-taek, they notified him orally of the incorporation, as if the incorporation was not a serious matter. The oral notification to the local official was made more than one year and two months late.

Regarding the process of the notification, even if the Korean government held extremely low standards, officials of imperial Japan should have officially visited Ulleung-gun county and notified the magistrate through a public process. However, the governor of Shimane Prefecture at that time, Matsunaga Takeyoshi, did not do so. He merely inspected Dokdo very briefly in August 1905.[348]

Nevertheless, the Japanese government today argues that the inspections described above were final steps taken in completing the incorporation of Dokdo into Japanese territory begun earlier. The Japanese government argued in *Japanese Government Opinion 2* that the on-the-spot surveys were "conducted to establish adequate power to control the territory in order to complete its possession."[349] This was after Japan had defeated Russia and transformed Korea into a dependent state. However, Japan did not have to worry any longer about the possible uprising of the Korean people if it notified or publicly announced the Dokdo possession. In other words, Japan found no need to keep the incorporation of Dokdo a secret.

However, the Japanese Ministry of Foreign Affairs argued in *Japanese Government Opinion 2*, submitted to the representatives of the Republic of Korea in Japan on February 10, 1954, that "a group of Japanese inspectors led by Secretary Kaminishi of the Shimane Prefecture government office visited Ulleung-gun county with lavish gifts including a seal caught near Takeshima, which the magistrate of Ulleung-gun county accepted with many thanks." He continued, "If at the time magistrate Sim Heung-taek had thought that Takeshima belonged to Ulleung-gun county, he

348 Lee Sang-Tae, "Ilbon ui Dokdo bulbeop gangjeom e gwanhan yeongu," 74.

349 Shin Yong-Ha et al., *Dokdo yeongyugwon jaryo ui tamgu*, vol. 4, 228–229.

would not have treated the group of inspectors with generosity."[350]

The Republic of Korea representatives in Japan disagreed with that argument. In *Korean Government Opinion 2*, which was delivered to Japan's Ministry of Foreign Affairs, the Korean government argued that there is no record indicating that magistrate Sim Heung-taek received such gifts. Further, he would not have accepted a greeting by a group led by Kaminishi. Therefore, it is a fabrication."[351]

The Government of the Korean Empire Does Not Acknowledge Japanese Possession of Dokdo

Once the magistrate Sim Heung-taek received the surprising news, he sent a report the next day, March 29, 1906, to the governor of Gang-won-do province and to the cabinet in Seoul. However, because of difficulties with communication and transportation, the report arrived nearly a month later. In his report, Sim used the interesting phrase, "Dokdo that belongs to Ulleung-gun county . . . ."

When the Korean side quoted this specific phrase from the report, the Japanese side reacted negatively. The Japanese Ministry of Foreign Affairs stated in *Japanese Government Opinion 2*, "The authentic text is not being quoted here. Thus, there is no way to express the opinion of the Japanese side." In response, the Korean side countered in *Korean Government Opinion 2* that "the original text is kept by the [Korean government]."[352]

Who was Sim Heung-taek? He was born in Hanyang in 1855 and grew up as a patriot. He not only attended Sangdong Church, known

---

350 Ibid., 221.
351 Ibid., 259.
352 Ibid., 220–221, 259.

for its anti-Japanese atmosphere, but also paid dues to the Korean Independence Club. He was appointed magistrate of Ulleung-gun county in April 1903, and one of his first acts as magistrate was to deport Japanese people and Japanese policemen for excessive illegal logging. These actions motivated Japanese officials to stage a commemorative photograph and label Dokdo as Japanese territory. In protest, Sim made local children stand next to him with a large Korean flag.[353] At the time, there was already a Korean flag at the Ulleung-gun county government office. Nevertheless, taking the picture with children holding up a large Korean flag was reaffirmation that the island belonged to the Korean Empire. After serving as the magistrate of Ulleung-gun county, Sim subsequently served as magistrate of Hoengseong-gun county but was removed from office by the Japanese colonial government in 1911.

The magistrate of Chuncheon-gun county, Yi Myeong-nae, realized the sensitivity of the matter and reported the issue to his superiors on April 29 of the same year, which was relayed to the State Council (K. *Uijeongbu*) on May 7. The original text of the report filed by Yi Myeong-nae is preserved at Gyujanggak, the royal library of Korea. The original text of Sim's report was discovered in 1947 by Shin Sok-ho in the Ulleung-gun county government office.[354]

First, Home Minister Yi Ji-yong affirmed that Dokdo was Korean territory, stating, "It simply does not make sense that Dokdo is Japanese territory, and it is certainly appalling to receive such [a] report." In addition, another cabinet member, Park Je-sun, via Order 3 composed on May 28, "ordered investigation of which stance Japan is taking on the groundless matter."[355] What stands out here is that both Yi Ji-yong and

353 Lee Sang-Tae, *Saryo ga jeungmyeong haneun Dokdo neun Hanguk ttang*, 196.

354 Song Byeong-Ki, *Ulleungdo wa Dokdo: Geu yeoksajeok geomjeung* [Ulleungdo and Dokdo: The historical verification] (Seoul: Yeoksa Gonggan, 2010), 246–251; Shin Yong-Ha et al., *Dokdo yeong-yugwon jaryo ui tamgu*, vol. 4, 175–176.

355 Shin Yong-Ha et al., *Dokdo yeongyugwon jaryo ui tamgu*, vol. 4, 176–177.

Park Je-sun were among the group of "traitors" who, six months before making the above remarks about Dokdo, stamped the royal seal on the Japan-Korea Treaty of 1905. It is clear that the island belonged to Korea when even these two officials denied the Japanese argument over the possession of Dokdo.

The *Daehan Maeil Sinbo*, one of the most prominent Korean newspapers at the time, wrote in the miscellany section of the May 1, 1906, issue, "It is needless for Japan to argue that Dokdo belongs to its territory. Therefore, it is strange for Japan to do so." Eight days later, the *Hwangseong Sinmun* shared the same line of thought in its miscellany section.

At the time, Hwang Hyeon, a distinguished apolitical scholar, recorded in *Ohagimun* and in *Maecheon yarok* that "there is an island 100 nautical miles east of Ulleungdo called Dokdo. Since ancient times, it belonged to Ulleungdo, but Japanese people forcefully called it their island."[356] It seems that Hwang Hyeon, who lived in Gurye-gun county, Jeolla-do province, acquired the information via his subscription to both of the newspapers mentioned above. In 1907, the jurisdiction of both Ulleungdo and Dokdo transferred from Gangwon-do province to Gyeongsang-do province.

All of the documents reviewed so far show Dokdo as a legitimate territory of the Korean Empire and also show that the producers of the documents did not acknowledge Japanese possession of the island. However, the government of the Korean Empire could not stand up against the government of Japan because it had been previously stripped of all diplomatic powers. The Korean side simply could not defend against the Japanese government on this matter, and yet the Japanese government declared the behavior of non-action as an acknowledgment of possession. Even after Korea lost its sovereignty in August 1910 to

---

356 Ibid., 178–180.

Japan, the Korean people have never forgotten the fact that Dokdo was seized. For example, the Provisional Government of the Republic of Korea, on March 1, 1920, during the ceremony in commemoration of the March First Movement, stressed the matter of the seized island.

Japan Includes Dokdo on Maps

In 1907, one year after Japan notified the government of the Korean Empire of the incorporation of Dokdo into its territory, Japan began to include Dokdo on maps. Images produced by the Department of the Navy did so as well. As mentioned above, the Department of the Navy admitted that Dokdo belonged to Joseon at the end of the Russo-Japanese War. It thereby included Dokdo on maps of Joseon but not on maps of Japan. However, from 1907, Japan included a small island north of Oki Island and labeled it Takeshima.[357]

On August 22, 1910, some five years and six months after imperial Japan had incorporated Dokdo, the Japanese government coerced the government of the Korean Empire to sign the Japan-Korea Treaty of 1910 and publicly announced the signing of the treaty on August 29. This coerced document made the entire Korean Empire a part of Japan. Less than six years after claiming the possession of the small island of Dokdo, Japan annexed all of Korea.

The Korean-Japanese Controversy over Japan's Logic

The Japanese government today sees Shimane Prefectural Notice No. 40

---

357 Shin Yong-Ha, *Dokdo ui minjok yeongtosa yeongu*, 177.

as evidence supporting the Japanese territorial right over Dokdo. This is akin to saying that Dokdo was terra nullius (an ownerless land) which was occupied by Japan, thereby making it Japanese territory. Such logic is overt in *Japanese Government Opinion 2*.[358]

The unfairness and the unjustness of this logic have been revealed and explained above, but to reiterate: (1) Dokdo was not in a state of terra nullius; and (2) the Japanese government did not make the act of possession public. In relation to the second point, in *Korean Government Opinion 3* issued on January 7, 1959, the representatives of the Republic of Korea argued that "local notification was stealthily made. Therefore, neither the people at home (in Korea) nor international society were aware of the matter. Thus, the local notification cannot be treated as an official claim made at the national level." [359]

But Japan's Ministry of Foreign Affairs presented a different but still unjust version of its logic in *Japanese Government Opinion 4* submitted to Korea on July 13, 1962.[360] This document stated that Dokdo has been a Japanese island from before the incorporation in 1905. Therefore, Japan has the historical and the original right over the territory. This argument and logic made in *Japanese Government Opinion 4* are contrary to the earlier logic that Dokdo was in a state of terra nullius. The change in the Japanese government's logic shows that Dokdo was not authentically Japanese territory.

There is not a single Japanese document that claims historical possession of Dokdo. The Japanese government itself proved this when it defined Dokdo as terra nullius. Then Japan attempted to claim legitimacy in the scope of international law through the doctrine of terra nullius. Yet, once Japan made Dokdo a Japanese island by that logic, the

---

358 Shin Yong-Ha et al., *Dokdo yeongyugwon jaryo ui tamgu*, vol. 2, 217–231.

359 Ibid., 251–268, 269–290.

360 Ibid., 424.

government committed a contradiction by proceeding with the logic of original and historical possession.

In relation to this, an article by Yamabe Kentarō, a scholar considered to be a "conscientious historian of Joseon," is considered a classic. In this paper, Yamabe clearly stated that when Japan was drafting the Imperial Constitution it only included "as written in the ancient legend that Honshu, Kyushu, Shikoku, and Awaji Island are Japan's historical and original territory." Awaji Island is part of Hyōgo Prefecture. Yamabe continued, "This is enough evidence to show that Japan has no clear foundation in arguing for historical possession of Takeshima."[361]

The contradictory logic of the Japanese government was pointed out and criticized by Koreans. Japan responded, as seen in *Japanese Government Opinion 4*, in a twofold manner: (1) the incorporation of Takeshima as part of Shimane Prefecture was merely an act of strengthening its original claim over Takeshima at an international level, abiding by the standards provided by international law; and, (2) the Japanese government publicly claimed possession of Takeshima as a modern state.[362]

The Japanese government's argument met with criticism even from people such as Shimojō. He claimed that it is only natural for Koreans to resist if the logic of terra nullius was switched to the logic of original and historical possession. In other words, it is obvious for Korea to resist if the Japanese government argues that Dokdo originally belonged to Japan, although it is clear that the uninhabited island was later incorporated into Japan. Unfortunately, and recently, Shimojō seems to support the latter logic.[363]

---

361 Yamabe Kentarō, "Takeshima mondai no rekishi-teki kōsatsu," *Koria hyōron* (February 1995), 4.

362 Summarized in Chung In Seop, "Ilbon ui Dokdo yeongyugwon jujang ui nolli gujo," 176–177.

363 Park Byoungsup, "Simojo Masao (下條正男) ui nonseol eul bunseok handa (2)," 145–146.

The Fall of Japan and the Restoration of Dokdo

Chapter 6

1 The Cairo and Potsdam Declarations Promise the Restoration of Korea to Its Original Setting

The Cairo Declaration

The Cairo Conference was held on November 20, 1943, or approximately thirty-three years after Dokdo and the entire Korean Peninsula fell under Japanese colonialism. The Allied forces, composed of the major powers at the time, included the United States, Great Britain, and China, and these countries were led by Franklin D. Roosevelt, Winston Churchill, and Chiang Kai-shek, respectively. These leaders met in Cairo to sign a united declaration to end World War II at the soonest possible moment and to lay out the postwar international order.

The declaration completed on November 27, commonly known as the Cairo Declaration, included content on the fate of the Korean Peninsula, as well as of Dokdo. The Allies determined that Korea shall become free and independent. Furthermore, the declaration read, "Japan shall be stripped of all the islands in the Pacific which she has seized or occupied since the beginning of the first World War in 1914, and . . . all the territories Japan has stolen from the Chinese, such as Manchuria, Formosa, and the Pescadores, shall be restored to the Republic of China." Lastly, the declaration concluded that the "Japanese will also be expelled from all other territories, which she has taken by violence and greed."[364] To summarize, the declaration ensured the independence of Korea and the restoration of all territories that Japan acquired during wartime to their rightful possessors.

What are the implications of this decision? How might the territories of the Korean people be dealt with? Korean territory is included as part of "all other territories, which [Japan] has taken by violence and greed." As illustrated in the clause detailing the restoration of Chinese territory seized by Japan during the Sino-Japanese War, all territories were to be restored, even the territories acquired by Japan prior to August 29, 1910—the day of the annexation of Korea. Henceforth, Dokdo, which Japan renamed as Takeshima and forcefully stole from the Korean Empire in February 1905, is included here.

While the above interpretation of territorial restoration is clear, Japan argued that Dokdo was rightfully and legally incorporated into Japanese territory in 1905 and that, therefore, there exists no need to restore Dokdo to Korean dominion. This was evident when Japan's Ministry of Foreign Affairs delivered *Japanese Government Opinion 4* to the Korean government. The *Opinion* contained the argument that international documents included within the Cairo Declaration do not specify the restoration of Japanese territory prior to the annexation of Korea.[365] However, as discussed in previous chapters, the incorporation was illegally implemented and therefore invalid. This thereby maintains Dokdo as a legitimate object of restoration.

The Cairo Declaration was a joint declaration made by the three Allied powers that excluded Japan, which does not, in essence, bind Japan to its mandate. However, as will be seen below in this chapter, the declaration was affirmed within Article 8 of the Potsdam Declaration, a declaration

---

364 Shin Yong-Ha et al., *Dokdo yeongyugwon jaryo ui tamgu*, vol. 3, 241–244.

365 Shin Yong-Ha et al., *Dokdo yeongyugwon jaryo ui tamgu*, vol. 4, 466.

to which Japan consented unconditionally. In short, upon accepting the Potsdam Declaration, Japan became bound to both declarations.

The Potsdam Declaration

Approximately one year and eight months after the Cairo Declaration, the Allied powers held a conference in Potsdam, Germany, near Berlin, from July 16 to August 2, 1945. Harry S. Truman, Clement Attlee, and Joseph Stalin were all present at the conference, and although the Chinese were not present, their interests were represented within the declaration, essentially making it a declaration among four parties.

The Potsdam Declaration reaffirmed the Cairo Declaration by stating that "the terms of the Cairo Declaration shall be carried out." Within Article 8, the Potsdam Declaration included the following clause: "Japanese sovereignty shall be limited to the islands of Honshu, Hokkaido, Kyushu, Shikoku and such minor islands as we determine."[366]

Like the Cairo Declaration, the Potsdam Declaration was a joint declaration with no binding power. However, Japan accepted this declaration unconditionally on August 15, 1945, bestowing binding powers upon the document. To assure the matter still further, on September 2 of the same year, Japan signed the Instrument of the Surrender of Japan in front of Douglas MacArthur, the Supreme Commander for the Allied Powers (SCAP), agreeing to abide by the articles written in both the Cairo and Potsdam Declarations. Furthermore, by signing this document, Japan forfeited its authority to SCAP.

Within the document of surrender, it is stated that Japan, the Japanese government, and its successor will faithfully carry out the duties stated

---

366 Ibid., 244–245.

in the articles of the Potsdam Declaration. This means that Japan has pledged not to raise objections to restoring ". . . all other territories, which she has taken by violence and greed." This is the context in which the Dokdo restoration was made. In short, Dokdo was part of ". . . all other territories, which she has taken by violence and greed," and therefore Japan must restore the island without objection.

Focusing Again on the Method of Japanese Territorial Management

There is a new common thread between the two declarations and the surrender document previously discussed. The method of handling the territory of a defeated state has dramatically changed from previous eras as Kim U-gyu, a Korean scholar of Dokdo, noted.[367] In previous eras, territorial management was generally accomplished through peace treaties and a potential armistice agreement that came prior. These documents commonly dealt with military matters. However, World War II was fundamentally different from all wars that preceded it in terms of its scale, participants, casualties, technology, damage, and other aspects. Therefore, the conventional way of making peace no longer remained conventional. World War II required a new way of peacemaking, which did eventually reveal itself: the unconditional surrender of the losing state or of the losing powers.

This is precisely why the surrender included not only military issues but territorial management as well. In this regard, the unconditional surrender that Japan accepted on September 2, 1945, had characteristics of an armistice, surrender, and reserve reinforcement treaty. As a result, what once was Japanese territory did not require additional agreements

---

367 Kim U-gyu, *Donghae ui pasukkun Dokdo* [Dokdo: Protector of the East Sea] (Seoul: Sidae Munhak, 1996), 194–197.

because the unconditional surrender included the character and authority of a peace treaty. Thus, in addition to the four main islands of Japan and the other "minor islands" left for decision, the remainder of the Japanese holdings became divorced from Japanese authority.

The consequences of the unconditional surrender appeared as follows. First, Taiwan was restored to China on October 25, 1945. In addition, South Sakhalin and the Kuril Islands had already been restored to the Soviet Union as Sakhalin state on September 20, 1945. The United Nations Security Council mandated on April 2, 1947, to create a trust territory under the authority of the United States covering the Pacific Rim north of the equator.

Moreover, as per "General Order 1" issued by SCAP, Korea was divided along the 38th parallel on August 15, 1945. The land south of the 38th parallel remained under American control, while the northern half was controlled by the Soviet Union. Immediately after the order, the United States installed an American military government, the United States Army Military Government in Korea (USAMGIK).

Three years later, on May 10, 1948, in accordance with a United Nations mandate, the first election was held in South Korea, and the Republic of Korea was founded on August 15, 1948, which was recognized by the United Nations on December 12, 1948. In the north, the Democratic People's Republic of Korea (DPRK) was founded on September 9, 1948, in a decision made by the Soviet Union completely independent of the United Nations.

The postwar Japanese territorial restoration was accomplished within the jurisdiction of the Cairo and Potsdam Declarations, as well as the unconditional surrender. The Treaty of Peace with Japan, more commonly known as the Treaty of San Francisco, signed on September 8, 1951, took effect on April 28, 1952, and reaffirmed the status quo. Was this a unique occurrence and mandate applicable only to Japan? No, the same method of territorial management applied to all other defeated states. Following are several examples of their application.

First, the armistice among the Soviet Union, Great Britain, and Finland signed on September 19, 1944, included regulations for territorial management and military bases. The Paris Peace Treaties that followed three years later on February 10, 1947, reaffirmed the regulations outlined by the armistice itself. Second, the armistice between Romania and the Allied powers signed on September 12, 1944, included regulations on territorial management, which were reaffirmed by the peace treaty signed on February 10, 1947. Last, the armistice between Bulgaria and the Allied powers, and the agreement between Hungary and the Allied powers each followed the same pattern.

In this context, Japan's argument that the postwar territorial management was only tentative until the peace treaty was signed, and also its argument that Korean independence before the signing of the peace treaty is unacceptable by international law, cannot be established. Furthermore, Japan's claim that articles relating to the independence of Korea in the Potsdam Declaration were a "list of hysterical words made during wartime by the Allied powers" was unreasonable.[368]

---

[368] This statement was made by Kubota Kanichirō during the second property and right of claim committee meeting at the third Korea-Japan Meeting held in Tokyo on October 16, 1953. This statement became one of the reasons for breaking off the meeting. Detailed discussion may be found in Chee Choul Keun, *Pyeonghwaseon* [The peace line] (Seoul: Bumwoosa, 1979), 318–327. Chee participated in this meeting.

2 Three Documents Related to the Allied Occupation of Japan Published after the Japanese Surrender, and Dokdo

We have pointed out that Article 8 of the Potsdam Declaration limits the Japanese territory to the four main islands and the minor islands as dictated by the Allied powers. This presents the obvious question: is Dokdo included among the minor islands? The Potsdam Declaration did not specify which minor outlying islands it referred to because the Allied powers wished to postpone restoration of the minor islands. Accordingly, the matter was only discussed within the boundaries of the general occupation of Japan during the Allied powers' talks. In relation to this, the following three documents should be examined.[369]

United States Initial Post-Surrender Policy for Japan

The General Headquarters Supreme Commander for the Allied Powers (GHQ) issued the United States Initial Post-Surrender Policy for Japan.

---

369 Nah Hong-ju, *Dokdo ui yeongyugwon e gwanhan gukjebeopjeok yeongu: Dokdo neun Ilbon ui in-jeop sodoseo "smaller adjacent islands" ga anida* [Study on Dokdo territorial rights in view of international law: Dokdo is not "smaller adjacent islands" next to Japan] (Seoul: Beopseo Chulpansa, 2000), Chapter 5; Lee Sang Myeon, "Dokdo yeongyugwon ui jeungmyeong," 302–305.

First, the importance of this order must be addressed. Prior to the establishment of the Japanese occupation organization that created the Far East Commission as the supreme decision-making body, the United States nearly had a monopoly over the other Allied powers. That is precisely why the way in which the United States interpreted the Potsdam Declaration was extremely important. In this sense, the order concretely shaped the plans laid out by the Potsdam Declaration and the surrender.

How did this order shape the territorial management of Japan? To summarize, it limited Japan's sovereignty to "Honshu, Hokkaido, Kyushu, Shikoku" and the "minor islands" already included in the Cairo Declaration and by future Allied mandate. Generally, the limits set up by this order are the same as that of the Potsdam Declaration. However, there are two key differences here.

First, in the order, the clause, "islands decided by the Allied powers" in the Potsdam Declaration became "as decided by the Cairo Conference [and] other agreements that the US has already signed." The new verbiage refers to the Yalta Agreement. At the Yalta Conference, the Allies decided to restore the Kuril Islands and South Sakhalin to the Soviet Union, so the GHQ order merely reaffirmed this restoration.

Second, "minor islands" in the Potsdam Declaration was changed to "minor outlying islands." In reference to this, Kim U-gyu wrote as follows:

In the Potsdam Declaration, the adjacent islands and the other minor outlying islands were not differentiated. However, in the GHQ order, it included the word "outlying," thereby making it clear that only the minor islands within the vicinity of the main islands are included as part of Japanese territory. Therefore, what will remain of Japan included only those acknowledged by the Allied powers and it is only natural that the other islands not specified by the Allied powers are to be separated from the former territory of the Japanese Empire.[370]

How does this apply to Dokdo? Originally, Dokdo did not belong to any of the four main islands of Japan. Geographically, Dokdo is closer to Korea than to Japan. It is only 92 kilometers away from Ulleungdo, whereas it is about 160 kilometers away from the closest Japanese island of Okishima. Dokdo is closer to Korea by 68 kilometers. Thus, it is clear that Dokdo is not one of the "minor outlying islands." Unless the Allies or GHQ decides otherwise, Dokdo must be separated from the former Japanese territory.

What is also interesting here is that, in the GHQ order, the Cairo Declaration was referenced with great importance. As previously discussed, the range of territorial restoration decided at the Cairo Conference included "all other territories which [Japan] has taken by violence and greed." With confidence, the Korean government argues that Dokdo is included here.

"Basic Initial Post-Surrender Directive to the Supreme Commander for the Allied Powers for the Occupation and Control of Japan"

This was a basic order delivered to the GHQ by the United States government on November 1, 1945, thirty-nine days after the first order was issued. This basic order further specified the range of territorial restoration in the previous order. It stipulated that Japan's territory included only the four main islands and approximately 1,000 "smaller adjacent islands."

---

370 Kim U-gyu, *Donghae ui pasukkun Dokdo*, 203.

First, this order specified that the Tsushima Strait is part of Japan. Second, what was written in the first order as "minor outlying islands" was changed to approximately 1,000 "smaller adjacent islands." By "adjacent," this order meant islands very close to the main islands.

Where is Dokdo in this context? Dokdo is located neither near nor adjacent to the four main islands. Therefore, it is right to conclude that Dokdo is excluded from the "smaller adjacent islands" clause. Shin Yong-Ha interpreted the order similarly when stating that "Dokdo is located too far from the four main islands; therefore, it does not fall under the category of 'smaller adjacent islands.'" Also, because Japan took this island by "violence and greed," the island has no possibility of being part of Japan's territory.[371]

MacArthur's Order of December 19, 1945

General MacArthur reaffirmed the previous documents by issuing them as a specific order on December 19, 1945. MacArthur's orders, however, do not necessarily regulate the understanding of Japan. As Lee Han-key points out,[372] this was not a decision made by the Allied powers, nor does it hold legal weight. However, the fact that MacArthur reaffirmed the resolutions in the two previous documents illustrates his understanding of Japanese territory.

How did MacArthur's order issued on December 19, 1945, delineate the extent of Japanese territory? It repeated the previous document by referring to "the four main islands and Tsushima, and approximately 1,000 smaller adjacent islands." The slight difference in this order from the previous document lies in the description of "Japanese territory"

---

371 Shin Yong-Ha, *Dokdo ui minjok yeongtosa yeongu*, 258.

372 Lee Han-key, *Hanguk ui yeongto*, 265 footnote 68.

as "Japanese sovereignty." In this context, the order represents that the Allied powers, or at least the United States government, limits Japan's territorial extent, which removes any probability of Dokdo remaining a part of Japan.

3 "Memorandum for Governmental and Administrative Separation of Certain Outlying Areas from Japan" and Dokdo

A document far more important than those discussed above is the "Memorandum for Governmental and Administrative Separation of Certain Outlying Areas from Japan." This memorandum is more commonly known as SCAPIN (Supreme Commander for the Allied Powers Instruction) No. 677.[373]

The Exclusion of the Liancourt Rocks

Why is this document more important than the previous three? The answer is threefold.

First, this memorandum is a document relayed by GHQ to the government of imperial Japan to implement the plans for post-war Japan as per the Potsdam Declaration and the surrender document. In detail, this document is legally binding in its requirements as per the surrender document that places the Japanese emperor and Japanese government

---

373 Shin Yong-Ha et al., *Dokdo yeongyugwon jaryo ui tamgu*, vol. 4, 248–253; Kim Byungryull, *Dokdo nya Dakkesima nya*, 206–215; Lee Sang Myeon, "Dokdo yeongyugwon ui jeungmyeong," 300–310.

functions under suitable bounds as determined by the GHQ.

Second, unlike the previous documents, this memorandum was extremely detailed in describing the territory of post-war Japanese sovereignty. The following is an excerpt from Article 3 of the memoranda:

For the purpose of this directive, Japan is defined to include the four main islands of Japan (Hokkaido, Honshu, Kyushu and Shikoku) and the approximately 1,000 smaller adjacent islands including the Tsushima Islands and the Ryukyu (Nansei) Islands north of 30° North Latitude (excluding Kuchinoshima Island); and excluding (a) Utsuryo (Ullung) Island, Liancourt Rocks (Take Island) and Quelpart (Saishu or Cheju Island), (b) the Ryukyu (Nansei Islands) south of 30° North Latitude (including Kuchinoshima Island), the Izu, Nanpo, Bonin (Ogasawara) and Volcano (Kazan or Iwo) Island Groups, and all other outlying Pacific Islands (including the Daito [Ohigashi or Oagari] Island Group), and Parece Vela (Okinotori), Marcus (Minamitori) and Ganges (Nakano-tori) Islands, and (c) the Kurile (Chishima) Islands, the Habomai (Hapomaze) Island Group (including Suisho, Yuri, Akiyuri, Shibotsu and Taraku Islands) and Shikotan Island.

Third, this document excluded Korea from "the governmental and administrative jurisdiction of the government of imperial Japan." This was a reiteration of the Cairo, Potsdam, and surrender declarations. However, the memorandum is special because this was the first document to simultaneously exclude Ulleungdo, Dokdo, Jeju Island, and Korea. What is the significance of Article 3? Within Article 3, Section (a) defines "Liancourt Rocks (Take Island)" as Dokdo. All scholars, Japanese and Korean alike, know Liancourt Rocks as Dokdo.

The Importance of Grouping

SCAPIN No. 677 has another important aspect, that of grouping. It divided the areas exempt from "the governmental and administrative jurisdiction of the Government of Imperial Japan" into three categories, (a), (b), and (c). Ulleungdo, Dokdo, and Jeju Island belong to group (a).

As mentioned earlier, this document excluded Korea simultaneously with the abovementioned islands from "the governmental and administrative jurisdiction of the Imperial Japanese Government." One might interpret this as the memorandum authors' understanding that the contents of group (a) and Korean territory are linked.

This becomes more evident by referring to *Chizu kuiki ichiranzu* (地圖區域一覽圖), composed in 1936 by the Japanese navy. According to this map, Jeju Island, Ulleungdo, and Dokdo were all included as part of Korean territory. It may be inferred that this map was referenced during the making of SCAPIN No. 677. In other words, GHQ understood that Dokdo was a Korean island, and that understanding was directly reflected in the groupings in the memorandum.[374]

Interpreting Article 6

Article 6 of this memorandum states, "Nothing in this directive shall be constructed as an indication of Allied policy relating to the ultimate determination of the minor islands referred to in Article 8 of the Potsdam Declaration." Pointing this out, the Japanese Ministry of Foreign Affairs claimed to the Korean government on April 25, 1952, that the decisions made in this memorandum were not final.[375] This explains Japanese

---

374 Shin Yong-Ha, *Dokdo ui minjok yeongtosa yeongu*, 1996, 251–253.
375 Shin Yong-Ha et al., *Dokdo yeongyugwon jaryo ui tamgu*, vol. 3, 405–407.

intransigence with regard to accepting the argument that Takeshima (Liancourt Rocks) is excluded from Japan's territory.

The Japanese government went further in *Japanese Government Opinion 2*, delivered to the Korean government on February 10, 1954. The Japanese Ministry of Foreign Affairs presented the argument that Japan's sovereignty over islands north of 29 degrees north latitude and the islands south of 30 degrees north latitude were all restored as of December 5, 1951, according to the GHQ directive, which included the Ryukyu Islands and other outlying islands.[376]

In response to the Japanese claim, Lee Han-key countered, "SCAPIN No. 677 did not decide anything on the matter of postwar Japanese territorial management with finality. The document did, however, order the restoration of smaller islands, including Dokdo. Yet the lack of finality was due to a built-in flexibility to allow for further alterations should such be deemed necessary by the Allies. As a result, some smaller islands were restored, and for some others, residual sovereignty was acknowledged." Yi stated further:

> However, it is right that there was no future action taken on the matter of Dokdo after the decision was made that it was separated from the former Japanese territory. No decision was made on the matter of Dokdo, neither claiming restoration back to Japan, nor acknowledging residual sovereignty of Japan on Dokdo.
>
> Therefore, Dokdo greeted the San Francisco Treaty in the same state it was in after SCAPIN No. 677. In this context, unless it was specified in the San Francisco Treaty, Dokdo is deemed to have been completely separated from Japan's territory.[377]

---

376 Shin Yong-Ha et al., *Dokdo yeongyugwon jaryo ui tamgu*, vol. 4, 224–225.
377 Lee Han-key, *Hanguk ui yeongto*, 266.

On the same note, Shin Yong-Ha stated:

Article 5 of SCAPIN No. 677 reads, "The definition of Japan contained in this directive shall also apply to all future directives, memoranda and orders from this Headquarters unless otherwise specified therein." That is, the Allied powers could have amended the memorandum, as it was not an ultimatum. However, in order for the definition of Japan to be modified, the GHQ must issue special orders.

Ulleungdo, Dokdo, and Jeju islands were excluded from Japanese territory as of January 29, 1946, through SCAPIN No. 677. If in the future, Dokdo is to be included as part of the definition of Japan, then GHQ or the Allied powers must specify so in an extra memorandum, unless the contents of SCAPIN No. 677 are valid.

The GHQ or the Allied powers did not give extra orders or specify the restoration of Dokdo in the definition of Japan. Therefore, this suggests that Dokdo was completely excluded from Japan's territory and forever restored to Korean territory.[378]

Kim Byungryull interpreted SCAPIN No. 677 in the same vein. First, Kim analyzed Article 5, saying that it was necessary to do so in order to completely understand the meaning of Article 6. Kim reiterated that unless specified in an extra document by GHQ or the Allied powers, the definition of Japan does not change from what is stated in SCAPIN No. 677. Connecting Article 6 to this interpretation, Kim stated, "This memorandum is not an ultimatum. However, in order to reverse a portion of the contents specified in SCAPIN No. 677, there must be an extra document stating so by GHQ or the Allied powers." In sum, Kim

---

378 Shin Yong-Ha, *Dokdo, bobaeroun Hanguk yeongto: Ilbon ui Dokdo yeongyugwon jujang e daehan chongbipan* [Dokdo, precious Korean territory: Criticism of the Japanese claim to territorial rights over Dokdo] (Seoul: Jisik Sanup Publications, 1996), 189–190.

concluded, "The GHQ did not give such orders nor did it specify the restoration of Dokdo to Japan's territory. Therefore, Dokdo was forever restored as Korean territory."[379]

What must be kept in mind here, along with SCAPIN No. 677, is that Dokdo was separated from Japan and in the territory belonging to South Korea under the occupation of the United States at the time. But four days before the official founding of the Republic of Korea, on August 11, 1948, the "agreement between the government of the Republic of Korea and the government of the United States of America concerning the Transfer of Authority to the Government of the Republic of Korea and the Withdrawal of the United States Occupation Forces" was signed. Accordingly, official American governing authority in South Korea ended and the Republic of Korea assumed full authority to govern itself. As Yu Ha-young pointed out, "Therefore, the authority over Dokdo given to the United States government by [SCAPIN] No. 677 was transferred to the government of the Republic of Korea."[380]

---

379 Kim Byungryull, *Dokdo nya Dakkesima nya*, 207–208.

380 Yu Ha-young, "Geundae Hanguk beopchegye eseo ui yeongto" [Territory in the modern Korean legal system] (Seoul: Northeast Asian History Foundation, 2009), 86.

4 The MacArthur Line, the Korea Air Defense Identification Zone, and Dokdo

The MacArthur Line and Dokdo

After SCAPIN No. 677, the GHQ delivered another SCAPIN memorandum to the Japanese government. The so-called SCAPIN No. 1033, the Memorandum on Area Authorized for Japanese Fishing and Whaling, drew boundary lines in which Japanese fishermen could fish. The delineation came to be known as the "MacArthur Line," and the memorandum assumed a similar moniker as the "MacArthur Line Memorandum."

This boundary clearly limited the Japanese fishing industry. Japanese people were left devastated after the war, especially economically, and the Japanese relied heavily on fish for food. When they were given restrictions, they mounted strong resistance. Thus, the Japanese government attempted to negotiate with GHQ on the expansion of the MacArthur Line. The GHQ eventually left the supervision of the boundary to the Japanese government. The Americans thereby placated the Japanese by keeping quiet when Japanese fishing boats crossed the line. Naturally, Japanese and Korean fishermen clashed often.

With this in mind, SCAPIN No. 1033 should be reviewed in relation to Dokdo. Article 3, Clause (b) of the memorandum states, "Japanese vessels or personnel thereof will not approach closer than twelve (12) miles to Takeshima (37 degrees 15 minutes north latitude, 131 degrees 53 minutes east longitude) nor have any contact with said island."[381] The distance was changed to three miles on September 19, 1949. Again, Takeshima in this document refers to Dokdo.

Article 5 of the memorandum states, "The present authorization is not an expression of Allied policy relative to ultimate determination of national jurisdiction, international boundaries or fishing rights in the area concerned or in any other area." However, explicitly excluding Takeshima, this reflects the GHQ understanding that Takeshima belongs to Korea. In other words, SCAPIN No. 1033 proclaimed that all Japanese fishermen are banned from trespassing in waters closer than twelve miles from Takeshima. Furthermore, Shin Yong-Ha argued that SCAPIN No. 1033 "states that Dokdo, along with Ulleungdo and Jeju Island, was completely excluded from Japan's geographical boundary and was included as part of Korea."[382] Lee Sang Myeon, an international legal expert, had a similar interpretation. Yi stated that "according to SCAPIN No. 1033, Dokdo was in the hands of the USAMGIK, and as of August 15, 1948, with the founding of the Republic of Korea, it was properly returned to Korea."[383]

The Japanese side argued against the above interpretations. For instance, Kawakami Kenzō objected that the Korean government's interpretation of Article 5 was overly biased in favor of the Korean argument.[384] However, it is impossible to interpret the contents of Article 5 as temporal. It is natural to interpret the contents of Article 5 as valid until either revoked or amended. This point will be returned to below.

---

381 Shin Yong-Ha et al., *Dokdo yeongyugwon jaryo ui tamgu*, vol. 3, 257–259.

382 Shin Yong-Ha, *Dokdo ui minjok yeongtosa yeongu*, 261.

383 Lee Sang Myeon, "Dokdo yeongyugwon ui jeungmyeong," 306.

384 Kawakami, *Dakesima ui yeoksa jirihakjeok yeongu*, 251.

The Korea Air Defense Identification Zone and Dokdo

Around March 1951, when the MacArthur Line took full effect, the United States Pacific Air Forces (PACAF) drew the Korean Air Defense Identification Zone (KADIZ) and included Dokdo in the zone. This has never been acknowledged by international law. However, in terms of common law and practice, the trend leans toward general acknowledgment. PACAF's inclusion of Dokdo in KADIZ is interpreted within the same boundaries of SCAPIN No. 677 and SCAPIN No. 1033.[385]

Japanese Territory and Dokdo

The documents showing that the Japanese government accepted MacArthur's commands (or perhaps even the UPSACOM) are Prime Ministerial Ordinance No. 24 and Financial Ministerial Ordinance No. 4, both proclaimed in 1951. First, Financial Ministerial Ordinance 4 (a special ordinance determining the annexed islands based on Article 4 Clause 3 of the special exceptions to tax laws act) clearly indicated that Ulleungdo, Takeshima, and Jeju islands are excluded from the list of Japan's annexed islands. In other words, the Japanese government clearly admitted that Ulleungdo, Takeshima, and Jeju islands are not Japan's annexed islands. Moreover, Prime Ministerial Ordinance No. 24 (Prime Ministerial Ordinance 24 on the Adjustments to the Japanese Property Owned by the Mutual Benefits Association under the Ministry of Transportation of the Japanese Government-General of Korea), which took effect on June 6, 1951, also excluded the three aforementioned islands from the list of Japan's annexed islands.[386] The Japanese

---

385 Shin Yong-Ha et al., *Dokdo yeongyugwon jaryo ui tamgu*, vol. 3, 262–263.
386 Hong Seong-keun, "Ilbon ui Dokdo yeongto baeje jochi ui seonggyeok gwa uimi," 113–114.

government and Japanese scholars argue that such exclusion had no relation to the territory issues. Rather, they argue that the ordinances were merely written within the limits and boundaries of the SCAPIN No. 677 memorandum. The Japanese government and Japanese scholars argue that this had no relation to the territorial issue at all. The substance of their arguments lay in the fact that the ordinances were made only within the boundaries of the two SCAPIN memoranda.

5 The San Francisco Treaty and Dokdo

The Differing Views of Korea and the United States on Korea's Participation in the San Francisco Treaty

As mentioned above, forty-seven Allied nations, excluding the Soviet Union, signed a peace treaty with Japan on September 8, 1951, in San Francisco. On the same day, the Security Treaty between the United States and Japan was signed.[387] These treaties went into effect on April 28, 1952, and this meant that SCAPIN No. 677 was no longer valid. Foreseeing this, the GHQ invalidated the MacArthur Line on April 25, 1952. Therefore, as Lee Han-key suggested, "Legally, Dokdo could not have been affected by the MacArthur Line in the peace treaty."[388] Nevertheless, in case of uncertainty regarding the status of Dokdo in the treaty, it becomes problematic not to consider that the MacArthur Line excluded Dokdo from the list of islands under Japan's administrative jurisdiction.

It is in this context that the process of the San Francisco Treaty will

---

387 Ronald McGlothlen, "Japanese Peace Treaty," in *East Asia and the United States: An Encyclopedia of Relations since 1784*, vol. 1, ed. James I. Matray (Westport, CT: Greenwood Press, 2002), 271–272.

388 Lee Han-key, *Hanguk ui yeongto*, 267.

be reviewed. The Korean government spent great diplomatic effort attempting to participate in the process of drafting and signing the San Francisco Treaty. This fact was clearly noted by the United States Department of State in the report *Participation of the Republic of Korea in the Japanese Peace Settlement*, drafted by the Division of Research for the Far East of the Department of State, on December 12, 1949.[389] Although this document is partially lost, it is not difficult to grasp the general gist and flow of the argument.

First, this report clearly indicated that "Koreans" showed deep interest in the peace settlement treaty. A specific example in the report was the case of President Rhee Syngman's public statement that MacArthur guaranteed a seat for the Korean representative at the peace talks. Furthermore, this report indicated that the United States embassy in Seoul reported to the Department of State that the Republic of Korea showed great interest, in both official and unofficial roles, in participating in the conference "either in a negotiating or consultative capacity."

What justification did the Korean government offer to be considered as participants in the peace conference? The Korean government argued that Koreans had fought against Japan in Manchuria and other regions of China. It also argued that the provisional government of the Republic of Korea, which was located in Shanghai, fought alongside China, an Allied power, and therefore was "a belligerent against Japan."

However, the United States government denied the request made by the Korean government for the following four reasons. First, the Provisional Government of the Republic of Korea had not yet received international recognition. Second, while "Koreans" were distressed, they ultimately accepted Japanese occupation. Third, the primary interest of the Korean government was in securing compensation from Japan. Fourth, there

---

[389] Shin Yong-Ha et al., *Dokdo yeongyugwon jaryo ui tamgu*, vol. 3, 257–283.

was fear that, should the Republic of Korea be granted participant status, the Democratic People's Republic of Korea would then demand the same status. Nevertheless, the United States government decided to offer an unofficial opportunity to Korea, which resulted in the Republic of Korea gaining observer status.

Unlike the Korean government, Japan participated in the peace talks as a state directly involved in the war. Naturally, the Republic of Korea was not offered a chance to comment, whereas Japan was given all possible chances to speak. As Cho Sung Hun revealed, from March 1947 the Japanese government was open to the passage of submitting documents related to the peace talks to the United States. Among the documents were those that pertained to Dokdo. Japan used this opportunity. The Japanese delegation was led by the veteran diplomat and politician Prime Minister Yoshida Shigeru. At the time, the Japanese government relied heavily on William J. Sebald, an American. A graduate of the Naval Academy, Sebald practiced law and taught English in Japan. He grew familiar with Japanese culture and domestic politics. His skills were acknowledged at the end of World War II when MacArthur recruited him as a political adviser. His influence grew significantly within the GHQ, to a level at which people began to refer to him as the United States ambassador to Japan.

Prime Minister Yoshida himself showed hopes that Sebald would play a "central role" between Japan and the United States. In fact, Sebald exercised a great deal of influence over the Department of State, especially John F. Dulles, who was the foreign policy advisor at the time. In this process, Sebald took measures that were very favorable to Japan to the point of being called "pro-Japan."[390]

---

[390] John Swenson-Wright, "Sebald William J.," in *East Asia and the United States* 1, ed. James I. Matray, 538–539.

Preparation of the San Francisco Treaty and Dokdo

Dokdo was not a central topic during the process of preparing the San Francisco Treaty, but it also was never completely outside the interest of the Allied powers. This was apparent in the drafting of the treaty. The first draft on March 20, 1947, the second on August 5, 1947, the third on January 2, 1948, the fourth on October 13, 1949, and the fifth draft on November 2, 1949, all included a clause excluding the "Liancourt Rocks" (Dokdo) from Japanese territory and including it in Korean territory. In other words, these drafts included Dokdo in the list of islands to be restored along with Jeju Island, Geomundo, and Ulleungdo.[391]

When Sebald learned of the drafts, he sent a telegram to the Secretary of State on November 14, 1949, twelve days after the fifth draft was written. The substance of his message railed against constructing the character of the peace treaty as a mechanism for bullying Japan. If the peace treaty were to gain such a reputation in the international community, it would "[become] a psychological barrier to the prompt, orderly and progressive re-entry of Japan into a dignified place within the community of nations."

With regards to this, Sebald recommended eliminating some clauses that pertained to the redrawing of Japan's borders. In the list of territories to be reconsidered, he included the Liancourt Rocks. He suggested excluding Dokdo from the list of islands to be restored to Korea. He surmised that, firstly, "Japan's claim to these islands is old and appears valid" and, secondly, "security considerations might conceivably envisage weather and radar stations thereon."[392]

On November 19, Sebald submitted his requests officially to the Department of State. In the request, Sebald was more aggressive about

---

391 Shin Yong-Ha et al., *Dokdo yeongyugwon jaryo ui tamgu*, vol. 3, 284–300.

392 Ibid., 302–305.

242

removing Dokdo from the list of islands. He added, "It is difficult to regard them as islands off the shore of Korea."[393] His reasons for the removal of Dokdo, in particular, that "Japan's claim to these islands is old and appears valid," suggests that he was lobbied by the Japanese government. We can infer here that Sebald wanted every advantage in the creation of an East vs. West-dominated Cold War world. November 14, 1949, was approximately forty-five days after the creation of the People's Republic of China, a communist state, and, therefore, the value of Japan as an "anti-communist base" in East Asia was never greater. The Yoshida cabinet in Japan emphasized these facts.

The American government accepted Sebald's request and immediately reflected it in the sixth draft of the treaty compiled on December 29, 1949. In this draft, the Liancourt Rocks were eliminated. What is interesting to note is that, from the first draft to the sixth draft, the name "Dokdo" never appeared. Rather, Liancourt Rocks, a Japanese rendition of the name in English, appeared in all six drafts. Why? This will be explored next.

The United States Department of State composed a commentary on the sixth draft in July 1950, explaining, "There is a Japanese name for the island, however, not a Korean one. The Korean government did not take any action when the island was forcefully incorporated into Japanese territory."[394] However, the content of the commentary is not true. As already explored in the previous chapters, the island had multiple Korean names, ranging from Usando, Gajido, Seokdo, and Dokdo. As discussed in Chapter 5, the island was discretely taken from Korea and secretly incorporated into Japan's territory. Thus, when the Korean government took action, it was at a much later date when Koreans discovered the wrongdoings of the Japanese government. The Korean government was

---

393 Ibid., 310.
394 Ibid., 317–324.

certain that the Department of State relied solely on the explanations given by the Japanese side without examining the full story of Dokdo.

Great Britain, Australia, New Zealand, and other Allied states proposed issues upon receiving the sixth draft. The New Zealand representatives accurately pointed out that the handling of the Liancourt Rocks, as proposed in the draft, would only lead to conflict with the Republic of Korea. Influenced by this warning, the United States decided to completely remove the clause containing the list of Korean islands, including Ulleungdo, Jeju Island, and Geomundo, in the seventh draft, which was composed on August 7, 1950. The eighth draft, composed on September 11, 1950, was the same as its immediate predecessor. Eventually, the Allied states all agreed that the islands to be restored to Korea were to be named in the actual treaty. However, that list excluded the Liancourt Rocks and only included Jeju Island, Geomundo, and Ulleungdo. This was a decision based on the "United States-United Kingdom Joint Draft Treaty of Peace," which was composed by these two parties on June 14, 1951. Ultimately, this was Sebald's work. As will be seen below, the Japanese government uses this document as its basis of argument, claiming that the Liancourt Rocks, or Takeshima, was never restored to Korea.

The Embassy of the Republic of Korea Belatedly Learns that Dokdo was Excluded from the San Francisco Treaty

Was the Korean government aware of the fate of Dokdo at the hands of the Allied powers? According to Kim Dong-jo, a Korean diplomat who was present in San Francisco and a figure who later became minister of foreign affairs under the Park Chung-hee administration, claimed, "The Korean representatives were aware that the final draft of the peace treaty announced on July 7, 1951, did include Jeju Island, Geomundo, and

Ulleungdo, but not Dokdo. We were uneasy about this, and knowing that Dokdo is our territory, we requested that Dokdo be added in Article 2."[395] Kim Dong-jo's recollection recognizes that it was on and after July 7, 1951, that the Korean government discovered Dokdo's exclusion from the final draft.

The records from the US Department of State support this claim. First, in the "Comments on Korean Note Regarding US Treaty Draft May 9, 1951," Dokdo is not included among the eleven requests made by the Korean side. The Korean side only requested the return of Tsushima. In response, the Department of State wrote, "Korea's claim to Tsushima is extremely weak."[396] Second, records from the meeting of Yang Yu-chan, the Korean ambassador to the United States at the time, and Dulles, show that Dokdo was never mentioned.[397] Ambassador Yang merely requested restoration of Tsushima again while complaining that Korea did not get to participate in the signing of the San Francisco Treaty. Dulles refused again.

When Ambassador Yang spoke of Dokdo to Dulles for the first time on July 19, 1951, according to Department of State records, he omitted the argument pertaining to Tsushima but did in fact mention Dokdo and Parangdo. After reading, "the Korean government requests that the islands be returned along with Jeju, Geomundo, and Ulleungdo," Dulles asked the location of the abovementioned islands. The secretary of Ambassador Yang answered, "These were two small islands lying in the Sea of Japan." The Department of State records indicated that the "secretary seemed to have believed that the islands were near Ulleungdo."[398]

395 Kim Dong-jo, *Hoesang 30 nyeon: Han-Il hoedam* [Recollecting 30 years: Korea-Japan summit meeting] (Seoul: Joongang ilbosa, 1986), 157.

396 Shin Yong-Ha et al., *Dokdo yeongyugwon jaryo ui tamgu*, vol. 3, 362.

397 Ibid., 364–369.

398 Ibid., 370–371, 379–381.

However, according to another record from the Department of State, when Dean Rusk, the second assistant secretary for Far East affairs, asked the Korean diplomats the same question, the Korean delegation answered that the islands are located next to Ulleungdo or "Takeshima Rock."[399]

If this record is indeed accurate, the Korean diplomats will surely receive harsh criticism for providing a false location for the islands. However, Dokdo is not located next to "Takeshima Rock." And Parangdo is not located near Ulleungdo. Rather, it is located south of Jeju Island and is more commonly known as Ieodo in Korean. The island takes its name from the first Western ship to have found it, and which named it Socotra in 1905. The island thus is known as the Socotra Rocks in the West.

Rusk confirmed that what the Korean party called Dokdo was the same as what the Japanese called Takeshima. He concluded that "according to our records, this island has never been treated as Korean territory, and after 1905, it has been under the jurisdiction of the Oki Islands Branch Office of Shimane Prefecture of Japan." Simultaneously, the Korean government withdrew its request for Parangdo. This allowed Rusk to conclude that there was no need to include Dokdo and Parangdo.[400]

Unfortunately, the Korean embassy in the US was not aware of Dokdo having been removed from the list of islands to be restored to Korea because the Department of State never notified the Korean embassy. This illuminates why Ambassador Yang never mentioned Dokdo to Secretary of State Dean Acheson on August 2, 1951.[401] The Department of State finally responded to Ambassador Yang, notifying him that Dokdo had been removed on August 9. The letter of response from the

---

399 Ibid., 381–382.
400 Ibid., 371.
401 Ibid., 377–378.

Department of State repeated the earlier wording: (1) "Takeshima, or Dokdo known as Liancourt Rocks . . . according to our records, has never been a Korean territory; (2) this island has been under the jurisdiction of Shimane Prefecture of Japan since 1905; and (3) this island has never been claimed as territory by Korea."[402]

Kajimura, one of the few Japanese scholars arguing that Dokdo belongs to Korea, stated, "The Japanese government, although minor, had an opportunity to speak at the negotiation, whereas the Korean side did not have a single opportunity to argue that Dokdo was stolen from them."[403] He admitted that the Department of State was not objective in their decision-making concerning Dokdo.

In fact, the Department of State drafted an internal report criticizing Rusk's letter of response on August 26, 1954. The report was discovered by Kim Chai-hyung in 2008 at the National Archives and Records Administration in the United States. The report stated that "Rusk's letter of response may not have been based upon historical facts."[404] In addition, Rusk's letter of response was written about one year after North Korea invaded South Korea on June 25, 1950. The government of the Republic of Korea could not have spent a great deal of time and effort on this matter at the provisional capital of Busan while preoccupied with the war.

The Korean-Japanese Controversy over the Exclusion of Korea from the San Francisco Treaty

Article 2, Section (a) of the San Francisco Treaty stated, "Japan,

402 Ibid., 379–380.

403 Kajimura, "Ilbon ttang jujang eun paengchang – singminjuui sosan," 625.

404 Hosaka, *Uri yeoksa Dokdo*, 29–32.

recognizing the independence of Korea, renounces all rights, title, and claim to Korea, including the islands of Quelpart, Port Hamilton, and Dagelet."[405] Quelpart, Port Hamilton, and Dagelet are Western names for Jeju Island, Geomundo, and Ulleungdo, respectively. The names were given during the late Joseon period.

To reiterate, Article 2 of the San Francisco Treaty explicitly ensured the separation of Korea from Japan. This was a legal mandate of Japan's surrender. In that sense, the San Francisco Treaty confirmed the validity of the GHQ orders within the San Francisco Treaty. Article 19, Section (d) adds evidence to this fact in stating that "Japan recognizes the validity of all acts and omissions done during the period of occupation under or in consequence of directives of the occupation authorities or authorized by Japanese law at that time, and will take no action subjecting Allied nationals to civil or criminal liability arising out of such acts or omissions." As Yu Ha-young pointed out, Japan agreed to abide by all decisions and acts made during the period of the GHQ occupation, which meant that Japan admitted to the validity of SCAPIN No. 677.[406]

The Japanese has a different interpretation. The Japanese side claimed in *Japanese Government Opinion 1*, dated July 13, 1953, that the statement "Japan recognizes the independence of Korea" in Clause 7 of the San Francisco Treaty acknowledges the separation of Korea so that its status may return to that previous to Japanese annexation in August 1910. The Japanese government added that any meaning to the effect of "the land which was a part of the Japanese territory before the annexation" must be "ced[ed]" is not included.[407]

Japanese scholars such as Kawakami Kenzō largely supported the Japanese government's argument and offered an additional point of

405 Shin Yong-Ha et al., *Dokdo yeongyugwon jaryo ui tamgu*, vol. 3, 420.

406 Yu Ha-young, "Geundae Hanguk beopchegye eseo yeongto," 87.

407 Shin Yong-Ha et al., *Dokdo yeongyugwon jaryo ui tamgu*, vol. 3, 440–441.

discussion. Based on the fact that Dokdo was not mentioned in the San Francisco Treaty but was included in earlier documents such as SCAPIN No. 677 along with Jeju and Ulleungdo islands, they argued that such exclusion indicates that the island was separated from Korean territory for good.

The Korean government countered immediately. In *Korean Government Opinion 1*, delivered to Japan on September 9, 1953, Korea claimed that it "cannot recognize" the interpretation of the Japanese government. The opinion stated that if one's interpretation that Dokdo's exclusion from the list of islands Japan must relinquish translates to Dokdo remaining a part of Japan, then all of the other islands of Korea, which were not explicitly included in the list must also remain part of Japan. Korea harshly criticized the logic presented by Japan for essentially pushing Japanese territorial rights over all other Korean islands.[408]

The Korean government repeated its argument in *Korean Government Opinion 3*. The document concluded, "Japan agreed to abide by Article 2 of the San Francisco Treaty, which guaranteed the independence of Korea from Japan, and it promised the restoration of the entire territory of Korea, therefore the Republic of Korea can claim benefits of Article 2 as its inherent right."[409] In that context, Park Kwan-Sook, an international legal expert and the first individual to earn a doctorate for research on the territorial right over Dokdo, essentially supported the argument presented in "Korean Government Opinion 2." Park stated that just because the numerous islands belonging to Korea were not explicitly mentioned in the San Francisco Treaty does not mean that they do not belong to Korea.[410]

---

408 Shin Yong-Ha et al., *Dokdo yeongyugwon jaryo ui tamgu*, vol. 4, 384–385.

409 Ibid., 267–268.

410 Park Kwan-Sook, "Dokdo ui beopjeok jiwi" [Legal status of Dokdo], *Gukjebeop hakhoe nonchong* (February 1956), 29–49. This article was also published in *Dokdo*, ed. Daehan Gongnonsa (Seoul: Daehan Gongnonsa, 1965), 39–69, and *Hanguk ui Dokdo yeongyugwon yeongusa*, ed. Dokdo Insti-

Lee Han-key, who received a doctorate for his research on Dokdo at approximately the same time as Park Kwan-Sook, had the same interpretation.[411]

Japanese scholars such as Ueda Toshio and Taijudō Kanae refuted such views of the Korean government and Korean scholars. Taijudō published an article in English on this issue to appeal to Western scholars. The main ideas of that article are summarized below:

> Jeju Island, Geomundo, and Ulleungdo are not only Korea's most representative islands but also are islands located near the Japanese border. Therefore, if Takeshima is located closer to mainland Korea than the three islands mentioned above, then it is beyond doubt that the island belongs to Korea regardless of explicit mention in the San Francisco Treaty or not. Yet, Takeshima is located closer to Japan than the three islands mentioned. It does not make sense that it might belong to Korea. If it did belong to Korea just because of its location, it should have been explicitly mentioned in the Treaty. Takeshima was nowhere to be found in the San Francisco Treaty. And so, Takeshima was left as Japanese territory.[412]

In response, Lee Han-key criticized the statements above by arguing that because Dokdo is located closer to Japan than Jeju Island, Geomundo, and Ulleungdo, and not explicitly mentioned in the San Francisco Treaty, does not mean that it belongs to Japan.[413]

Kim Byungryull had the same idea. First, he criticized the extreme

---

tute, pages 13–34. Also see Park Kwan-Sook, "Dokdo ui beop-jeok jiwi e gwanhan yeongu" [Studies on the legal status of Dokdo], unpublished PhD dissertation, Yonsei University, 1968.

411 Lee Han-key, *Hanguk ui yeongto*, 267–268.

412 Taijudō Kanae, "The Dispute Between Japan and Korea Respecting Sovereignty over Takeshima," *The Japanese Annals of International Law* 10 (1966), 105–136.

413 Lee Han-key, *Hanguk ui yeongto*, 269.

stubbornness of Japan with his statement that Jeju Island, Geomundo, and Ulleungdo are not located at Korea's periphery. If one assumes that they are, then what about Marado, and all the other islands off the shores of Mokpo? These islands are farther away from mainland Korea than Jeju Island or Geomundo. Kim argued that while it is right that Jeju Island, Geomundo, and Ulleungdo are Korea's most representative islands, they are not the most distantly located islands. Therefore, the Japanese argument that Dokdo is Japanese territory because of its territorial location is invalid.[414]

As Kim stated, if the United States had intended to leave Dokdo as Japanese territory, then Dokdo should have been excluded from SCAPIN No. 677 as well. The Korean argument is in fact supported by Japanese evidence. The *Mainichi Shimbun*, a prominent newspaper in Japan, published a map of Japan in 1952 to explain the San Francisco Treaty to the Japanese people. This map clearly locates Dokdo outside of Japanese territory.[415]

A Department of State internal report composed on August 26, 1954, also weakens the Japanese argument. This document notes that it is "unclear" whether excluding Dokdo from Article 2 of the San Francisco Treaty will lead to the legal conclusion of Dokdo remaining Japanese territory.[416]

414 Kim Byungryull, *Dokdo nya Dakkesima nya*, 214–215.

415 Kwon Chae-Hyun, "'Dokdo neun Hanguk ttang' Ilbon do injeong" ["Dokdo is Korean land," even Japan admits it], *Dong-A Ilbo*, February 24, 2005.

416 Hosaka, *Uri yeoksa Dokdo*, 31.

The Republic of Korea Assigns a Postal Code to Dokdo

Dokdo was never a part of the "minor outlying islands," nor was it a part of Japanese territory under American jurisdiction. Furthermore, its administrative jurisdiction was already restored to the Republic of Korea on August 15, 1945, the day of Korea's liberation, and the parties associated with the San Francisco Treaty acknowledged Korea as an independent state. This fact shows that Dokdo is internationally recognized as Korean territory.[417]

Accordingly, Korean fishermen who had lost fishing grounds for forty years following 1905 returned to the waters of Dokdo. Beginning in 1947, Korea sent envoys to conduct various research and investigations on Dokdo. A prominent example of such is the Dokdo Academic Research conducted by the Corean Alpine Club. The group visited Ulleungdo and Dokdo from August 16 to 25, 1947. This investigation included numerous scholars from a wide range of disciplines, such as the linguist Bang Jong-hyeon, the archeologist Kim Won-yong, the entomologist Seok Joo-myung, and the historian Shin Sok-ho. Upon completing their work, they installed a sign on Dongdo that read, "Dokdo, Nam-myeon, Ulleungdo, Joseon." This sign was the first sign to show that Dokdo belonged to Korea and to show the exercise of Korea's right over Dokdo.[418]

On June 8, 1948, the GHQ, through SCAPIN No. 1778 on July 6, 1947, assigned Dokdo as a drill area for the United States Far East Command. The information was passed only to Japan. Korean fishermen thus were left unaware of this fact and fell victim to the United States military bombing drills. Among the thirty fishermen, sixteen died immediately

---

417 Lee Han-key, *Hanguk ui yeongto*, 269.

418 *Dokdo munje gaeron* [Introduction to the Dokdo issue] (Seoul: Ministry of Foreign Affairs, 1955), 34.

and six sustained heavy injuries.[419] In response, the Far East Command acknowledged its failure to notify Korea and later apologized.

On August 15, 1948, the Republic of Korea was founded, and simultaneously the Korean government assigned a postal address to Dokdo: Do-dong 1, Nam-myeon, Ulleung-gun county, Gyeongsangbuk-do province. On June 8, 1950, the governor of Gyeongsangbuk-do province erected a memorial statue in commemoration of the victims of the American bombing incident.[420]

419 According to the July 1948 issue of the monthly magazine *Sincheonji*, which was published in Seoul at that time, casualties included sixteen dead and three people with critical injuries. There also was damage to twenty-three boats, including seven motorboats. According to a Korean Foreign Ministry record dated to 1955, there were fifty-five casualties. Ministry of Foreign Affairs, *Dokdo munje gaeron*, 38. Reporter Lee Jeong-hoon of the Dong-A Press recorded fourteen casualties and eleven damaged boats. Lee Jeong-hoon, "'Dokdo munje' Ilbon ui jankkoe e malliji malla" [Don't be fooled by Japan's trickery on the Dokdo issue], *Weekly Dong-A,* vol. 476, March 15, 2005, 33.

420 Lee Jeong-hoon, "Dokdo munje" [Dokdo issue], *Dong-A Ilbo*, March 24, 2005, 10. This statue was erected in June 1951. However, it was later revealed in a series of photographs sent to President Rhee Syngman from Governor Cho Jae-cheon that the date was June 8, 1950. I hereby acknowledge and thank President Rhee's daughter in law, Cho Hye-ja, who graciously sent these photographs to the *Dong-A Ilbo*.

Japan Attempts to Make Dokdo a Subject of "Legal Dispute"

Chapter 7

1 Korea's Proclamation of the Peace Line and the Restoration of Japan's Sovereignty Leads to the Korean-Japanese Controversy over Dokdo

Korean Government Includes Dokdo Within its Peace Line

As discussed above, the San Francisco Treaty was signed on September 8, 1951. When the treaty came into effect on April 28, 1952, the sovereignty of Japan was fully restored.

The Korean government was forced to pay special attention to two aspects of the evolving reality. First, once Japan regained its sovereignty, the MacArthur Line used to protect Korean fishing rights would be abolished. The abolishment of the MacArthur Line would become a large obstacle for the growth of the Korean fishing industry. Predicting this, the Korean government requested that the MacArthur Line be maintained, but the request was denied. Second, the Korean government was worried over the possibility of the Japanese government attempting to exercise jurisdiction over Dokdo, which the Japanese understood to be their island.

The Korean government began work on a grand strategy. This resulted in the creation and proclamation of the Peace Line, which was officially announced on January 18, 1952.[421] President Rhee, Prime Minister

---

421 Shin Yong-Ha et al., *Dokdo yeongyugwon jaryo ui tamgu*, vol. 1, 398–400; Chee Choul Keun, *Pyeonghwaseon*, chapter 3.

Heo Jeong, Minister of Defense Lee Ki-poong, Minister of Foreign Affairs Pyun Yong-tae, and Minister of Commerce Kim Hun signed the proclamation. Through this proclamation, the Korean government publicly announced that it would exercise its sovereignty over its waters. The proclamation outlined that the purpose of the Peace Line was to protect natural resources and the Korean fishing industry. Needless to say, Korea included Dokdo on its side of the line. While it is true that the protection of Korea's natural resources, the fishing industry, and its people are without doubt important, it is the protection of sovereignty that is deemed inviolate. This became one of the most prominent achievements of President Rhee.

Resisting Japan versus Refuting Korea

Resisting the implementation of the Peace Line, Japanese strongly criticized the Peace Line. Newspaper articles and opinion essays in the January 24 issue of the *Mainichi Shimbun* and in the January 25 issue of the *Yomiuri Shimbun* informed the Japanese public of the Peace Line and guided their response. The Japanese media sarcastically labeled the line the "Rhee Line."

The Japanese government responded immediately. On January 24, Japan's Ministry of Foreign Affairs stated, (1) as the agreement on fishing rights made among the United States, Canada, and Japan set a precedent for ensuring the freedom of the sea, the freedom of the sea must also be respected between Japan and Korea; and (2) there exists no case in which a country proclaimed national sovereignty over the seas. This statement concluded that the issue must be addressed and reviewed with extreme care and attention for the bettering of Japanese and Korean relations.[422]

The response from the Japanese government continued. On January 28, 1952, Japan delivered a written statement of protest to the Korean government. The note stated that the Korean proclamation goes against "the long internationally established principle of the freedom of the seas." In the note, the Japanese government complained that the proclamation restricts Japanese fishing practices and mentioned Takeshima (Dokdo) as well. Japan further argued that the Korean proclamation "assumes" territorial rights over Takeshima, of which "any such assumption or claim" will not be tolerated nor be acknowledged by the Japanese government.[423]

The Korean government sent a counterargument on February 12, 1952. First, the Korean government began by stating that there was no need to quarrel over the territorial rights of the Liancourt Rocks (Dokdo). The Korean government continued that Japanese territorial rights over Dokdo were "clearly excluded as explicitly stated in SCAPIN No. 677 of January 29, 1946. The island was also located outside of the MacArthur Line."[424]

Japan immediately refuted this. The Ministry of Foreign Affairs delivered a note to the representatives of the Republic of Korea in Japan on April 25, 1952, claiming that "Takeshima has always been Japanese territory." Furthermore, Japan provided its own opinion regarding SCAPIN No. 677 and the MacArthur Line. A summarized version of Japan's claim follows below.

First, the first section of SCAPIN No. 677 only ordered a temporal ban on "governmental or administrative authority." SCAPIN did not exclude

---

422 Ibid., 172–173.

423 Ibid., 401–402.

424 Ibid., 403–405.

this island from "Japanese territorial possession."

Second, Article 3 of SCAPIN No. 677 reads, "For the purpose of this directive, Japan is defined to include the four main islands of Japan (Hokkaido, Honshu, Kyushu and Shikoku) and the approximately 1,000 smaller adjacent islands, including the Tsushima Islands and the Ryukyu (Nansei) Islands north of 30 degrees north latitude (excluding Kuchinoshima Island); and excluding (a) Utsuryo (Ullung) Island, Liancourt Rocks (Take Island) and Quelpart (Saishu or Cheju) Island," but Article 8 reads, "All records of the agencies referred to . . . above will be preserved and kept available for inspection" by the GHQ.

Third, the Liancourt Rocks were left on the Korean side of the MacArthur Line, but this was not evidence that it belongs to Korea. That is because Article 6 of SCAPIN No. 2046 of September 19, 1949, read, "Present authorization is not an expression of Allied policy relative to ultimate determination of national jurisdiction, international boundaries, or fishing rights in the area concerned or in any other area." Furthermore, the MacArthur Line has been abolished. Therefore, this argument is futile.[425]

The day that Japan's Ministry of Foreign Affairs submitted this message was the same day on which the MacArthur Line was abolished, and four days prior to the restoration of Japanese sovereignty. In this context, Japan quickly established a posture to assimilate Dokdo into its territory. On May 16, 1952, Shimane Prefecture amended the "Shimane Prefecture Adjustment of Fisheries," which authorized Japanese citizens to fish in the waters of Takeshima.

---

425 Ibid., 406–407.

The Korean-Japanese Controversy over Dokdo as Part of the United States Air Force Air-Maneuvering Zone

Two months prior to the signing of the San Francisco Treaty, on February 28, 1952, the United States and Japan signed the "United States-Japan Executive Agreements." Article 2 of this agreement made the Liancourt Rocks a "facility and area," which meant that the United States was able to practice bombing drills in the area. Eventually, on July 26, 1952, the island became a United States Air Force air-maneuvering zone. The Japanese government and many Japanese scholars argued that this designation is proof that "the United States acknowledged Takeshima as Japanese territory."[426]

However, at the request of the Korean government, the United States Air Force excluded Dokdo from its list of air-maneuver zones on February 27, 1953, which contradicts the Japanese argument. On September 9, 1953, the Korean government delivered *Korean Government Opinion 1* to Japan stating, "The Japanese government must understand that the United States government exempted Dokdo from its air-maneuver zones as of February 27, 1953, at our behest."[427] The Korean government interpreted the exemption of Dokdo as an act of the United States recognizing Dokdo as Korean territory.[428] However, according to a Department of State internal report dated August 26, 1954, and discovered in 2008, "There is no need to judge that the 'United States-Japan Executive Agreement' acknowledged Dokdo as Japanese territory."[429]

---

426 Kawakami, *Dakesima ui yeoksa jirihakjeok yeongu*, 252–256.

427 Shin Yong-Ha et al., *Dokdo yeongyugwon jaryo ui tamgu*, vol. 4, 433–442.

428 Hong Seong-keun, "Dokdo pokgyeok sageon ui gukjebeopjeok jaengjeom bunseok" [Analysis of the Dokdo bombing incident through the lens of international law] in *Hanguk ui Dokdo yeongyugwon yeongusa*, ed. Dokdo Institute (Seoul: Dokdo Research Conservation Association, 2003), 397–398.

429 Hosaka, *Uri yeoksa Dokdo*, 29–30.

The Boycott of the Peace Line in Japan

On July 13, 1952, approximately two months after the Japanese were authorized to fish in the Dokdo area, the Japanese government announced the installment of the "ABC Line." This line was intended to act as a security line. It included not only Dokdo but also Jeju Island. Clearly, it was an aggressive maneuver aimed at resisting Korea's implementation of the Peace Line.

On September 27, 1952, during the war raging on the Korean Peninsula, the Commander of the United Nations Forces Mark Clark declared the Clark Line in effect as a preventive measure against communist incursion and combat material smuggling. Dokdo was included within this boundary.[430]

The Clark Line was very similar to Korea's Peace Line, and while giving Korea an advantageous position, it also effectively nullified Japan's ABC Line. This was precisely why Japan rejected the implementation of the Clark Line. Japan began an aggressive campaign against both the Clark Line and the Peace Line. The Japanese government's logic concluded, "Takeshima has been Japanese territory, but Korea seized it." Borrowing the words of Kajimura, until the end of the boycott movement in 1954, this period became the "first intensification of the contentious period."[431]

According to Kajimura, the Korean argument was never made public to the Japanese people, and the aforementioned logic of Dokdo as "inherently Japanese territory" was the sole assertion promoted within Japanese society. Kajimura recalled that this movement became the watershed moment in Japanese history when Takeshima became remembered as part of the collective memory considered inherently Japanese among its people. He continued, "Japan promoted fictional stories and based them

---

430 Chee Choul Keun, *Pyeonghwaseon*, 178–181.

431 Kajimura, "Ilbon ttang jujang eun paengchang – singminjuui sosan," 626.

on its imperialist experiences. To this day, the Japanese government has not apologized, which is highly problematic."[432]

The national Peace Line boycott continued until 1954. Just as Kajimura pointed out, the boycott campaign was used not only as a means to promote the rebuilding of Japan's military but also as a measure to implement provocative steps toward Dokdo's acquisition. To expand upon this, on April 1, 1953, a large ship moored near Dokdo and a group of Japanese erected a sign reading, "Takeshima, a Japanese territory."[433] From then on, groups of Japanese trespassed in a flurry of instances: May 28, June 11, June 17, June 25, June 27, and June 28. According to Korean fishermen present at Dokdo during that time, these Japanese used the deceptive technique of sailing under the American flag each time they trespassed.

Needless to say, the Japanese government supported those trespassing. This was evident on June 25 when a ship belonging to the Japanese government moored at Dokdo. Six people went ashore gathering up and taking photographs of Koreans present for the trespassing. This was repeated on June 27. On June 29, however, events escalated. Two Japanese Coast Guard vessels carried thirty government workers and policemen ashore and erected two border signs and two bulletin boards. The Japanese also issued threats to the Korean people using the Korean language, saying, "This island belongs to Japan. If you are caught operating on this island from this point on, Japanese police will arrest you."[434]

---

432 Kajimura, Ibid., 626.

433 Choi Gyu-jang, "Dokdo subidae bisa" [Undisclosed history of the Dokdo Volunteer Garrison], in *Dokdo*, ed. Daehan Gongnonsa (Seoul: Daehan Gongnonsa, 1965), 313–322.

434 Kim Myungki, *Dokdo Uiyong Subidae wa gukjebeop* [Dokdo Volunteer Garrison and international law] (Seoul: Damul Chulpansa, 1998), 29–31; Hong Sun-chil, "Jeonjaesan gwa onmom bachyeo Dokdo jikyeotta" [I protected Dokdo with everything I had], *Shindonga* (April 1996), 632–634.

The Dokdo Protection Movement in Korea

It was only natural for Koreans to retaliate by creating protection movements of their own as Japan attempted to seize Dokdo again. The most prominent Dokdo protection movement was the Dokdo Volunteer Garrison. Hong Sun-chil, whose family had been Ulleungdo residents for the three generations after Hong Jae-hyeon, became the head of the first Dokdo volunteer guards and protected Dokdo for more than three years. He began his duties on April 30, 1953.[435]

It was only after August 1953 that the Korean government began its involvement. Police units of Gyeongsangbuk-do province installed radio communication on Dokdo. According to Korean law, radio operators must be current police officers. Thus, two of the voluntary guards were appointed as policemen.[436] The Japanese government complained to Korea. For example, on June 22, 1953, Japan's Ministry of Foreign Affairs argued that fishermen originating from Ulleungdo were illegally trespassing on Dokdo and requested that Korea prevent future trespassing. On June 26, Korea rejected the request by concluding that there is no more to discuss regarding the matter because Dokdo belongs to Korea and Japan has no right to dictate anything concerning Korean territory.[437]

Amid the controversy, on July 8, 1953, the Korean government passed the "Resolution on Japan's Trespassing on Dokdo." This resolution was intended to protect Dokdo from Japanese incursion. A similar resolution was passed at local levels as well. For example, on July 10, the

---

435 Hong Sun-chil, "Jeonjaesan gwa onmom bachyeo Dokdo jikyeotta," 632–659; Hong Sun-chil, *I ttang i nwi ttang inde! Dokdo Uiyong Subidae Hong Sun-chil daejang sugi* [Who do you think this land belongs to? Memoirs of Commander Hong Sun-chil of the Dokdo Volunteer Garrison] (Seoul: Hyean, 1997); Kim Myungki, *Dokdo Uiyong Subidae wa gukjebeop*, 19.

436 Kim Myungki, *Dokdo Uiyong Subidae wa gukjebeop*, 84.

437 Shin Yong-Ha et al., *Dokdo yeongyugwon jaryo ui tamgu*, vol. 3, 408–409, 409–410.

Gyeongsangbuk-do Provincial Congress passed identical wording.[438] During the period of October 15 to 16, 1953, the Corean Alpine Club and the Dokdo Research Commission visited Dokdo aboard navy vessel no. 905 to dispose of the signs that Japanese fishermen had previously erected. Upon removing the Japanese signs, the group installed a granite sign reading "Dokdo" and "Liancourt." On the back of the sign, there is a short description noting the planned installation date of August 15, 1952, with the actual date of installation engraved on the side as October 15, 1953.

Despite this, Japan's provocations continued. On October 23, 1953, the Japanese Coast Guard, along with Japanese government officials, landed on Dokdo to tear down the granite sign and again erected the Japanese signs. In February 1954, the Japanese government authorized phosphate mining on Dokdo. From this point on, the Japanese government publicly announced that it would not hesitate to exercise its right to self-defense in order to protect Japan.

The Korean government had no other choice but to confront Japan face-to-face. In April 1954, Prime Minister Baek Du-jin delivered a hand-written message to the Gyeongsangbuk-do Provincial police ordering warning shots to be fired toward Japanese vessels nearing Dokdo and to sink trespassing ships. President Rhee delivered 100 rounds of mortars and cannon shells. The Dokdo guards crafted one fake cannon from wood and painted it gunmetal grey in order to threaten trespassing Japanese ships.[439] Korea maintained its hardline stance. On May 18, 1954, a group of Korean government officials and stonemasons arrived on Dokdo to remove all Japanese signs. The group carved a sign reading "Korean Territory" in hangeul script and a Korean flag in a cliffside rock

---

438 Ibid., 412–413.

439 Kim Myungki, *Dokdo Uiyong Subidae wa gukjebeop* [Dokdo Volunteer Garrison and international law] (Seoul, Damul Chulpansa, 1998), 85–94.

on the southeast end of the island.

The Japanese government confirmed Korea's actions and sent a letter of protest to the Korean government. Japan continued to send investigation scout ships to Dokdo. Korea did not remain idle and installed a lighthouse on the island. This matter was discussed in Japan's House of Representatives. A number of house members requested that the Japanese government take action in response to the Korean installation of the lighthouse. Officials from the Ministry of Foreign Affairs refused to make lengthy remarks on the subject, arguing that the Japanese stance that Dokdo belongs to Japan will not change.[440]

---

440 *Ilbon Gukhoe Dokdo gwallyeon girok moeumjip*, vol. 1, 259–260.

2 Japan's Proposal to Take the Matter to the International Court of Justice and Korea's Refusal

Japan's Proposal

Japan suspended provocations after realizing that the Korean government refused to yield. The government instead changed tactics by pursuing international legal arbitration. On September 25, 1954, the Japanese government proposed to take the Dokdo issue to the International Court of Justice. In the proposal, Japan wrote, "The issue is a dispute on territorial rights involving [the] interpretation of the fundamental principles of international law." The proposal continued by arguing that "the only equitable solution" toward a "peaceful solution of the dispute" would be to take the matter before the International Court of Justice.[441]

Korea's Refusal

Korea flatly refused the offer from Japan. Korea's Ministry of Foreign

---

441 *Ilbon Gukhoe Dokdo gwallyeon girok moeumjip*, vol. 4 [Collection of Japanese National Diet records on Dokdo] (Seoul: Northeast Asian History Foundation, 2009), 300–302.

Affairs announced the decision on September 28, 1954.[442] On October 28, 1954, the representatives of the Republic of Korea argued that the Japanese proposal is a "judicial disguise" attempting to make fictitious arguments to illegally seize Dokdo. This is explained further below.

> Korea has inherent rights over Dokdo, and it finds no need to prove it "before any international court of justice." Japan is the party that wishes to create a fictitious scenario from the imagination of "a quasi territorial dispute where none should exist." By presenting "the Dokdo problem" to the International Court of Justice, Japan is attempting to stand on the same level as the Republic of Korea on "the so-called territorial dispute over Dokdo." Japan is attempting to establish its own version of Korea's claim to "the complete and indisputable territorial rights of Korea over Dokdo."[443]

The representatives of the Republic of Korea announced the following statement, similar to that submitted to Japan's Ministry of Foreign Affairs. The statement clearly indicates the firm stance of the Korean government.

> Dokdo was the first victim of the Japanese invasion of Korea. With liberation, Dokdo was rightfully restored to the hands of Korea again. Dokdo symbolizes the independence of Korea. Anyone who dares to touch this island must be prepared to stand up to the resistance of the Korean people. Dokdo is not merely a few rocks standing in the middle of the sea. Rather, it is an anchor of Korean glory. How can independence be protected after losing this? Japan's act of stealing Dokdo signifies the reinvasion of Korea.

---

442 *Dong-A Ilbo*, September 30, 1954, 1.

443 *Ilbon Gukhoe Dokdo gwallyeon girok moeumjip*, vol. 4, 304–306.

The Logic of the Korean Government and Korean Scholars

How can one judge Japan's proposal to take the matter before the International Court of Justice? Japan attacks Korea for refusing the proposal, stating that Korea is not confident enough to stand before an international organization that adjudicates international disputes. Is that the case? Korea has several ways of confronting this charge.

First, Dokdo has been Korean territory from the beginning and will be so to the end. Dokdo is not a disputed territory nor is it up to legal contestation. Korea simply does not see a need to prove what is already theirs in front of the international society. The burden of proof lies with Japan. Would Japan accept to go before the International Court of Justice if Korea wishes to dispute the territorial rights to Tsushima? The answer is a resounding no.

In fact, numerous scholars argue that Tsushima is Korean territory. For instance, Yang Tae-jin, who carried out in-depth studies on Korean territory and border claims, insists that Tsushima is historically and geographically Korean.[444] Some scholars go further, arguing that the Korean government has the right to officially dispute the matter. A Korean international legal expert, Loh Kye-hyun, has been arguing this for some time. He came to that conclusion after objectively examining many pieces of evidence.[445]

The plan is not pure imagination. Jung Il-young, a Korean scholar of international law who participated in the Korea-Japan summit meetings from 1960 to 1962, recalled the following:

[During the meeting,] a Japanese representative asked me, "Would it not

---

444 Yang Tae-jin, *Hanguk yeongtosa yeongu* [Research in the history of Korean territory] (Seoul: Beopgyeong Chulpansa, 1991), chapter 6.

445 Loh Kye-hyun, *Joseon ui yeongto* [Joseon territory] (Seoul: KNOU Press, 1997), chapter 7.

be nice to take the Dokdo matter to the International Court of Justice?" I answered, "Yes, this would be great, but only under one condition, only if the matter of reinstating Korean sovereignty over Tsushima and Kyushu also were to be discussed." He became angry. All I meant was not to make such blunt statements.[446]

Second, as Kajimura pointed out, the reason why Korea does not accept the proposal to take the matter before the International Court of Justice is due to "an inherent distrust [of] the international judicial organization."[447] This issue will be discussed in detail below. The international standard of arbitrating similar "territorial disputes" has been based on the principle of effective possession. The International Court of Justice favors this principle, which became the backbone of Western imperialists' seizure of territory in the past. Aware of this, the Japanese government and Japanese scholars offer Shimane Prefecture's incorporation of Dokdo in 1905 as evidence of effective possession.

Lee Han-key concluded that "as long as Japan's 1905 incorporation of Dokdo can be used as evidence of effective possession, one cannot help but conclude that that is legitimizing imperialistic colonial rule." He also claimed that it is only natural for Korea to refuse that kind of a trial, explaining as follows:

The political character of the Dokdo issue is integral to Korea's refusal to abide by what it believes to be an unjust and dangerous law. Any sovereign nation has this right, and it is neither illegal nor unethical to exercise such a right.[448]

446 Jung Il-young, "Dokdo yeongyugwon yeongu ui hyanghu gwaje" [Future tasks of Dokdo territorial rights research], unpublished paper presented at the Commemorative Seminar for Professor Shin Dong Wook, 2009, 1.

447 Kajimura, "Ilbon ttang jujang eun paengchang – singminjuui sosan," 628.

448 Lee Han-key, Hanguk ui yeongto, 303.

Kim Myungki proceeded with a similar argument. He concluded "The actions taken by the Korean side to refuse the Japanese offer [were] never a violation of some sort."[449] This is not to say that Korea will exclude any and all international adjustments. Lee Han-key states that if an "International Court of Justice for Asia" is created, then Korea can safely present the matter to such an organization. Lee's idea aroused international sympathy and interest. Kajimura commented that this idea is "worth attention."

One should not mistake Korea's decision as a fear of losing the case at the International Court of Justice. As the Korean international law scholar Shin Dong Wook stated, despite the Korean government's refusal to take the case to the International Court of Justice, the evidence and the situation are favorable for Korea. Thus, if this issue ever reaches the International Court of Justice, it will most likely end well for Korea.[450] The Korean government was as tough with its actions. On November 30, 1954, it fired on a Japanese scout ship approaching Dokdo and showed its resolve not to hesitate to order an airstrike if Japan continued to trespass. On December 25, 1956, the Korean government dismissed the guards of the Dokdo Volunteer Garrison and officially ordered the Gyeongsang-buk-do province police to assume the duty. Simultaneously, it issued Dokdo stamps, affirming Korean territorial rights over Dokdo.[451]

A Temporary Pause in the Controversy

Japan halted the presentation of the matter officially in light of the strong

---

449 Kim Myungki, *Dokdo wa gukjebeop*, 122.

450 Shin Dong Wook, *Dokdo yeongyu e gwanhan yeongu* [Study on Dokdo territorial rights] (Seoul: Eomungak, 2008), chapter 8.

451 Kim Myungki, *Dokdo Uiyong Subidae wa gukjebeop*, 116.

Korean resistance. The Dokdo matter stagnated, temporarily frozen.

The Dokdo issue was never selected as a formal item for a Korea-Japan meeting. Specifically, as a result of Kubota Kanichirō's reckless comment on October 15, 1953, that "Japanese colonial rule was beneficial to Korea. . . . Korea would have been colonized by other countries anyway, which would have led to harsher rule than Japanese rule." The topic at the summit meetings between the two countries remained in a stalemate until the fourth summit meeting in 1957. The Dokdo issue was never officially discussed at the fifth summit meeting held in 1960 either.[452]

The Van Fleet Delegation's Report

Starting in April 1954, the American government ordered retired general James A. Van Fleet to lead a group to Korea, Taiwan, Japan, and the Philippines. The aptly named Van Fleet Delegation's primary purpose was to conduct an inspection of the American military aid plan among countries receiving military or economic aid, or both. The delegation reported directly to President Dwight D. Eisenhower on September 30, 1954.

The report included remarks on the Liancourt Rocks. The statement revealed that the American government had made an internal decision to conclude that the Liancourt Rocks belong to Japan. The Japanese government uses this fact even to this day as evidence of the American recognition of Takeshima as Japanese territory. However, the remark in the Van Fleet Report amounted to no more than a reiteration of Sebald's opinion discussed above. On the other hand, the report included the

---

452 Kajimura, "Ilbon ttang jujang eun paengchang – singminjuui sosan," 626–628.

Korean government's opinion that Dokdo is an adjacent island to Ulleungdo that belongs to Korea and that historically and legally the island is a Korean territory.[453]

Japanese Governmental Ordinances

The Japanese government issued General Ordinance No. 43 in 1960. This ordinance excluded Ulleungdo, Jeju Island, and even Dokdo from its annexed islands. The same exclusion was made on General Ordinance No. 37 issued in 1968. In the midst of the Dokdo issue emerging again, these ordinances were discussed. The Japanese government clarified that "these ordinances are no more than amendments made to the ordinances issued in 1951 dealing with settlement of corporations in the annexed territory."

---

453 Cho Sung Hun, "1954 Baen Plit sajeoldan bogoseo wa Miguk ui Dokdo insik" [The report of Gen. Van Fleet mission in 1954 and America's recognition on Dokdo Island], *Dongyanghak* ([Oriental studies] 46 (August 2009), 199–218.

3 Dokdo Discussed at the Korean-Japanese Summit Meetings between 1962 and 1965

Japan Suggests Exploding Dokdo

On May 16, 1961, Park Chung-hee and Kim Jong-pil led a coup d'état and eventually installed a military government in power. This altered the chain of events dramatically. The Japanese government, interested in improving Korean-Japanese relations, proposed again to take the Dokdo issue before the International Court of Justice. The offer was made in March 1962, but the Korean side refused again.[454]

The Japanese government seemed persistent about this proposal. At the 6th Korean-Japanese Summit, the Japanese government brought up the Dokdo issue once again. The first preliminary meeting to the sixth summit meeting was held at the Ministry of Foreign Affairs in Japan on August 21, 1962. Dokdo was discussed during the fourth meeting, which was held on September 3, 1962. At the meeting, Iseki Yujirō, the director of General Asian Affairs stated that "Takeshima has no value. It is about the size of Hibiya Park, and it would make no difference even if we bomb it to get rid of it."[455]

---

454 Park and Naitō, *Dokdo=Dakesima nonjaeng*, 178.

455 Lee Do-seong, *Sillok Park Chung-hee wa Han-Il hoedam* [Park Chung-hee and the Korea-Japan sum-

There is a point to be clarified here. For several decades a rumor has circulated in Korea that Kim Jong-pil, the head of the Korean Central Intelligence Agency at the time, offered to bomb Dokdo. However, if one reads the official document from the abovementioned meeting, it was Iseki who publicly offered the idea. When Kim Jong-pil visited Tokyo and met with Foreign Minister Ōhira Masayoshi on October 20, 1962, approximately seven weeks after the fourth preliminary meeting, Kim delivered the response to Japan's offer to take the Dokdo matter before the International Court of Justice. He stated that "the Dokdo matter bears no relevance to the summit meeting. Therefore, it should be discussed after the normalization of relations between the two countries." The Japanese side understood this as a refusal.

President Park Chung-hee Orders No Discussion of Dokdo

Kim Jong-pil met with Minister Ōhira again on November 12, 1962. At the time, acting-president Park Chung-hee gave Kim five emergency orders. One of these was an order pertaining to Dokdo, which read, "If Japan brings up Dokdo again, point out that the matter was not immediately relevant, and simultaneously warn Japan that it will remind the Korean people of Japan's invasion, which will most likely stifle the atmosphere of the meeting." Despite President Park's direct orders, Kim could not help but respond to Minister Ōhira, who insisted on settling the Dokdo issue before the International Court of Justice.

---

mit meeting] (Seoul: Hansong, 1995), 341–348. The compilation *Sillok Park Chung-hee wa Han-Il hoedam* by Lee Do-seong of the *Dong-A Ilbo* recorded this in detail. At that time, Choi worked as a councilor to the South Korean government representative stationed in Japan, who belonged to a central government office as a same-year graduate of the Army Officers School. He had graduated in its eighth graduating class with Kim Jong-pil, who at that time was the second-ranking official in the government. In Japan, Kōno Ichirō was one of the leading figures in Japanese politics and the head of one of the eight major factions within the Liberal Democratic Party.

Kim's response was third-party arbitration, which can be verified in the fifteenth preliminary meeting notes.

What drove Kim to go against his superior's orders? What made him devise the plan of third-party arbitration? Kim could have thought that delaying the meeting because of the Dokdo issue went against their respective national interests, or he could have thought that third-party arbitration would have ended in favor of Korea. However, as Yi Do-seong, a reporter, pointed out, "Kim Jong-pil's plan could not avoid criticism for its immature character."[456] The Korean government immediately realized that Kim's suggestion of third-party arbitration was not wise. Therefore, the Dokdo issue was dealt with separately from that point on. The Japanese government was also not fond of the suggestion. It informed Korea that it is developing plans that would seek to share Dokdo or jointly administer the island. The Korean government turned these offers down as well.

Japanese media reported on the Dokdo issue from time to time. The Korean Minister of Commerce Kim Yong-sik conducted an interview with Japanese reporters at an airport on July 25, 1963. A group of reporters asked Kim whether Dokdo would be discussed with Minister Ōhira. Kim was firm that "Dokdo will not be discussed as it is clear that it belongs to Korea."[457]

The Second Intensification of the Contentious Period

After the October 1963 presidential election, Park Chung-hee became the president of the Republic of Korea. The November congressional

---

456 Lee Do-seong, *Sillok Park Chung-hee wa Han-Il hoedam*, 343.

457 Kim Yong-sik, *Huimang gwa dojeon: Kim Yong-sik oegyo hoegorok* [Hope and defiance: Kim Yong-sik's diplomatic memoir] (Seoul: Dong-A Ilbosa, 1987), 78.

elections marked the beginning of the Third Republic. The media and the opposition, who had been suppressed under military rule, became active again. Naturally, the public grew weary of the direction the government was heading toward with regard to the Korea-Japan summit talks. A boycott movement that started at Seoul National University on March 24, 1964, spread nationwide by June. Park was forced to declare martial law.

Meanwhile, a rumor began to circulate that the Korean government would give up Dokdo in exchange for economic aid. A boycott movement spread in Japan as well, and Dokdo was discussed there, too. This was the beginning of the "Second Contentious Period." The Korea government promised that there would be no such exchange. Nevertheless, on February 18, 1965, the Japanese government proposed to discuss the matter at the Korean-Japanese commerce ministerial meeting. Yi Dong-won, the minister of commerce at that time, recalled that the Japanese raised the Dokdo issue first. Yi joked that they could "exchange that island with Japan's Tsushima." The joke ended the conversation immediately.[458]

Japan did not seem to have lingered on the topic, but each initiation of the issue on the international level was met with a Korean refusal to discuss the matter. On June 22, 1965, the day on which the "Treaty on Basic Relations between Japan and the Republic of Korea" was signed, Japanese representatives raised the issue again.[459]

According to Minister Yi Dong-won, Satō Eisaku, then the Japanese prime minister, "pressured [him] that Japan will not sign the treaty if Takeshima is not returned to Japan." Ultimately, the Treaty on Basic Relations between Japan and the Republic of Korea did not include

---

458 Lee Dong-won, *Daetongnyeong eul geurimyeo* [In memory of the president] (Seoul: Goryeowon, 1992), 220–221.

459 This point was confirmed at a press conference held by Yi Dong-won with the L'Agence France-Presse in Seoul on February 10, 1977.

content regarding Dokdo. Kajimura commented that the exclusion of the Dokdo issue from the treaty meant that the Korean governmental objective of no discussion had been achieved. The Korean government interpreted this as a treaty respecting Korean sovereignty over Dokdo. Yet, Korea's Peace Line was abolished, a much decried mistake among Koreans. There are numerous people critical of its abolishment, and they argue that the disposal gave Japan room to continue arguing rights over Dokdo.[460]

As Kajimura pointed out, fishermen from both countries in the island region seemed to have a tacit agreement to operate in peace, which calmed the situation.[461] From the Korean perspective, was the Dokdo issue disregarded? Not necessarily. On June 22, 1965, a exchange of notes concerning the settlement of disputes between the government of the Republic of Korea and the Government of Japan declared that both countries will first make every effort to resolve issues in a respectful, diplomatic manner. This declaration seemed to have Dokdo in mind. However, the Korean government's understanding is that the Dokdo matter was already resolved with the normalization treaty and is therefore not part of the "dispute" mentioned within the exchange.[462]

---

460 Hyeon Seung-il, then a junior studying in the political science department at Seoul National University, published an editorial titled "Concession of the Peace Line is Disposal of National Territory" in the university newspaper. As far as I know, Hyeon's paper was among the earlier papers arguing that under no circumstances should the Peace Line be yielded. At the time, Hyeon had already predicted that unless Park Chung-hee's military administration did not change its approach to the Korea-Japan summit meeting, then there would be great damage to national pride and interest. Hyeon was responsible for a large student demonstration nine months after publishing his editorial, on March 24, 1964. As a consequence, he was jailed twice for two years. Later, he received a doctorate in sociology at Utah State University, was president of Kookmin University in Korea, and served as an elected official.

461 Kajimura, "Ilbon ttang jujang eun paengchang – singminjuui sosan," 628.

462 Kim Myungki, and Lee Dong-won, *Ilbon Oemuseong Dakesima munje ui gaeyo bipan: Dakesima 10-pointeu bipan* [Criticism of introduction to Takeshima issue by Japan's Ministry of Foreign Affairs: Criticism on Takeshima 10 key points] (Seoul: Chaek gwa Saramdeul, 2010), 247.

Prime Minister Fukuda's Statements and the Beginning of the Third Phase of the Intensification of the Contentious Period

On February 5 and February 9, 1977, Japan's Prime Minister Fukuda Takeo made the reckless statement that "Takeshima is without doubt Japanese territory."[463] Kajimura evaluated this as the starting point of the "Third Intensification of the Contentious Period." Why did Prime Minister Fukuda make such a comment?

From the mid-1970s onward, international society faced new concerns with respect to the fishing industry arising from the development of underwater resources. As a result, a new trend pervaded globally. Many governments advocated territorial limits extending to 200 nautical miles from shore. The Japanese government paid close attention to this in relation to Dokdo. If both Korea and Japan set a territorial limit of 200 nautical miles from Dokdo, this would garner large gains of seafloor. One could assume that this provided the context for Fukuda's gaffe regarding Dokdo.

Fukuda's statement eventually resulted in very heated and very negative repercussions. The Korean people were angry, but the two governments acted responsibly, blocking physical conflict. The Japanese government enforced the 200 nautical mile law but did not apply the law to Dokdo. The Korean government limited its sea territory to twelve nautical miles from Dokdo and unofficially tolerated Japanese fishermen in the waters off Dokdo periodically.

---

463 *Ilbon Gukhoe Dokdo gwallyeon girok moeumjip*, vol. 2, 48, 51.

Korea Expands its Sovereignty over Dokdo

While the two governments were facing off over Dokdo, other Korean citizens volunteered to inhabit the island. Choi Jong-deok became the first person to build a house on Dokdo. In 1987, his son-in-law Jo Jun-gi and his family of four, plus Song Jae-uk, moved to Dokdo. In 1991, Kim Seong-do and his wife Kim Sin-yeol changed their address to Dokdo. In 1989, a civilian environmentalist group called "Green Dokdo Gardening" was formed and planted trees on Dokdo annually. In December 1991, President Roh Tae-woo installed telephone cables between Ulleungdo and Dokdo. Ever since, regular phone service functions there. Kajimura evaluated the series of events by stating, "The Japanese argue that Koreans have abandoned Dokdo for a long time, but Korea never neglected Dokdo. Of course, the people are confident in their intent to restore sovereignty, something that was stolen from them by Japan. As many Japanese people believe today, it was wrong to steal in the first place."[464]

---

464 Kajimura, "Ilbon ttang jujang eun paengchang – singminjuui sosan," 625.

4 The Dokdo Issue Resumes as the United Nations Convention on the Law of the Sea Takes Effect

The Korean-Japanese Controversy over the Exclusive Economic Zone

The United Nations Convention on the Law of the Sea was adopted on December 10, 1982, going into effect on November 16, 1994. This convention laid a foundation upon which Japan was able to bring the Dokdo issue back to the surface. From its adoption and implementation, nearly twelve years passed. The convention ruled that rocks or islands unable to provide economic activities and habitation would not be regarded as an exclusive economic zone. The text reads, "Rocks, which could not sustain human habitation or economic life of their own, would have no economic zone or continental shelf."[465]

It is true that many people view Dokdo as a rock that cannot "sustain human habitation or economic life of [its] own." However, there are probably more people that understand Dokdo to be capable of sustaining human habitation and economic life. Accordingly, Dokdo must be regarded as an exclusive economic zone. Thus, could Dokdo

---

[465] Baek Bong-heum, *Dokdo wa baetajeok gyeongje suyeok* [Dokdo and the exclusive economic zone] (Seoul: Kyongsaewon Publishing Company, 2003).

become the point of delineation for a border at sea? As Kim Chan-gyu, a Korean international law scholar, pointed out, if the rule of 200 nautical miles were to be used in the East Sea, it is inevitable that the two borders would overlap. In this matter, however, the United Nations convention rules that "States Parties shall settle any dispute between them . . . by peaceful means" on their own.[466]

The water of Dokdo includes Oki Island, a Japanese territory. Would it be equitable to draw the border somewhere between Dokdo and Oki Island? Or would it be more so to draw the line somewhere between Ulleungdo and Oki Island? There are many precedents in arbitrating the delineation of sea boundaries. Nevertheless, the most critical aspect is a settlement based on mutual considerations of the geographic situation. On this point, the Japanese government once again argued, "Takeshima inherently belongs to Japan," and decided to declare an exclusive economic Zone extending 200 nautical miles.[467] This declaration motivated Korean President Kim Young-sam to declare that he would "fix the Japanese manner."

Japan repeatedly iterated that Takeshima is inherently Japanese territory. On the other hand, the Japanese government relayed to Korea that it would not choose Dokdo as the point to apply the 200 nautical miles rule as long as Korea did the same. Shin Yong-Ha interpreted this point by saying, "It is clear that Japan wishes to prevent Korea from setting Dokdo as an exclusive economic zone so that it can take the matter to the international community and have it be acknowledged as a 'disputed territory.'" So far, Korea has argued that Dokdo is neither disputed nor a subject of negotiation over a potential territorial dispute.

---

466 Kim Chan-gyu, "Dokdo wa EEZ seonpo ui sumeun geurim" [The hidden picture of Dokdo and the EEZ Declaration], *Saemulgyeol* (April 1996), 36–38.

467 For the Japanese government's decision and the discussions surrounding it in the House of Representatives and House of Councilors, see *Ilbon Gukhoe Dokdo gwallyeon girok moeumjip*, vol. 2, 873–877, 888–893.

Here, the Japanese government is attempting to systematically weaken the Korean argument. Shin concluded that in order to settle the issue in the most objective manner possible, the Japanese government must acknowledge that Dokdo belongs to Korea and draw the boundary line between Dokdo and Oki Island.[468]

The New Korean-Japanese Fishing Agreement Leads to a New Round of Controversy

The controversy intensified again as the two parties began negotiations over the "New Korea-Japan Fishing Agreement" in 1996. The issue of Dokdo resurfaced in the process. The subject spilled over into the public. In 1997, the Dokdo Research Commission and the Takeshima Research Commission were launched in Korea and Japan, respectively. On November 28, 1998, President Kim Dae-jung of Korea and Prime Minister Obuchi Keizō of Japan provisionally signed the "New Korea-Japan Fishing Agreement." The two governments exchanged instruments of ratification on January 22, 1999. The agreement replaced the previous fishing agreement dating from December 18, 1965. The new agreement initiated a heated discussion within Korea focusing primarily on Dokdo.[469]

According to Article 1 of the new agreement, Dokdo is thought to be located in the central waters of the East Sea. Some scholars, such as Shin Yong-Ha, Kim Young-Koo, and Lee Sang Myeon, criticized the language of the agreement for being too vague, arguing that the words "in the

---

[468] Shin Yong-Ha, "Dokdo jugwon sahwal geollin minjok munje ida" [Dokdo sovereignty is an important national matter], *Shindonga* (April 1996), 608.

[469] This debate is described well by Youngshik D. Bong in his PhD dissertation submitted to the University of Pennsylvania, "Flashpoints at Sea? Legitimization Strategy and East Asian Island Disputes."

central waters" threaten Korean sovereignty over Dokdo. Kim Myungki admitted that effective control of an island located in the center of the sea is no longer guaranteed.[470] These scholars all considered this agreement to be flawed.

Nevertheless, other scholars including Park Choon-ho, a former judge at the International Tribunal for the Law of the Sea, and Paik Jin-Hyun of Seoul National University argued the opposite. "'Central waters' is an area of the water where exclusive administrative rights are not applied by either country. Therefore, it is absolutely necessary for Dokdo to remain in the central waters in order to maintain the status quo of the Dokdo issue." They finally concluded that "the new agreement will neither be beneficial nor damaging to the Dokdo matter." Park cautioned that the Korean government should commit to silent diplomacy concerning Dokdo because a noisy scene is exactly what Japan seeks.[471] Ultimately, the Ministry of Foreign Affairs and Trade shared the view of Park and Paik and provided a nearly identical interpretation of the matter.[472]

An issue arising from the controversy concerns the fishing agreement's relation to the territorial rights of Dokdo. Scholars who argue the former consider the judgment rendered in the Minquiers and Ecrehos incident very seriously. The incident was a territorial dispute between Great

---

470 Kim Young-Koo, "Han-Il eoeop hyeopjeongsang Donghae junggan suyeok gwa Dokdo yeongyu-gwon munje" [The middle line and the Dokdo territorial rights issue in the Korea-Japan fishing agreement], in *Dokdo yeongyugwon wigi yeongu* [Study on the Dokdo territorial rights crisis], ed. Dokdo Yeoksa Chatgi Undong Bonbu (Seoul: Baeksan Seodang, 2003), 77–138; Kim Myungki, "Shin Han-Il eoeop hyeopjeong gwa Dokdo yeongyugwon hweson yeobu" [The new Korea-Japan fishing agreement and its impact on Dokdo territorial rights], in *Dokdo yeongyugwon wigi yeongu* [Study on the Dokdo territorial rights crisis] (Seoul: Baeksan Seodang, 2003), 139–168; Lee Sang Myeon, "Shin Han-Il eoeop hyeopjeongsang Dokdo wa geu jubyeon suyeok ui beopjeok munje" [The new Korea-Japan fishing agreement and legal issues of the surrounding waters of Dokdo], in *Dokdo yeongyugwon wigi yeongu* [Study on the Dokdo territorial rights crisis] (Seoul: Baeksan Seodang, 2003), 169–200.

471 Lee Jeong-hoon, "'Dokdo munje' Ilbon ui jankkoe e malliji malla," 35.

472 Lee Seo-hang et al., "Shin Han-Il eoeop hyeopjeong ui pyeongga" [Evaluation of the new Korea-Japan fishing agreement], Oegyo Tongsangbu Oegyo Anbo Yeonguwon jeongchaek bogoseo [Policy Report, Institute of Foreign Affairs and National Security, Ministry of Foreign Affairs and Trade], November 4, 1998, 7–8.

Britain and France. The final ruling was to the effect that the geographic location of islands, whether inside or outside of the joint fishing zone, has no relation to territorial rights. The diplomat and international legal expert Shin Gak-su supports this interpretation.[473]

However, some scholars, such as Kim Myungki, argue that (1) the Minquiers and Ecrehos ruling is about administrative rights within the "joint fishing zone," whereas the new fishing agreement between Korea and Japan is not; (2) the Minquiers and Ecrehos ruling is one of many judgments, yet it is in no way a precedent; and (3) even if it had set a precedent, this ruling still could not be applied internationally as such.[474] Despite the differences in interpretations, essentially, all of the scholars mentioned above based their arguments upon the common understanding that Dokdo belongs to Korea.

Advocating to Prepare for a Trial at the International Court of Justice

During this time, Korean public opinion grew in favor of Korean preparation against a possible International Court of Justice arbitration case with Japan. Japan was transforming Dokdo into a matter that had to be dealt with by the International Court of Justice, thus the pervading logic moved them to prepare for such an occurrence. Public opinion shifted from its previous form, in the sense that it sought the possibility of capitulation to International Court of Justice arbitration.

Kim Byungryull supported the International Court of Justice path as

---

473 Ministry of Foreign Affairs and Trade, "Shin Han-Il eoeop hyeopjeong" [New Korea-Japan fishing agreement], announced on November 25, 1998, 2.

474 Kim Myungki, "Shin Han-Il eoeop hyeopjeong gwa Dokdo yeongyugwon hweson yeobu," in *Dokdo yeongyugwon wigi yeongu*, 160.

he explained in detail in his book.[475] His line of thought spread among other scholars, such as Park Hyun-jin, an international law scholar.[476] Below is a summarized version of their argument.

First, the Republic of Korea joined the United Nations in September 1991. A United Nations member state is automatically eligible to pursue legal arbitration before the International Court of Justice. The Republic of Korea may engage on a level footing with Japan, which gained this eligibility in 1956. However, if Korea refuses to accept Japan's proposed arbitration, there will never be a trial.

Second, if the United Nations Security Council passes a resolution to resolve a specific legal issue via the International Court of Justice, then that resolution applies to all United Nations member states. Although one may refuse trial, the act of defying a resolution to go before the International Court of Justice would undoubtedly be criticized by the international community.

Third, Japan is attempting to facilitate a favorable international atmosphere concerning the Dokdo issue by transforming Dokdo into a disputed territory. If the situation escalates to military action, then it would be reported to the Security Council, which would in turn refer the case to the International Court of Justice.

Fourth, although unlikely, the international political situation may make a trial before the International Court of Justice unavoidable.

Fifth, the Japanese government could offer to jointly administer Dokdo at any time.

Within the last fifteen years, the character of the Dokdo issue has

---

475 Kim Byungryull, *Dokdo nya Dakkesima nya*, 218–233.

476 Park Hyun-jin, "Dokdo munje wa gukje sabeop jaengsong" [The Dokdo question and international adjudication: Possibility, precaution and procedure in an age of litigation proliferation], *Gukjebeop hakhoe nonchong* (*Korean Journal of International Law*) 50, no. 2 (October 2005), 125–156.

changed into that of a "territorial dispute" between Japan and Korea.[477] This trend will continue, especially if Japanese people are taught from a young age to accept Dokdo's inherent Japanese character. In such a situation, the inevitability that the United Nations Security Council will interfere will increase greatly. It is fascinating, however, that contrary to greater acceptance of the International Court of Justice path among Koreans, there seems to be growing public disfavor in Japan regarding the same path.[478]

---

477 Professor Je Seong-ho's comment, September 7, 2006, quoted in *Dokdo hannun e bogi* [Dokdo at a glance], ed. National Assembly Library of Korea (Seoul: National Assembly Library of Korea, 2010), 68.

478 Park Byoungsup, and Naitō Seichū, Hosaka Yuji, ed., *Dokdo = Dakesima nonjaeng*, 174.

5 Heightened Tension After Shimane Prefecture Establishes "Takeshima Day"

The Shimane Prefectural Assembly Establishes "Takeshima Day"

The Korean-Japanese controversy over Dokdo flared again in 2005 when the Shimane Prefectural Assembly established February 22 as "Takeshima Day." As may be recalled, February 22, 1905, was the day that Shimane Prefecture "incorporated" Takeshima into the prefecture. The Korean public was angered by the decision. On February 23, 2005, Ambassador Takano Toshiyuki held a press conference at the Seoul Foreign Correspondents' Club. In response to a series of questions by journalists, he answered, "Clearly there is a difference of perception regarding the Takeshima matter between the two countries. However, historically and legally, Takeshima belongs to Japan." This repeated the Japanese government's argument. This, too, angered the Korean public. On March 1, 2005, Korean National Liberation Day, President Roh delivered a speech on anti-Japanese imperialism that harshly criticized Japan's colonial rule. The speech aroused anti-Japanese sentiment nationwide.

Korea Announces the "New Doctrine of Korean-Japanese Relations"

On the day that Shimane Prefecture established "Takeshima Day," the Ministry of Foreign Affairs and Trade spokesperson Lee Kyu-hyung announced once again that Dokdo is Korean territory. The statement also warned that Japan's action violated Korean sovereignty in what would severely damage the relations between the two countries. Lastly, the statement concluded that Shimane Prefecture's establishment of "Takeshima Day" has no international legal authority nor would it affect the current status of Dokdo.

On the same day, Director Yu Hong-jun of the Cultural Heritage Administration held an urgent press conference in which he informed the public that the limit on visitors to the island had been removed and that domestic media was allowed to cover stories relating to Dokdo. Until 2005, the Cultural Heritage Administration had placed a cap of thirty people per visit since 1999 in order to preserve the marine ecosystem of Dokdo and its environs. The Cultural Heritage Administration had administered Dokdo since its designation as Natural Monument No. 336 in 1982.

The Korean government went a step further and declared a New Doctrine of Korean-Japanese Relations on March 17. Minister of Unification Chung Dong-young publicly stated that Dokdo is "our territory, which has been coercively incorporated into Japanese territory during the process of colonial pillage but restored to us after the liberation." In response to Chung's statement, Minister of Foreign Affairs Machimura Nobutaka stated, "Since early times, there has been a division between the two countries on the issue of Takeshima but becoming emotional regarding the issue will not help anyone. There is a need to treat the matter from an objective perspective with the entirety of Japanese-Korean relations in mind."

The Korean public was angered again at the response of the Japanese government and right-wing figures. Numerous civic groups began anti-Japan protests while the general public facilitated the spread of anti-Japanese sentiment. On this issue, the ruling and opposition parties in Korea were united. Yeungnam University, in Gyeongsan, Gyeongsangbuk-do province, founded the Dokdo Institute (K. *Dokdo Yeonguso*), and since December 2005, the institute has published the biannual academic journal *Dokdo yeongu* (*The Journal Of Dokdo*).

North Korea shared the same position as its southern neighbor. The South Korean prime minister at the time, Lee Hae-chan, and the president of the Presidium of the Supreme People's Assembly of North Korea, Kim Yong Nam, agreed at the Asia-Africa summit meeting held on April 22, 2005, that "South and North must come together, at least for the Dokdo issue." It seemed that an era of anti-Japanese nationalism was imminent throughout the Korean Peninsula.

To make matters worse, on April 15, 2005, Japan's Ministry of Foreign Affairs issued a public statement claiming, "Takeshima is both histor-ically and legally inherently Japanese territory." This heated situation continued throughout 2006. In fact, in April 2006, the Japanese govern-ment notified Korea that it would conduct an investigation into marine resources around Dokdo. The two countries were steps away from likely military conflict. Luckily, the tension eased after discussions were held, but the incident motivated many Koreans to advocate the amendment of the "New Fishing Agreement" in order to set Dokdo as the boundary for an exclusive economic zone. The Roh administration acknowledged the public sentiment and requested that Japan hold talks in order to change the exclusive economic zone boundary from Ulleungdo to Dokdo on June 12 to 13, 2006, in Tokyo and on September 4 to 5, 2006, in Seoul. The Japanese government refused the request. Instead, Japan intensified its promotion of Takeshima as "inherently Japanese."

New Evidence Found Supporting Dokdo as Korean Territory

The heightening tension between the two countries led to the discovery of new evidence supporting claims that Dokdo is indeed Korean. This section will briefly share six points.

First is a map that the government of Great Britain published which Jung Byung-joon discovered at the National Archives and Records Administration. The map was compiled in March 1951, and it excluded Jeju Island, Ulleungdo, and Dokdo from Japanese territory.

Second, Naitō Seichū claimed in the March 17, 2005, issue of *Tōkyō Shimbun* that "to argue that Takeshima is inherently Japanese is a crude description." He later explained this opinion in further detail in his book published in 2008.[479]

Third, Hosaka argued that "old maps of Japan kept at the map center in Japan do not have Dokdo on them." He obtained eleven media files of old Japanese maps, among them a map composed by the Japanese government. Hosaka claimed that "Japan is extremely fearful that the maps will be available to the Korean public."

Fourth, Li Jin-mieung found many old maps that the French navy had compiled. These maps labeled Dokdo as Korean territory. Based on his findings, Li published a book and other research between 2005 and 2009.[480] All of the old maps presented in that book clearly document Dokdo as Joseon territory prior to its "incorporation."

Fifth, an employee of the Cheongju city government, Nam Yo-seop, who is also an avid book collector, shared a geography textbook

---

479 Naitō Seichū, *Takeshima = Dokutō mondai nyūmon: Nihon Gaimushō 'Takeshima' hihan* [Introduction to the Takeshima = Dokdo issue: Criticism of the Japan Ministry of Foreign Affairs' "Takeshima"] (Tokyo: Shinkansha, 2008).

480 Li Jin-mieung, *Dokdo: Jirisang ui jaebalgyeon*, 175; Li Jin-mieung, "Real Status of Dokdo: Administered by South Korea, Claimed by Japan," in *Territorial Issues in Europe and East Asia: Colonialism, War Occupation, and Conflict Resolution*, eds. Bae Chinsoo et al. (Seoul: Northeast Asian History Foundation, 2009), 84–135.

produced by the Japanese Government-General of Korea. Dokdo was not in the textbook's image of Japan.[481]

And sixth, Suh Jung-chul made public a book that he found in London in the 1980s. The book was a translation of Hayashi Shihei's *Sangoku tsūran zusetsu* composed in 1785 (discussed in Chapter 3) by Julius Klaproth, the most prominent Oriental scholar active in nineteenth-century Europe. Klaproth wrote that near Ulleungdo were Jukdo and Usando, which formed Usanguk. Specifically, he stated that Usando is located southeast of Ulleungdo and Jukdo. Klaproth clearly indicated that all three islands belong to Joseon.[482]

The Expulsion of the United States Board of Geographic Names and the Japanese Textbook Issue

In 2008 came a new wave of controversy over Dokdo. It became apparent to Korea that the United States Board of Geographic Names classified Dokdo as being under "undesignated sovereignty" by July 26. This enraged the Korean public. From 1977 on, this organization had labeled Dokdo as Liancourt Rocks under Korean jurisdiction but reversed course and labeled Dokdo as an ownerless island.[483] Han Seung-soo became the first Korean prime minister to visit Dokdo when he went to the island on July 29. He boasted that the Korean government and the Korean people will protect Dokdo from all evil. Additionally, Korean ambassador to the US Lee Tae-sik complained to the American

---

481 *Chosun Ilbo*, May 2, 2005, A6.

482 *Weekly Dong-A*, April 13, 2000, 44–45; Suh Jung-chul and Kim In-hwan, *Jido wiui jeonjaeng: Gojido eseo chajeun Han-Jung-Il yeongto munje ui jinsil* [War over maps: The truth of the Korea-China-Japan territorial issue found in ancient maps] (Seoul: Dong-A Ilbosa, 2010), 309–312.

483 For the background to this controversy and the process through which it unfolded, see Hosaka, *Uri yeoksa Dokdo*, 10–23.

government about the Board of Geographic Names. The American government immediately restored the previous status of Dokdo.

In light of these controversial events, on June 20, 2006, the Korean Ministry of Oceans and Fisheries established the Dokdo Research Center under the Korea Maritime Institute, which soon expanded to become the Korea Dokdo and Maritime Territory Research Center. Furthermore, Korea's Northeast Asian History Foundation established its Dokdo Research Institute on August 14, 2008. The dispute resumed in 2010 when the Japanese government accused Korea of illegally occupying Dokdo, while allowing the distribution of a fifth-grade textbook that labeled Takeshima as inherently Japanese. The Korean government resisted by criticizing Japan,[484] stating that "Japan is teaching its youngsters incorrect information. It is teaching them lies. A country teaching lies to its children, and dishonest in the face of history, has no future."

On April 2, the Korean National Assembly drafted a bill denouncing Japan. Four days later, President Lee Myung-bak stated that he would "actively review measures to strengthen effective control of Dokdo." Nevertheless, the Japanese government did not back down. On April 6, the Japanese government once again publicly announced a diplomatic document claiming that this island is inherently Japanese. Two days later, Prime Minister Hatoyama Yukio reaffirmed that the Japanese government had not changed its position regarding the Takeshima issue.

---

[484] For a detailed analysis of how Japanese textbooks, including primary school textbooks, describe Dokdo as well as the significance of these textbooks, see Shin Ju-bak, "Gyogwaseo wa Jukdo munje" [Textbooks and the Jukdo issue], *Dokdo yeongu* (*The Journal of Dokdo*) 2 (December 2006), 87–108.

Conclusion

Recapitulating the Controversy

To this point, we have examined the Korea-Japan controversy over territorial rights to Dokdo at both political and academic levels. Below is a recapitulation of the main points of the controversy.

The first point concerns which country's government acknowledged Dokdo first. Korea argues that Korea has acknowledged the existence of Dokdo and its sovereignty over Dokdo since the Silla Kingdom's rule in the seventh century. Furthermore, Korea acknowledged Dokdo at the latest from the early Joseon Dynasty, during the reign of King Sejong, and has claimed that Usan or Sambong in historical sources from the Joseon period is today's Dokdo. This explanation leads to the claim that Dokdo is inherently Korean territory.

Japan, however, rejects such an interpretation, speculating that Usan or Sambong must have been today's Ulleungdo or another rock near Ulleungdo.

In response, Korea offers the records of An Yong-bok's negotiations with Japanese elites. Such records include a transcript of a Japanese official acknowledging that both Dokdo and Matsushima belonged to Joseon. Japan does not shy away though. While admitting An

Yong-bok's negotiations, Japan argues that he was acting as a private entrepreneur and not as an official from the Korean government. Japan also belittles An as a liar who at the time was under interrogation by the Joseon government. Therefore, Japan argues that An did not represent the Joseon government and that any and all records related to An are invalid as evidence to be used in this case. Moreover, Japan argues that Dokdo is not found on Japan's old maps.

Korea repeatedly stresses that An's records show that Usan or Ulleungdo were called Matsushima and Takeshima in Japanese, which is written in the court records of Joseon. Korea has repeatedly claimed that An represented the Joseon government because his negotiations were reported in official records of the Joseon government.

Japan argues that Japanese people have been aware of this island "since ancient times" and that it had administered and utilized the island since the seventeenth century. Japan provided the fishing permit issued by the Edo shogunate as evidence to support its claim. This claim leads to the argument that the island has been considered as Japan's "original" territory.

Korea interprets such a fishing permit as having resembled a passport for Japanese people traveling overseas, which shows that the Edo shogunate considered Dokdo to be Joseon territory. Korea provides evidence to support its claim: it introduced an official Japanese local government record reporting to the shogunate that Ulleungdo and Dokdo do not belong to Japan.

Both Korea and Japan provided numerous pre-World War II documents to support claims. For instance, in *Japanese Government Opinion 2*, Japan argued that (1) the Korean map called *Daehan jiji* (originally published in 1901, reprinted in 1905) showed that the eastern border of the Korean Empire was east 130 degrees 35 minutes, which excludes Dokdo, and (2) a Korean independence activist who used the pen name Taebaek Gwangno (author's note: this is the pen name of Park Eun-sik, who served two terms as president of the Provisional Government of the Republic of Korea) wrote the same coordinates as Korea's farthest border, thereby excluding Dokdo from the official territory of Korea.[485] Korea responded in a similar manner. For example, in *Korean Government Opinion 1*, Korea offered a passage from Shimane Prefecture's official records from 1923 that Nakai Yōsaburō, a sea lion hunter and fisherman, acknowledged the island that Koreans call Dokdo as "territory of the Korean Empire."

Upon careful examination, one can see that most of the documents that Korea provided as evidence were government documents, whereas the majority of the documents that Japan provided were historical documents. Needless to say, government records hold more weight than mere historical documents.

The second point of controversy regards whether Dokdo is an annexed island of Ulleungdo or not. The Korean side argues that Dokdo is an annexed island of Ulleungdo, noting that Dokdo is only ninety-two kilometers away from Ulleungdo, whereas it is 160 kilometers away from Oki Island, and that Dokdo is visible to the naked eye from Ulleungdo. Also, the Korean side provided written records from the Joseon period that indicated the visibility of Dokdo from Ulleungdo. According to civic laws of many countries around the world, affiliation of an annexed island is determined by the affiliation of the main island. In this case, Ulleungdo belongs to Korea, therefore Dokdo does, too.

However, the Japanese side has a different interpretation. It argues that Dokdo is closer to mainland Japan than to mainland Korea. In fact, Dokdo is 215 kilometers away from the closest point on the Korean mainland, whereas it is 212 kilometers away from the closest point on Japan's mainland.

---

485 Shin Yong-Ha, ed., *Dokdo yeongyugwon jaryo ui tamgu*, vol. 4, 230.

However, the Korean government's method of calculating the distance to Dokdo from Ulleungdo is a justified and legitimate method. The Korean side argues that the water current from Ulleungdo naturally leads to Dokdo, and on good days a fishing boat can float to Dokdo on its own. Furthermore, the Korean side pays attention to the ways in which Japanese people write the names of Ulleungdo and Dokdo. In Japanese, Ulleungdo is written as 松島 (Matsushima) and Dokdo is written as 竹島 (Takeshima). It is ordinary for Japanese people to write a pair of something as 松 (*matsu*) and 竹 (*take*), which shows that Japanese people have thought of the two islands as a pair. All of the documents provided by the Japanese side that have been examined from Chapter 2 through Chapter 5 mentioned Matsushima and Takeshima as a pair. This shows that the Japanese side acknowledged Dokdo as a sister island of Ulleungdo.

The third point of controversy concerns the investigation report compiled by the Meiji government. For this report, an investigation of Takeshima and Matsushima was conducted, and it concluded that these islands are not related to Japan. The Korean side argues that this report is sufficient evidence that Dokdo has already been acknowledged as Joseon territory. In response, the Japanese side argued that just because the islands are not related to Japan does not mean that they belong to Joseon. This logic is flawed.

The fourth point of controversy is concerned with the imperial orders of the Korean Empire regarding Dokdo. On October 25, 1900, the emperor of the Korean Empire declared the name of the island as Seokdo and placed its jurisdiction under Ulleung-gun county. The Korean side provides this imperial order as evidence that clearly shows that Dokdo belonged to Korea. The prominent Korean international law scholar Kim Myungki pointed out that this imperial order also supports Korean sovereignty over Dokdo by the principle of acquisition by prescription.[486] Interestingly, the Japanese government has been silent about this imperial order, keeping its comments and arguments brief. Some Japanese scholars argued that Seokdo mentioned in the imperial order is not today's Dokdo but rather a small rock next to Ulleungdo. However, although a minority of Japanese scholars may argue in this way, the majority of Japanese scholars agree that Seokdo mentioned in the order is today's Dokdo.

The fifth point of controversy is over Japan's incorporation of the island, and the fact that Japan switched the names of Matsushima and Takeshima. For hundreds of years, Japan has been calling Ulleungdo as Takeshima and Dokdo as Matsushima. However, from February 2, 1905, Japan switched the two islands and their names, calling Dokdo as Takeshima and Ulleungdo as Matsushima. Also, a Japanese local government incorporated Takeshima as part of its territory, attempting to legitimize their actions by the principle of terra nullius. To this present day, the Japanese government has seen this act of incorporation as the strongest evidence in support of their unsupported argument that Dokdo belongs to them. However, in *Japanese Government Opinion 4*, submitted to Korea on July 13, 1962, the Japanese government officially claimed the inherent possession of Dokdo, which goes against their previous argument that Dokdo is historically Japan's territory because of the incorporation in 1905. Jung Il-young, a Korean international law scholar, criticized this contradiction of the Japanese argument as a breach of principle of estoppel.[487]

Korea argues that the incorporation was illegal and undertaken secretly, thus not even Japanese people were aware of the decision. Most importantly, Korea stressed that Dokdo was not an ownerless island. The Korean side criticized the contradiction in the Japanese argument,

---

486 Kim Myungki, *Dokdo Uiyong Subidae wa gukjebeop*, 116.
487 Jung Il-young, "Dokdo yeongyugwon yeongu ui hyanghu gwaje," 5.

as well.

The sixth point of controversy is concerned with the treatment of postwar Japan by the Allied powers. Korea argues that the American government and the United Nations Pacific headquarters ruled through a series of ordinances to restore the entire Korean Peninsula, including, of course, Dokdo. Japan, however, argues that only the territory that they acquired after the annexation of Korea is to be restored. The Korean side strongly criticizes this argument, claiming that the Japanese imperialists practically stole Dokdo by discreetly incorporating the island into their territory while stealing Korean diplomatic rights away from the Korean people.

The seventh point of controversy is concerned with the list of islands to be restored to Korea explicitly mentioned in the San Francisco Treaty. In that treaty, only Ulleungdo, Geomundo, and Jeju Island were included in the list. The Japanese side argues that the fact that Dokdo was excluded from the list is proof that the Allied powers acknowledged Dokdo as a Japanese island. In response, the Korea side argues that the three islands mentioned above are the most representative islands of Korea, thus the less representative islands were naturally omitted from the list, and that simply because Dokdo was not explicitly mentioned in the list does not mean that the island belongs to Japan.

The eighth point of controversy is concerned with the timing of governmental effective control of the island. The Korean side argues that the Korean Empire claimed control over Dokdo on October 25, 1900, at the latest. This is nearly four years and four months prior to the date that Japan conducted a discrete incorporation of Dokdo into its territory on February 22, 1905.

Clearly, Dokdo was restored to Korea at the conclusion of World War II with the end of Japanese imperialism. Moreover, Korea's effective control over Dokdo began again and continues to this day. Furthermore, the normalization treaty between Japan and the Republic of Korea, which went into effect on December 18, 1965, ruled that all treaties and agreements signed during the colonial era and between Japan and the Korean Empire are invalid. In this context, the Japanese incorporation of Dokdo should be considered illegal as well because incorporation was undertaken while Korean diplomatic authority was severely limited.

A Summary of the Controversy

In my opinion, the core of the controversy lies in the matter of how to evaluate the Shimane Prefecture notification of February 22, 1905, on the incorporation of Dokdo, and the Korean Empire's imperial order issued on October 25, 1900. The Korean imperial order was a justified act of assigning an administrative district to a Korean territory. Therefore, other countries, including Japan, did not raise objections.

In contrast, Shimane Prefecture's incorporation of Dokdo was clearly an illegal act of stealing a foreign island. On September 25, 1904, five months prior to the incorporation, the Japanese navy vessel *Niitaka Maru* clearly indicated that Dokdo is an island that belongs to the Korean Empire. The Japanese government incorporated what is clearly a foreign island to its territory after renaming it as "Takeshima." There is no other way to describe what has happened here: Japan exercised its imperialist, invasive power to steal Dokdo. This is the truth and a fact, but the Japanese side still argues that Dokdo is inherently Japanese with Shimane Prefecture's act of incorporation as evidence. Japan's stubbornness is interpreted as an attempt to legitimize the invasion of Korea and their long-lost imperialist practices.

As the discussion above shows, Dokdo clearly belongs to the Korean people. In addition, Dokdo is a strong protector of the Korean territory. This land cannot be lost to Japan or to any other. It is the responsibility of the Korean people to protect this land and pass it on to our future generations. To protect Dokdo is to protect Korean sovereignty. The most important duty of a nation is to protect its sovereignty. By protecting Dokdo, we are protecting our national sovereignty.

In this context, it is inappropriate to approach the matter of protection of Dokdo under a simple premise of maintaining a good relationship with Japan. This is not to say that Japan-Korea relations are less important than the protection of our territory, our sovereignty. But international relations require a multi-layered and multi-directional approach. Nevertheless, it is unwise to focus solely on that logic. In that case, the Korean government's temporary banning of the song "Dokdo is Our Land" was not a wise decision.

The most important point in the protection of Dokdo is to discover more documents and more evidence in support of the truth that Dokdo belongs to the Republic of Korea. As the Korean international legal scholar Park Hyun-jin stresses, we must work harder to discover more maps that prove Dokdo is Korean territory.[488] In this context, it is a relief to see that a number of Dokdo-related research institutions and organizations have been established. For instance, in February 1996, Shin Yong-Ha was a central figure in founding the Dokdo Institute. In January 1997, Shin led the founding of the Dokdo Yeongu Bojeon Hyeophoe (Dokdo Research Conservation Association). In May 2007, Kim Myungki and others founded the Dokdo Research and Studies Society. In addition, more academic meetings have been held recently and more scholarly research on Dokdo has been published in support of the Korean side's claim.

Beyond research and publication, it is important to spread the truth and facts of Dokdo to the Korean people. The Korean government should promote tourism to Dokdo and instill faith in the Korean people that Dokdo is truly the land that belongs to them, the Korean people. Seeing the island themselves and actually setting foot on Dokdo will most definitely deepen their love for the island. That is why I have been trying to convince the government to promote Dokdo tourism, though allowing too many tourists on the island will damage the natural habitat of the island. Therefore, the government must devise a way to minimize this risk.

In promoting tourism to Dokdo, President Kim Young-sam funded the construction of a modern dock on Dokdo and ordered cruise ships to sail regularly from Ulleungdo to Dokdo. The cruise is still in operation today. It is also wise to develop Dokdo to provide more residences. To do so, a drinking water source must be developed and a forestation would make a welcome addition. More people on Dokdo with drinkable water

---

488 Park Hyun-jin, "Dokdo yeongyugwon gwa jido, haedo ui jeunggeo neungnyeok, jeungmyeon-gnyeok" [Title to Dokdo as interpreted and evaluated chiefly from changing international juris-prudence on map evidence], *Gukjebeop hakhoe nonchong* (*Korean Journal of International Law*) 52, no. 1 (April 2007), 89–128; Park Hyun-jin, "Yeongto, haeyang gyeonggye bunjaeng gwa jido, haedo ui jeunggeo jiwi, gachi: Dokdo gwallyeon jido, haedo ui beop, jeongchaek, oegyo reul jungsim euro," 61–98.

and a forestation are three prominent characteristics of a natural island, and if all three developments are to be made, then Dokdo will finally become a natural island considered as a territory. In this context, it was wise that Korea's Kim Dae-jung administration promoted the administrative status of Dokdo from Do-dong, Nam-myeon, Ulleung-gun, Gyeongsangbuk-do to Dokdo-ri, Ulleung-eup, Ulleung-gun, Gyeongsangbuk-do with a new postal code on April 8, 2000. Currently, Seodo has postal codes of San 1 to 26, Dokdo-ri, and Dongdo has those from San 27 to 37.

The Korean public supported the government's Dokdo development campaign and some even changed their address to Dokdo. In fact, by September 25, 2000, 122 families had changed their address to Dokdo—that is to say, 438 people registered their address as Dokdo. This is regarded as a realization of Korean people's hopes of making Dokdo into a natural island. Some Korean citizens argue that the government should deploy its naval units to protect Dokdo. However, military protection is not a good idea given that Dokdo is not a disputed territory, and it is appropriate for police to protect undisputed territory. If the Korean government deploys its navy to protect Dokdo, then that is an act acknowledging Dokdo as a disputed territory. It must not be forgotten that continued warnings to Japan are necessary and crucial to protecting Dokdo. Germany sincerely apologized for its war crimes after World War II and gave the Oder-Neisse, an eastern territory larger than South Korea, to Poland as a sign of the postwar settlement. This also was a sign of the permanent end of imperialism and foreign invasion.[489] Meanwhile, the stance of postwar Japan remained completely different from that of Germany. Japan has not yet apologized for its war crimes.

---

489 Ju Seop-il, "Dokdo ui Odereunaise seon (線)" [Dokdo and the Oder-Neisse Line], *Jugan Naeil Shinmoon*, March 13, 1996; Hong Ki-Joon, "The Oder-Neisse Line: Contingency, Path Dependence and Emergent Property," in *Territorial Issues in Europe and East Asia: Colonialism, War Occupation, and Conflict Resolution*, eds. Bae Chinsoo et al. (Seoul: Northeast Asian History Foundation, 2009).

In fact, Japan is still caught up in invasive imperialist ideas.

Wakamiya Yoshifumi, a prominent Japanese opinion leader at the *Asahi Shimbun*, remains flexible yet rational about the stubbornness of Japan. In his opinion column of March 27, 2005, Wakamiya wrote these words under the premise of mere fancy: "Give Dokdo to Korea and make it an island of friendship." In a similar context, Serita Gentarō, a Japanese scholar, suggested the restoration of Dokdo as a sign of apology for Japan's war crimes.[490] Wada Haruki ultimately had the same perspective on Dokdo, saying that Japan must lose the historical burden it has against Joseon.

The Japanese government publicly apologized for its colonialism through Prime Minister Kan Naoto's speech on August 10, 2010. The Korean people and the international community will be able to accept that apology if the Japanese government makes explicit remarks acknowledging Korean territorial rights over Dokdo. Meanwhile, Korea must always be careful in dealing with Japan, which is anxious to take Korea to the International Court of Justice. Along with acknowledging the importance of protecting Dokdo, Koreans must realize the importance of Korea's unification as well. On this point, Park Yee-mun wrote:

> Japan's recent, reckless comments regarding Dokdo must have been made because it conceives Korean power to be weak, as it was during the coerced annexation of Korea. [. . .] This is the context in which Korea's division becomes more painful and sad. Dreams and hopes of the unification of Korea are harbored more desperately than ever. [. . .] In ensuring that we never lose our land again, it is clear that the unification of Korea is of utmost importance and necessity.[491]

---

490 The core argument of Wakamiya Yoshifumi's article, "The Only Solution is to 'Delete Takeshima,'" which was published in the November 2006 issue of *Chūō kōron*, may be found on pages 272–277 of that issue.

491 Park Yee-mun, "Tongil ui jeolsilham kkaeuchyeo jun Ilbon ui Dokdo gwallyeon mangeon [Japan's

Park's remarks give a teaching that we should all keep in our mind. Protection of Dokdo is ultimately a unification movement.

reckless remarks on Dokdo that remind us of how important unification is]," *Newsweek* (Korean-language edition), March 20, 1996.

Bibliography

Bae, Sung-joon. "Ulleungdo Dokdo myeongching byeonhwa reul tonghaeseo bon Dokdo insik eui byeoncheon" [Transition of Dokdo awareness seen through the name changes of Ulleungdo and Dokdo]. *Jindan hakbo* (*The Chin-Tan Society*) 30: 68–96.

Baek, Bong-heum. *Dokdo wa baetajeok gyeongje suyeok* [Dokdo and the exclusive economic zone]. Seoul: Kyongsaewon Publishing Company, 2003.

Bang, Jong-hyeon. "Dokdo ui haru" [A day of Dokdo]. *Gyeongseong daehak yegwa sinmun* 13, 1947.

Bong, Younshik D., "Flashpoints at Sea? Legitimization Strategy and East Asian Island Disputes," PhD diss., University of Pennsylvania, 2002.

Chee, Choul Keun. *Pyeonghwaseon* [The peace line]. Seoul: Bumwoosa, 1979.

Cho, Sung Hun. "1954 Baen Plit sajeoldan bogoseo wa Miguk ui Dokdo insik" [The report of Gen. Van Fleet mission in 1954 and America's recognition on Dokdo Island]. *Dongyanghak* (*Oriental Studies*) 46 (August 2009): 199–217.

Choe, Nam-seon. "Dokdo neun eomyeonhan Hanguk yeongto" [Dokdo is clearly Korean territory]. In *Dokdo*, edited by Daehan Gongnonsa. Seoul: Daehan Gongnonsa, 1965.

Choe, Nam-seon. "Ulleungdo wa Dokdo" [Ulleungdo and Dokdo]. *Seoul*

Shinmun, August 10–September 7, 1953.

Choi, Gyu-jang. "Dokdo subidae bisa" [Undisclosed history of the Dokdo Volunteer Garrison]. In *Dokdo*, edited by Daehan Gongnonsa. Seoul: Daehan Gongnonsa, 1965.

Chung, In Seop. "Ilbon ui Dokdo yeongyugwon jujang ui nolli gujo" [The logical structure of Japan's argument on Dokdo territorial rights]. In *Dokdo yeongyu ui yeoksa wa gukche gwangye*, edited by the Dokdo Institute. Seoul: Dokdo Research Conservation Association, 1997.

Chung, Tae-Man. "Dokdo munje ui suhakjeok jeopgeun: Dokdo neun wae jirijeok yeoksajeok euro uri ttang i doel su bak e eomneunga?" [A mathematical approach to the Dokdo issue: Why is it inevitable that Dokdo is our land geographically and historically?]. *Dokdo yeongu (The Journal of Dokdo)* 5 (December 2008): 167–199.

Dokdo Institute. Vol. 3 of *Dokdo yeongyugwon jaryo ui tamgu*. Seoul: Dokdo Institute, 2000.

"'Dokdo neun Hanguk ttang' Ilje sidae gyogwaseo balgyeon." *Chosun Ilbo*, May 2, 2005.

Dokdo Research Conservation Association. *Dokdo ingeun haeyeok ui hwangyeong gwa susan jawon bojeon eul wihan gicho yeongu* [Basic research on conserving environment and marine resources around Dokdo]. Seoul: Dokdo Research Conservation Association, 1998.

Fern, Sean. "Tokdo or Takeshima?: The International Law of Territorial Acquisition in the Japan-Korea Island Dispute." *Stanford Journal of East Asian Affairs* 5, no. 1 (Winter 2005): 78–89.

Hong, Kijoon. "The Oder-Neisse Line: Contingency, Path Dependence and Emergent Proprty." In *Territorial Issues in Europe and East Asia: Colonialism, War Occupation, and Conflict Resolution*, edited by Chinsoo Bae et al. Seoul: Northeast Asian History Foundation, 2009.

Hong, Seong-keun. "Dokdo pokgyeok sageon ui gukjebeopjeok jaengjeom bunseok" [Analysis of the Dokdo bombing incident through the lens of international law]. In *Hanguk ui Dokdo yeongyugwon yeongusa* [Research history of Korea's territorial rights over Dokdo], edited by the Dokdo Institute. Seoul: Dokdo Research Conservation Association, 2003.

Hong, Seong-keun. "Ilbon ui Dokdo yeongto baeje jochi ui seonggyeok gwa uimi" [Characteristics and meaning of Japan's territorial exclusion of Dokdo]. In *Dokdo wa Han-Il gwangye: Beop yeoksajeok jeopgeun* [Dokdo and Korea-Japan relations: From the standpoint of law and history], edited by the Northeast Asian History Foundation. Seoul: Northeast Asian History Foundation, 2009.

Hong, Sun-chil. "Jeon jaesan gwa onmom bachyeo Dokdo jikyeotda" [I protected Dokdo with everything I had]. *Shindonga*, April 1996.

Hong, Sun-chil. *I ttang i nwi ttang inde!: Dokdo Uiyong Subidae Hong Sun-chil daejang sugi* [Who do you think this land belongs to?: Memoirs of Commander Hong Sun-chil of the Dokdo Volunteer Garrison]. Seoul: Hyean, 1997.

Hori, Kazuo. "1905-nen Nihon no Takeshima ryōdo hennyū." *Chōsenshi kenkyūkai ronbunshū* 24 (1987).

Hosaka, Yūji. *Ilbon gojido edo Dokdo eopda* [There is no Dokdo even on ancient Japanese maps]. Seoul: Jaeum gwa moeum, 2005.

Hosaka, Yūji. *Uri yeoksa Dokdo: Han-Il gwangyesa ro bon Dokdo iyagi* [Dokdo, our history: The story of Dokdo from the perspective of Korea-Japan relations]. Seoul: BM Seongandang, 2009.

Hwang, Myong Chol. "1905 nyeon Dokdo-ui Simane hyeon pyeonip eun Ilje ui Joseon gangjeom jeongchaek gwa yeongto yamang ui beomjoejeok sanmul" [Shimane Prefecture's 1905 incorporation of Dokdo is a product of Japan's colonial practices and territorial ambition]. *Dokdo yeongu (The Journal of Dokdo)* 2 (December 2006): 29–38.

Hwang, Sang-gi. "Dokdo munje yeongu" [Study of Dokdo issues]. In *Dokdo*, edited by Daehan Gongnonsa. Seoul: Geullo Haksaengsa, 1954; Seoul: Daehan Gongnonsa, 1965.

Hwang, Sang-gi. *Dokdo yeongyugwon haeseol* [Dokdo territorial rights explained]. Seoul: Geullo Haksaengsa, 1954.

Ikeuchi, Satoshi. "Ilbon Edo sidae ui Dakesima, Masseusima insik" [Edo era recognition on Takeshima–Matsushima]. *Dokdo yeongu (The Journal of Dokdo)* 6 (June 2009): in Japanese, 181–197; in Korean, 199–221.

Japanese Government Opinion 2.

Japanese Government Opinion 3.

Japanese Government Opinion 4.

"Jaryo: 2005 nyeon e balgyeon doen An Yong-bok ui jinsul jaryo" [Document: Testimony of An Yong-bok, found in 2005]. *Dokdo yeongu (The Journal of Dokdo)* (December 2005): 231–310.

Jeungbo munheon bigo

Jo, Hwa-ryong. "Dokdo: Gaegwan, jayeon hwangyeong, eoeop hwangyeong" [Dokdo: The opening, natural environment, and fishery]. In vol. 7 of *Hanguk minjok munhwa daebaekgwa sajeon* (Encyclopedia of Korean Culture), edited by the Academy of Korean Studies. Seongnam, Republic of Korea: Academy of Korean Studies, 1991.

Ju, Seop-il. "Dokdo wa Odereunaise seon (線)" [Dokdo and the Oder-Neisse Line]. *Jugan Naeil Sinmun*, March 13, 1996.

Jung, Il-young. "Dokdo yeongyugwon yeongu ui hyanghu gwaje" [Future tasks of Dokdo territorial rights research]. unpublished paper presented at the commemorative seminar for Professor Shin Dong-wook, 2009.

Kajimura, Hideki. "Ilbon ttang jujang eun paengchang – singminjuui sosan." *Shindonga*, vol. 439, April 1996.

Kajimura, Hideki. "Takeshima = Dokutō mondai to Nihon kokka" [The Takeshima = Dokdo issue and the Japanese state]. *Chōsen kenkyū* 182 (September 1978).

Kang, Mangil. "Oeguk ui munheonsang e natanan Dokdo" [Dokdo in foreign literature]. In *Dokdo yeongu (Dokdo Research)*, edited by the Korea Modern History Research Committee. Seoul: Mungwangsa, 1985.

Kawakami, Kenzō. *Takeshima no rekishi chirigakuteki kenkyū* [Studies in the historical geography of Takeshima]. Tokyo: Kokin Shoin, 1966.

Kim, Byungryull. *Dokdo nya Dakkesima nya* [Dokdo or Takeshima]. Seoul: Dada Media, 1996.

Kim, Byungryull, "Ilbon gojido edo Dokdo neun Hanguk ttang ira myeongsi" [Dokdo labeled Korean on an ancient Japanese map]. *Hanguk nondan (Monthly Korea Journal)* 82, no. 1 (June 1996): 160–171.

Kim, Byungryull. "Dokdo yeongyugwon e daehan Ilbon cheuk ui jujang jeongni (整理)" [The collection of Japanese arguments on territorial rights over Dokdo]. Seoul: Dokdo Research Conservation Association, 2002.

Kim, Chan-gyu, "Dokdo wa EEZ seonpo ui sumeun geurim" [The hidden picture of Dokdo and the EEZ declaration]. *Saemulgyeol* (April 1996): 62–69.

Kim, Dong-jo. *Hoesang 30 nyeon: Han-Il hoedam* [Recollecting 30 years: Korea-Japan summit meeting]. Seoul: JoongAng Ilbosa, 1986.

Kim, Eui-hwan, ed. *An Yong-bok janggun: Butim, Ulleung-do·Dokdo ui yeoksa*, expanded edition. Translated by Taegil Yi. Seoul: An Yong-bok Janggun Ginyeom Saeophoe, 1996.

Kim, Hwa-hong. *Yeoksajeok siljeung euro bon Dokdo neun Hanguk ttang* [Dokdo is Korean territory in the perspective of historical evidence]. Seoul: Simon, 1996.

Kim, Hwa-kyong. "Kkeut eomneun wijeung ui yeonsok: Simane-hyeon Jukdo Munje Yeonguhoe 'choejong bogoseo' ui munjejeom" [Continuation of the endless perjury: Points of contention in the Shimane Prefecture 'Final Report' of the Takeshima Issue Research Group]. *Dokdo yeongu* (*The Journal of Dokdo*) 3 (December 2007): 1–36.

Kim, Myungki. "Dokdo ui yeongyugwon e gwanhan Ilbon jeongbu jujang e daehan beopjeok bipan" [Legal criticism of the Japanese government's opinion regarding the territorial rights over Dokdo]. In *Hanguk ui Dokdo yeongyugwon yeongusa* [Research history of Korea's territorial rights over Dokdo], edited by the Dokdo Institute. Seoul: Dokdo Research Conservation Association, 2003.

Kim, Myungki. *Dokdo Uiyong Subidae wa gukjebeop* [Dokdo Volunteer Garrison and international law]. Seoul: Damul Chulpansa, 1998.

Kim, Myungki. *Dokdo wa gukjebeop* [Dokdo and international law]. Seoul: Hwahaksa, 1987.

Kim, Myungki. "Sin Han-Il eoeop hyeopjeong gwa Dokdo yeongyugwon hweson yeobu" [The new Korea-Japan fisheries agreement and its impact on Dokdo territorial rights]. In *Dokdo yeongyugwon wigi yeongu* [Study on the Dokdo territorial rights crisis], edited by Dokdo Yeoksa Chatgi Undong Bonbu. Seoul: Baeksan Seodang, 2003.

Kim, Myungki, and Dong-won Lee. *Ilbon Oemuseong Dakesima munje ui gaeyo bipan: Dakesima 10-pointeu bipan* [Criticism of introduction to the Takeshima issue by Japan's Ministry of Foreign Affairs: Criticism on Takeshima 10 key points]. Seoul: Chaek gwa Saramdeul, 2010.

Kim, U-gyu. *Donghae ui pasukkun Dokdo* [Dokdo: Protector of the East Sea]. Seoul: Sidae Munhak, 1996.

Kim, Yong-shik. *Huimang gwa dojeon: Kim Yong-sik oegyo hoegorok* [Hope and defiance: Kim Yong-shik's diplomatic memoir], Seoul: Dong-A Ilbosa, 1987.

Kim, Young-koo. *Hanguk gwa bada ui gukjebeop.* Seoul: Korea Institute for Maritime Strategy, Hyoseong Chulpansa, 1999.

Kim, Young-koo. "Han-Il eoeop hyeopjeongsang Donghae junggan suyeok gwa Dokdo yeongyugwon munje" [The middle line and the Dokdo territorial rights issue in the Korea-Japan fisheries agreement]. In *Dokdo yeongyugwon wigi yeongu* [Study on the Dokdo territorial rights crisis], edited by Dokdo Yeoksa Chatgi Undong Bonbu, 77–138. Seoul: Baeksan Seodang, 2003.

Kim, Young-soo. "Geundae Dokdo wa Ulleungdo myeongching munje reul dulleossan nonjaeng gwa geu uimi" [Modern disputes over the issue of naming of Dokdo and Ulleungdo, and its significance]. In *Dokdo wa Han-Il gwangye: Beop yeoksajeok jeopgeun* (Dokdo and Korea-Japan relations: From the standpoint of law and history), edited by the Northeast Asian History Foundation. Seoul: Northeast Asian History Foundation, 2009.

Kitazawa, Shōsei. *Takeshima kōshō* [The historical investigation of Takeshima]. Tokyo: Ministry of Foreign Affairs, 1881.

Korean Government Opinion 1.

Korean Government Opinion 2.

Korean Government Opinion 3.

Kwak, Chang-kwon, "Simojo-ssi ui jujang busil, buranjeong gadeuk" [Shimojō's arguments, full of flaws and weaknesses]. *Hanguk nondan (Monthly Korea Journal)* 82, no. 1 (June 1996): 174–183.

Kwon, Chae-Hyun. "'Dokdo neun Hanguk ttang' Ilbon do injeong" ["Dokdo is Korean land," even Japan admits it]. *Dong-A Ilbo*, February 24, 2005.

Lee, Dong-won. *Daetongnyeong eul geurimyeo* [In memory of the president]. Seoul: Goryeowon, 1992.

Lee, Do-seong. *Sillok Park Chung-hee wa Han-Il hoedam* [Park Chung-hee and the Korea-Japan summit meeting]. Seoul: Hansong, 1995.

Lee, Han-key. *Hanguk ui yeongto: Yeongto chwideuk e gwanhan gukjebeopjeok yeongu* [Korean territory: International law on territorial acquisition]. Seoul: Seoul National University Press, 1996.

Lee, Jeong-hoon. "'Dokdo munje' Ilbon ui jankkoe e malliji malla." *Weekly Donga*, vol. 476, March 15, 2005.

Lee, Sang Myeon. "Dokdo yeongyugwon ui jeungmyeong" [Proof of territorial rights over Dokdo]. In *Hanguk ui Dokdo yeongyugwon yeongusa* [Research history of Korea's territorial rights over Dokdo], edited by the Dokdo Institute. Seoul: Dokdo Institute, 2003.

Lee, Sang Myeon. "Sin Han-Il eoeop hyeopjeongsang Dokdo wa geu jubyeon suyeok ui beopjeok munje" [The new Korea-Japan fisheries agreement and legal issues of the surrounding waters of Dokdo]. In *Dokdo yeongyugwon wigi yeongu* [Study on the Dokdo territorial rights crisis]. Seoul: Baeksan Seodang, 2003.

Lee, Sang-Tae. "Ilbon ui Dokdo bulbeop gangjeom e gwanhan yeongu" [A study on Japan's illegal occupation of Dokdo]. In *Dokdo yeongyugwon yeongu nonjip*, edited by the Dokdo Institute, Dokdo Territorial Right Research Collection. Seoul: Dokdo Research Conservation Association, 2002.

Lee, Sang-Tae. *Saryo ga jeungmyeong haneun Dokdo neun Hanguk ttang* [As evidence shows, Dokdo is Korean territory]. Seoul: Kyongsaewon Publishing Company, 2007.

Lee, Seo-hang et al. *Sin Han-Il eoeop hyeopjeong ui pyeongga* [Evaluation of the new Korea-Japan fisheries agreement]. Policy report, Institute of Foreign Affairs and National Security, Ministry of Foreign Affairs and Trade, November 4, 1998.

Lee, Sungun. "Ulleungdo mit Dokdo tamheom sogo" [Short journals on an expedition to Ulleungdo and Dokdo]. In *Dokdo*, edited by Daehan Gongnonsa. Seoul: Daehan Gongnonsa, 1965.

Li, Jin-mieung. *Dokdo: Jirisang ui jaebalgyeon* [Dokdo: New geographical findings]. Seoul: Samin Press, 1998 first printing; 2005 new edition.

Li, Jin-mieung. "Real Status of Dokdo: Administered by South Korea, Claimed by Japan." In *Territorial Issues in Europe and East Asia: Colonialism, War Occupation, and Conflict Resolution*, edited by Chinsoo Bae et al., 84–135. Seoul: Northeast Asian History Foundation, 2009.

Loh, Kye-hyun. *Joseon ui yeongto* [Joseon territory]. Seoul: KNOU Press, 1997.

McGlothlen, Ronald. "Japanese Peace Treaty." In vol. 1 of *East Asia and the United States: An Encyclopedia of Relations since 1784*, edited by James I. Matray. Westport, CT: Greenwood Press, 2002.

Ministry of Foreign Affairs. *Dokdo munje gaeron* [Introduction to the Dokdo issue]. Seoul: Ministry of Foreign Affairs, 1955.

Ministry of Maritime Affairs and Fisheries, and Korea Institute of Ocean Science & Technology. *Areumdaun seom Dokdo* [Beautiful island, Dokdo]. Seoul: Ministry of Maritime Affairs and Fisheries and Korea Institute of Ocean Science & Technology, 2000.

Nah, Hong-ju. *Dokdo ui yeongyugwon e gwanhan gukjebeopjeok yeongu: Dokdo neun Ilbon ui injeop sodoseo "smaller adjacent islands" ga anida* [Study on Dokdo territorial rights in view of international law: Dokdo is not "smaller adjacent islands" next to Japan]. Seoul: Beopseo Chulpansa, 2000.

Naitō, Seichū. "Jukdo munje boyu (竹島問題補遺): Simane-hyeon Jukdo Munje Yeonguhoe choejong bogoseo bipan" [The Takeshima issue on hold: Criticism of the final report by the Shimane Prefecture Takeshima Issue Research Group]. *Dokdo yeongu* (*The Journal of Dokdo*) 3 (December 2007): 37–80.

Naitō, Seichū. *Takeshima = Dokutō mondai nyūmon: Nihon Gaimushō 'Takeshima' hihan* [Introduction to the Takeshima = Dokdo issue: Criticism of the Japan Ministry of Foreign Affairs' "Takeshima"]. Tokyo: Shinkansha, 2008.

National Assembly Library of Korea, ed. *Dokdo hannun e bogi* [Dokdo at a glance]. Seoul: National Assembly Library of Korea, 2010.

Northeast Asian History Foundation, ed. Vol. 1 of *Ilbon Gukhoe Dokdo gwallyeon girok moeumjip* [Collection of Japanese National Diet records on Dokdo]. Seoul: Northeast Asian History Foundation, 2009.

Northeast Asian History Foundation, ed. Vol. 2 of *Ilbon Gukhoe Dokdo gwallyeon girok moeumjip* [Collection of Japanese National Diet records on Dokdo]. Seoul: Northeast Asian History Foundation, 2009.

Northeast Asian History Foundation, ed. Vol. 4 of *Ilbon Gukhoe Dokdo gwallyeon girok moeumjip* [Collection of Japanese National Diet records on Dokdo]. Seoul: Northeast Asian History Foundation, 2009.

Ōkuma, Ryōichi. *Takeshima shikō: Takeshima (Dokutō) to Utsuryūtō no bunkenshi-teki kōsatsu.* Tokyo: Hara shobō, 1968.

Ōnishi, Toshiteru. *Dokdo.* Translated by O-yub Kwon and Jung Kwon. Seoul: JENC, 2004.

Park, Byoungsup, "Simojo Masao (下條正男) ui nonseol eul bunseok handa (2)." *Dokdo yeongu (The Journal of Dokdo)* 4 (2008): 101–131.

Park, Byoungsup, and Seichū Naitō. *Dokdo=Dakeshima nonjaeng: Yeoksa jaryo reul tonghan gochal.* Seoul: Bogosa, 2008.

Park, Hyun-jin. "Dokdo munje wa gukje sabeop jaengsong" [The Dokdo question and international adjudication: Possibility, precaution and procedure in an age of litigation proliferation]. *Gukjebeop hakhoe nonchong (Korean Journal of International Law)* 50, no. 2 (August 2005): 125–156.

Park, Hyun-jin. "Dokdo yeongyugwon gwa jido, haedo ui jeunggeo neungnyeok, jeungmyeongnyeok" [Title to Dokdo as interpreted and evaluated chiefly from changing international jurisprudence on map evidence]. *Gukjebeop hakhoe nonchong (Korean Journal of International Law)* 52, no. 1 (April 2007): 89–128.

Park, Hyun-jin. "Yeongto, haeyang gyeonggye bunjaeng gwa jido, haedo ui jeunggeo jiwi, gachi: Dokdo gwanllyeon jido, haedo ui beop, jeongchaek, oegyo reul jungsim euro" [The legal status and probative value of maps and charts in international adjudication on territorial/boundary disputes]. *Gukjebeop hakhoe nonchong (Korean Journal of International Law)* 53, no. 1 (April 2008): 61–98.

Park, Kwan-Sook. "Dokdo ui beopjeok jiwi" [Legal status of Dokdo]. *Gukjebeop hakhoe nonchong (Korean Journal of International Law)* 1 (February 1956): 29–49.

Park, Kwan-Sook. "Dokdo ui beopjeok jiwi e gwanhan yeongu" [Studies on the legal status of Dokdo]. Unpublished PhD dissertation, Yonsei University, 1968.

Park, Yee-mun. "Tongil ui jeolsilham kkaeucheyojun Ilbon ui Dokdo gwallyeon mangeon" [Japan's reckless remarks on Dokdo that remind us of how important unification is]. *Newsweek* (Korean-language edition), March 20, 1996.

Seonwoo, Yeong-jun. "Dokdo yeongtogwon ui yeongu: Dokdo yeongto jugwon jedohwa gwanjeong ui bunseok" [A study of territorial title to Dokdo: An analysis of institutionalization process of territorial sovereignty of Dokdo]. PhD diss., Sungkyunkwan University, 2006.

Shimojō, Masao. "Jeunggeo reul deuleo siljeung hara" [Verify with evidence]. *Hanguk nondan* (*Monthly Korea Journal*) (August 1996): 226–235.

Shimojō, Masao. "'Jukdo' ga Hanguk ryeong iraneun geungeo neun waegok dwaeeo itda" [Evidence of Korean possession of "Jukdo" is fabricated]. *Hanguk nondan* (*Monthly Korea Journal*) (May 1996): 148–150.

Shimojō, Masao. "Zoku: Takeshima mondai kō (jō)." *Gendai Koria* 371 (May 1997): 62–78.

Shimojō, Masao, "Zoku: Takeshima mondai kō (ge)." *Gendai Koria* 372 (June 1997): 38–57.

Shin, Dong-wook. *Dokdo yeongyu e gwanhan yeongu* [Study on Dokdo territorial rights]. Seoul: Eomungak, 2008.

Shin, Ju-back. "Gyogwaseo wa Dokdo munje" [Textbooks and the Dokdo issue]. *Dokdo yeongu* (*The Journal of Dokdo*) 2 (December 2006): 87–108.

Shin, Sok-ho. "Dokdo ui naeryeok" [The origin of Dokdo]. In *Dokdo*, edited by Daehan Gongnonsa. Seoul: Daehan Gongnonsa, 1965.

Shin, Yong-Ha. *Dokdo, bobaeroun Hanguk yeongto: Ilbon ui Dokdo yeongyugwon jujang e daehan chongbipan* [Dokdo, precious Korean territory: Criticism of the Japanese claim to territorial rights over Dokdo]. Seoul: Jisik Sanup Publications, 1996.

Shin, Yong-Ha. "Dokdo jugwon sahwal geollin minjok munje ida" [Dokdo sovereignty is an important national matter]. *Shindonga,* April 1996.

Shin, Yong-Ha. *Dokdo ui minjok yeongtosa yeongu* [Research on Dokdo national territorial studies]. Seoul: Jisik Sanup Publications, 1996.

Shin, Yong-Ha. "Dokdo – Ulleungdo ui myeongching byeonhwa yeongu: Myeongching byeonhwa reul tonghae bon Dokdo ui Hanguk goyu yeongto jeungmyeong" [Study on Dokdo and Ulleungdo name transformation: Proof of Korean territorial right of Dokdo through name transformation]. In vol. 2 of *Dokdo yeongyugwon jaryo ui tamgu* [Research on the territorial rights of Dokdo], edited by Yong-Ha Shin et al. Seoul: Dokdo Research Conservation Association, 1999.

Shin, Yong-Ha. *Hanguk gwa Ilbon ui Dokdo yeongyugwon nonjaeng* [Korea and Japan's Dokdo territorial rights controversy]. Seoul: Hanyang University Press, 2003.

Shin, Yong-Ha et al. Vol. 1 of *Dokdo yeongyugwon jaryo ui tamgu* [Research on the territorial rights of Dokdo]. Seoul: Dokdo Research Conservation Association, 1998.

Shin, Yong-Ha et al. Vol. 2 of *Dokdo yeongyugwon jaryo ui tamgu* [Research on the territorial rights of Dokdo]. Seoul: Dokdo Research Conservation Association, 1999.

Shin, Yong-Ha et al. Vol. 3 of *Dokdo yeongyugwon jaryo ui tamgu* [Research on the territorial rights of Dokdo]. Seoul: Dokdo Research Conservation Association, 2000.

Shin, Yong-Ha et al. Vol. 4 of *Dokdo yeongyugwon jaryo ui tamgu* [Research on the territorial rights of Dokdo]. Seoul: Dokdo Research Conservation Association, 2001.

Song, Byeong-Ki. *Gochyeo sseun Ulleungdo wa Dokdo* [Rewritten Ulleungdo and Dokdo]. Seoul: Dankook University Press, 2005.

Song, Byeong-Ki. *Ulleungdo wa Dokdo: Geu yeoksajeok geomjeung* [Ulleungdo and Dokdo: The historical verification]. Seoul: Yeoksa Gonggan, 2010.

Suh, Jong-hak. "'Dokdo,' 'Seokdo' eui jimyeong pyogi e gwanhan yeongu" [A study on the place names of "Dokdo" and "Seokdo"]. *Eomunyeongu* 36, no. 3 (2008): 39–62.

Suh, Jung-chul, and In-hwan Kim. *Jido wiui jeonjaeng: Gojido eseo chajeun Han-Jung-Il yeongto munje ui jinsil* [War over maps: The truth of the Korea-China-Japan territorial issue found in ancient maps]. Seoul: Dong-A Ilbosa, 2010.

Swenson-Wright, John. "Sebald William J." In vol. 1 of *East Asia and the United States*, edited by James I. Matray. Westport, CT: Greenwood Press, 2002.

Taijudō, Kanae. "The Dispute Between Japan and Korea Respecting Sovereignty over Takeshima." *The Japanese Annals of International Law* 10 (1966): 105–136.

Taijudō, Kanae. "Takeshima funsō." *Kokusaihō gaikō zasshi* 64 (March 1966).

Tamura, Seizaburō. *Shimane-ken Takeshima no shin kenkyū* [New research on Takeshima, Shimane Prefecture]. Matsue: Shimane-ken, 1963.

Ueda, Toshio. "Dakeshima ui gwisok eul dulleossan Il-Han bunjaeng" (in Japanese) [Japan-Korea controversy over the return of Dokdo], 29.

Wakamiya, Yoshifumi. "The Only Solution is to 'Delete Takeshima.'" *Chūō kōron*, November 2006.

Yamabe, Kentarō. "Takeshima mondai no rekishi-teki kōsatsu." *Koria hyōron*, February 1995.

Yang, Tae-jin. *Hanguk dongnip ui sangjing Dokdo* [Symbol of Korean independence, Dokdo]. Seoul: Baeksan, 2004.

Yang, Tae-jin. *Hanguk yeongtosa yeongu* [Research in the history of Korean territory]. Seoul: Beopgyeong Chulpansa, 1991.

Yi, Geun-taek. "1693-1699 nyeon An Yong-bok ui Ulleungdo – Dokdo suho hwaldong: Sutoje (搜討制) silsi wa gwallyeonhayeo" [An Yong-bok's Ulleungdo and Dokdo protection, 1693–1699: In relation to Sutoje [搜討制] implementation]." In *Dokdo yeongyu ui yeoksa wa gukje gwangye* [History of Dokdo territorial rights and international relations], edited by Dokdo Research Conservation Association. Seoul: Dokdo Research Conservation Association, 1997.

Yi, Pyong-do. "Dokdo ui myeongching e daehan sajeok gochal: Usan, Jukdo myeongchinggo" [Historical contemplation of different names of Dokdo: The study of names: Usando and Takeshima]. In *Cho Myeong-gi Parksa hwagap ginyeom Bulgyo sahak nonchong*. 1963. This article was re-published in *Dokdo*, edited by Daehan Gongnonsa, 67–76. Seoul: Daehan Gongnonsa, 1965. It was republished again in *Hanguk ui Dokdo yeongyugwon yeongusa* [Research history of Korea's territorial rights over Dokdo], edited by the Dokdo Institute, 40–41. Seoul: Dokdo Research Conservation Association, 2003.

Yoo, Mirim. "Ilbon eui Seokdo = Dokdo-seol bujeong e daehan bipanjeok gochal" [Critical review on the Japanese denial of "Seokdo indicates Dokdo" doctrine]. *Haesang jeongchaek yeongu* (*Ocean Policy Research*) 23, no. 1 (2008): 173–197.

Yoon, So-young. "Ilbon Meiji sidae munheon e natanan Ulleungdo wa Dokdo insik" [Japanese perception of Ulleungdo and Dokdo shown in the Japanese literature of the Meiji period], *Dokdo yeongu* (*The Journal of Dokdo*) 1 (December 2005): 115–158.

Yu, Ha-young. "Geundae Hanguk beop chegye eseo yeongto" [Territory in the modern Korean legal system]. In *Dokdo wa Han-Il gwangye: Beop yeoksajeok jeopgeun* [Dokdo and Korea-Japan relations: From the standpoint of law and history], edited by the Northeast Asian History Foundation. Seoul: Northeast Asian History Foundation, 2009.

Yu, Hong-yeol. "Dokdo neun Ulleungdo ui sokdo: Yeongyugwon eul jungsim euro." In *Dokdo*, edited by Daehan Gongnonsa. Seoul: Daehan Gongnonsa, 1965.

Yu, Jong-hyeon. *Daemado yeoksa munhwa gihaeng: Daemado neun bonsi uri ttang inga* [Historical and cultural trip to Daemado: Is Daemado originally a part of Korea?]. Seoul: Hwasan Munhwa, 2008.

Index

The index omits entries for "Dokdo," "Ulleungdo," "Matsushima," "Takeshima," "Joseon," and "Japan."

S